Beer Drinkers and Hell Raisers
The Rise of Motörhead

by Martin Popoff

Published by ECW Press
665 Gerrard Street East, Toronto,
Ontario, Canada M4M 1Y2
416-694-3348 / info@ecwpress.com

Cover design: Michel Vrana
Cover images: © Fin Costello/Redferns/Getty
    Images International
Interior images: Unless otherwise stated, all images are
    from the author's personal collection
Type: Rachel Ironstone

Library and Archives Canada
Cataloguing in Publication

Popoff, Martin, 1963–, author
Beer drinkers and hell raisers : the rise of Motörhead /
Martin Popoff.

Issued in print and electronic formats.
ISBN 978-1-77041-347-4 (paperback)
ISBN 978-1-77305-033-1 (pdf)
ISBN 978-1-77305-032-4 (epub)

1. Motörhead (Musical group). 2. Rock musicians—
Great Britain—Biography. 3. Heavy metal (Music)–
Great Britain—History and criticism. I. Title.

ML421.M918P82 2017   782.42166092'2   C2016-906409-3
C2016-906410-7

MIX
Paper from
responsible sources
FSC® C016245

The publication of *Beer Drinkers and Hell Raisers* has been generously supported by the Government of Canada through the
Canada Book Fund. *Ce livre est financé en partie par le gouvernement du Canada.* We also acknowledge the support of the Government of Ontario through the Ontario Book Publishing Tax Credit and the Ontario Media Development Corporation.

Ontario Media Development
Corporation

Printed and bound by Friesens in Canada   5   4   3   2   1

Table of Contents

Introduction ix

Chapter 1 *1*
"Hang on, what drugs were we doing that day?"

Chapter 2 *17*
"A bullet belt in one hand and a leather jacket in the other."

Chapter 3 *38*
Motörhead: "Like a fucking train going through your head."

Chapter 4 *65*
Overkill: "He was a bit of a lad, old Jimmy."

Chapter 5 *95*
Bomber: "They saw us as noisy, scary people."

Chapter 6 *126*
Ace of Spades: "It wasn't that it was the best we did; it was that it was the best they heard."

Chapter 7 *152*
No Sleep 'til Hammersmith: "The bomber, the
sweat, the noise—it was an event."

Chapter 8 *182*
Iron Fist: "It was hard work getting Lemmy out of
the pubs."

Chapter 9 *197*
Eddie's Last Meal: "A bottle of vodka on the table,
a glass, and a little pile of white powder."

Chapter 10 *217*
The Aftermath: "God bless him, little fella."

Selected Discography 249
Credits 253
About the Author 257

Is aging a bad topic with you?
"No, I don't care, you know? I'm all right."
No big health problems right now?
"No, no small ones either."

Introduction

First thing to get off my chest is that I'd been formulating plans for a Motörhead book months before even dear Phil Taylor had died, and I had signed the papers with the good folks at ECW Press three weeks before Phil passed on, let alone any time after the tragic demise of Mr. walkin' talkin' Motörhead itself, Ian "Lemmy" Kilmister. I would hate for people to think I was glorifying or capitalizing on death—when I was finishing up this book, everybody was very much still with us, and it's only the stretched timelines and strict sales schedules of publishers that make it look otherwise.

Which, incidentally, speaks well of ECW themselves, having the sophisticated taste to order up a book on Motörhead before anybody died (and I happen to know for a fact that there are deep-track Motörhead fans on the staff of that fine institution).

Okay, that little bit of unpleasantness dispensed with, I have to say that I'm proud to avow that I was a Motörheadbanger from somewhere around the beginning. I can't find my materials or membership card, so I'm not sure what my number was, but I'm pretty sure I would've been in the first handful of Canadians ever to sign up, having joined the Saxon Militia Guard or whatever it was called at the same time. It was like magic sitting in my bedroom in Trail, B.C., receiving newsletters and black-and-white glossy photos from and about Motörhead and Saxon, materials that looked very much like the stuff I got from being part of the Buffalo Sabres fan club a little earlier than that, I suspect. Not sure who my favorite power trio was, Motörhead or the French Connection, but we don't have to fight that battle.

But yes, Motörhead came to me as a lad of 14, with the imported debut album, and I can't say I got it right away. Sure, hearing that tangled mass of distortion, I couldn't help but like them, clinging to anything heavy that crossed my path (and of course nothing that was not heavy). But on the strength of *Motörhead*, who in their right mind would call these squatters and street rats their favorite band? At 14 years old, I liked *Motörhead* exactly as much, and for the same reasons, as I liked *Raw Power*, not the least of which was I partly felt sorry for the bands that had to live with these records as the best that they could do.

It wasn't until my purchase of *Overkill* that Motörhead would indeed lodge themselves forever into my list of favorite 10 or so bands. But I suppose, one should clarify and not lie: Motörhead would be one of my favorite bands two times and with a gap: one, the period covered by this book, namely the classic lineup (you will notice throughout the following chapters that for expediency I also use the term original lineup although, of course, there was an original, transitional lineup that we do indeed recognize in this book), and then very much the band as it existed for about the last 15 years.

Now, we don't talk throughout this book about the heroic and heartbeating music that Lemmy, Mikkey Dee and Phil Campbell slammed together like a hundred clap push-ups, so I just want to say, in the here and now, it does cause me some pain not to extol and explain the great records that version of the band made, especially sort of the last half-dozen (and *Bastards*) before Lemmy's death at the very end of 2015. So yes, in summary, I love and appreciate and I am inspired by Motörhead as it existed in the 2000s, and as it existed in the late '70s and early '80s, and not particularly so much in between, the nadir being the band's cover of "Cat Scratch Fever." And yes, for the goddamn record, *Another Perfect Day* is my favorite Motörhead album of all time.

So to reiterate, this book celebrates what is known as the classic Motörhead lineup, and the six records—five studio and one live—that Lemmy Kilmister, Phil "Philthy Animal" Taylor and Fast Eddie Clarke created between 1977 and 1982.

Joining the Motörheadbangers is a filmy memory, but the fondest memory of these three guys and what they meant to me as an angry headbanger, exclusively headbanging during their reign, was the purchase of *Overkill*.

My fellow encyclopedic buddy, Forrest Toop, and myself had embarked upon one of our life-highlight trips to Spokane Washington, from our homes just north of the border in Canada, in Trail, B.C. We were by this point egregiously obsessed and knowledgeable metalheads, and we lived for these purchasing excursions into the Mecca that was shelves-stocked America. Spokane was just big enough to have a few tiny, perfect record stores that could fulfill our every obsession concerning our hobby. There was Eucalyptus Records, a bright and airy place walled with windows, a welcoming headquarters that had all the new domestic releases and a few imports. It was a cheery, somewhat corporate stand-alone building on Division, and it just made you feel good to be there—like Peaches must have been, or even Tower at its peak. But more important were the paired head shop/record emporia known as Magic Mushroom and Strawberry Jams, each, as I recall, with two locations during their incense-fumed reigns as the places we could buy *Sounds* and the *NME* and Tygers of Pan Tang singles with the patch still in them.

Now, I'm positive that I bought *Overkill* in the original, somewhat cramped location of Strawberry Jams. But I'm not sure that this is the time that I jumped up and let out a howl in the store and almost hit my head on a crossbeam, or if that happened when I flipped through the racks and found The Damned's *Music for Pleasure* a year and a half earlier. But I know for sure that the endorphin rush was the same. With *Music for Pleasure*, there was the added delayed reaction of making out the fact, through Barney Bubbles's vision, that this was a copy of a new Damned album. With the Motörhead record, it was more like being whacked in the face with an exploding baseball filled with paint. The debut album's front cover was almost miserable in its black-and-white-ness, and a little bit scary in that it looked like a biker patch, which was actually Lemmy's intention with the design. *Overkill*, on the other hand, was like *Motörhead*—and Motörhead—coming to life with a roar and a flurry of karate moves. It was Snaggletooth suddenly rendered in dramatic and violent color, and Motörhead as a trio of malnourished moochers in leather jackets was off to the races.

Soon would come the equally awesome *Bomber* and *Ace of Spades* (both, again, on import) and a live album that I really didn't give a shit about, and then *Iron Fist*, which I, as it turned out, clutched to heart more than most people did. By this point, Motörhead had insidiously become part of my sullen teenage personality, getting me through lonely high school years, serving as a body core-strengthener, knocking me out of the encouraging family home into university at 18 years old, and then onward into . . . whatever, quite a bit of life as a fan who, like the 99%, did other things for a living, and then, for a good 15 years now, a fan who gets to think about and fawn over all sorts of bands like Motörhead as his full-time job, if you can call it that.

And then Phil dies, and seven weeks later, Lemmy dies, and there's only Fast Eddie left to provide comfort and connection back to those magical days when Motörhead were the baddest bad-asses in heavy metal.

The tale of those great years, essentially, for purposes and purloin of this intimate and happy book, 1976 to 1982, was for the most part whacked together when all three of these hot-rod rock heroes were still alive. The finishing of it, with two of them dead, was much more of a mixed feeling experience. I have no idea if the reading of this book is going to make you happy with punk pride or sad with heavy metal heaviness, but I would hope that the communion with these words serves as a great re-living of those times, or for the youngsters, an entry point to six full-stride, widestance classics plus "Please Don't Touch" and assorted B-sides that inflamed our imaginations as teens.

Of note, you certainly are going to be cast right back into the making of all this great music, and through much first-hand accompaniment from the guys themselves, Eddie very much alive and telling me great stories, with Phil and Lemmy coming to life, because I've talked to all of them at length. The other reason why, hopefully, you will wind up feeling well inside this hurricane of great recorded music is that the recorded canon is my main concern; it's of the utmost importance and it's is all we have, plus our memories if we were ever there with them in the flesh. Writing the book, it was very much like sitting around the pub with these sociable, smart, funny guys perennially plunked into a surreal world lacking in REM sleep, and it is my hope that reading the book feels that way as well to you, rather than creeping you out from all the death.

So let's move on, shall we? I've never had any idea what these introductions are supposed to be for, specifically. I've certainly written enough of them, having bulldozed through close to 60 books now (and here I have to use a bit of time travel, because I know before this book actually hits the shelves, barring my own death, I'll write another four or five). And so I think I've knocked down all those conversational, reminiscing, bookkeeping, clarification-type things I usually want to knock off. So yeah, let's get started. Without further ado, here's the tale of the classic Motörhead lineup, with the overarching theme being very much an exploration of why these three guys were loved so much, why, in effect, no one has a bad word for the original Motörhead, and in fact, really, anything denigrating to say about Motörhead at all, excepting scrutiny perhaps of those too corporate and commercial albums from '87 to '92.

In other words, I think it's safe to say that with the death of Lemmy went any possible chance that Motörhead would go to its grave with anything other than an unassailable reputation as the purest expression of the magic of hard rock—and, yes, heavy metal—that we're ever likely to experience ever again in our lifetimes.

Martin Popoff
martinp@inforamp.net

BEER
DRINKERS

CHAPTER 1

"Hang on, what drugs were we doing that day?"

Born on the dole, born in the land of misfit rockers and always—always—born to lose, Motörhead was also born of a burn, its rank figurehead, Lemmy Kilmister, on fire to avenge his firing from the ranks of Hawkwind through the assemblage of a sonic force that would deafen all naysayers. Its name would be Motörhead, and the classic lineup this book celebrates—Fast Eddie Clarke, Phil "Philthy Animal" Taylor and lynchpin Lemmy his bad self—would grind up seven years' worth of posers and pretenders. Motörhead would create a contrast against the industry, one that will live forever as the potent realization of punk ethics applied to original rock 'n' roll and a bastard format called heavy metal, a genre nomenclature curiously dismissed by all three soldiers as mirage, but ultimately so much a part of their legacy, their home and hearth, their final resting place against a pop culture that rarely cared.

One mustn't forget or diminish the accomplishments of line-ups after the classic trio—most notably the band as it existed for the near quarter-century with Phil Campbell and Mikkey Dee—but one also mustn't forget that the classic lineup was not the original, and that the original . . . well, this is one of those happenstances where technically the original, or most salient, "lineup" just might consist of an army of one, namely Lemmy Kilmister.

Born on Christmas Eve in 1945 (and dead three days after Christmas 70 years later) in Stoke-on-Trent, England, Ian Fraser Kilmister, an only child, seemed destined for a life of independence and defiance. His father, an ex–Royal Air Force chaplain, left his mother when Lemmy was but three months old, and his mother, after nine years of single motherhood, took up with a footballer and washing machine factory worker who arrived with a couple of kids of his own, neither of whom Lemmy cooperated with. Stridently resentful of his father, conversely of his mother, Lemmy says, "She was a good mum. She was fair enough. She had a lot of good ideas."

Later, living on a farm in north Wales, Lemmy says he "used to breed horses when I was younger, before I got into rock 'n' roll." He also was an enthusiastic reader, having been encouraged by his English teacher, and he worked the carnival when it was in town. But he soon discovered girls and rock 'n' roll, at its birth in the '50s. The only English kid among seven hundred Welsh children, Lemmy needed an edge against the inherent territorial resentment he suffered there. Always strategizing, Lemmy took his mother's Hawaiian guitar to school to impress the girls. "It worked like a charm too," recalled Kilmister to *Classic Rock Revisited*. "I saw this other kid with a guitar at school. He was immediately surrounded by chicks and I thought, 'Oh, I see.' Luckily, my mother had one laying around the house, so I grabbed it and took it to school. I couldn't play it. Eventually, they expected me to play so I had to learn a couple of chords. It turned out all right."

Lemmy recalls how, as a young boy, he used to have to go to the "electrical appliance" store and order records, after which they would arrive in three weeks' time. Early favorites included Jerry Lee Lewis, Buddy Holly, Tommy Steele, Eddie Cochran, Elvis and Little Richard, who he always called the greatest rock 'n' roll singer of all time.

But it was the Beatles that really lit the fire—Lemmy, all of 16, hitchhiked to Liverpool to see what the fuss was about and watched them live at the Cavern Club before they even had a record out. Our hero soon would play guitar in bands like the Sundowners, the Rainmakers, the Motown Sect and the mildly legendary Rocking Vickers (sometimes spelled Rockin' and some-times spelled Vicars), who managed to tour Europe and distinguish themselves as the first western band ever to play Yugoslavia.

"The Beatles had an influence on everybody," Lemmy told *Goldmine* magazine. He admired the Beatles as hard men from Liverpool against the Stones, suburban Londoners in his estimation. "You have to realize what an incredible explosion the Beatles were. They were the first band to not have a lead singer in the band. They were the first band to write their own songs in Britain because we always just covered American songs before that. Everybody was singing at the same time and the harmonies were great. Daily papers in England used to have an entire page of the paper dedicated to what the Beatles had done the day before. When George died, the guards at Buckingham Palace played a medley of George's songs during the changing of the guard; that sort of thing never happens."

Lemmy says that his Rocking Vickers were as famed and respected in Northern England, north of Birmingham, as the Who and the Kinks were down in London, but that the other guys in the band seemed to content themselves with playing a predictable circuit, while he had grander plans. But even though the money was good, at £200 a week each, they couldn't get a foothold in London themselves. And so, dispensing with the

Rocking Vickers—which Lemmy ultimately describes as less of a garage band, more of a show band—he left the band house in Manchester empty-handed. "When I left the Vickers, the guitar stayed," noted Lemmy to *Classic Rock Revisited*. "It was a band guitar. When people left that band then the instruments stayed and I think that really made a lot of sense. If you need a guitar player but he hasn't got a guitar then you have one for him to use. When he leaves, you have one for the next guy so you don't have to run around." Traveling light not for the last time in his life, Lemmy found his way to London where his mind was about to get expanded through his apocryphal internship as a Jimi Hendrix roadie, living for a brief spell with bassist Noel Redding and road manager Neville Chesters.

"Lemmy has been my friend since 1963," explains Chesters, who also worked with both the Who and Cream. "The story goes, and I can tell you, we have a different one on how the story goes but it ends up the same. I actually took Lemmy to London. He came to see us at the Odeon in Liverpool. He wanted to go to London; he asked me if I could give him a ride to London and I said yes. He slept on the floor of my room and then the next day I took him down to London via his house, which was inconvenient. He grabbed a few things. Gone to London, I said, 'Where do you want to go?' And he said, 'Well I don't really have anywhere; I was wondering if I could stay with you?' His band then had been the Rocking Vickers, and I'd known him since then. So I happened to have a basement hovel that had three beds. One of them was given over to Noel when he was supposed to share the rent. And I had a spare bed, so Lemmy was in there. And then the next day it was . . . he couldn't get a job at all. He couldn't get anything, so I got him a job as my assistant to roadie for Jimi. And that was, at the time, his big claim to fame. In fact for years it was his claim to fame. It was a story that used to come out in many of his radio and TV interviews. But we have a different way of describing how he got to London."

"I mean, I used to say he did his work," says Chesters, unwittingly helping to establish Lemmy's reputation as unsuitable for any gainful employment other than the haphazard helming of his own shambolic show. "I did an interview for a documentary, and they say to him, 'Didn't you roadie with Hendrix at one time?' And he goes, 'Speak to Neville about that.' So I get a phone call. So, 'Yes, he came in supposedly to help me' and they said, 'Did he work? Did he do anything?' And I said, 'Yeah.' And they said, 'Are you sure?' And I said, 'Well what do you mean?' 'Because most people said he just hung out with the band.' And I said, 'Actually, come to think of it, yeah, that's what he did.'"

"It was very confusing because we were tripping all the time," reminisced Lemmy in October 2006. "[Hendrix] came over to England from America and there was this guy named Owsley Stanley the Third. He was one of those guys who had a laboratory and he gave Hendrix about ten thousand tabs of acid. It was even legal back then. Hendrix put it in his suitcase and gave it out to the crew—there were only two of us. We had the best acid in the world in 1967 and most of 1968. After a while it doesn't affect your work because you learn to function. I drove the van from London to Bletchley, which is about 150 miles, on acid with a pair of those strobe sunglasses on. They had the vision of a fly, where you would see eight times around. I drove the van with those on for 150 miles on acid, and we got there."

Lemmy's also been known to say that he would score drugs for Mitch Mitchell as well, but when obtaining acid for Jimi, he said his pay came in the three tabs of ten that he would have to take on the spot, while Jimi took seven.

But working for a genius must have been a trip of its own. "Oh yeah, everybody knew it as soon as he came to England," continued Lemmy. "When he came to the States, you had Monterey and everybody knew about it. It was like that in England. He played one show and everyone knew. It went around like a wildfire. Pete Townshend came out of a club where Hendrix was playing and

Eric Clapton was going in. Eric asked Pete, 'What is he like?' and Pete replied, 'We are in a lot of trouble.' We used to get Clapton sitting in a chair behind the stack with his ear pressed up against it trying to figure out what he was doing. But I was just hired part time while he was in England. When he went abroad, I was not invited. I was living at Noel Redding's house and he needed an extra pair of hands. I have been really lucky. I have been in a few of the right places at the right time. My street credibility is incredible. I saw the Beatles at the Cavern, too. It ends up that I was on hallowed ground but it was actually a filthy hole."

,•

"Lemmy was there about three months maximum," laughs Chesters. "Somewhere between two and three months. After that I really only saw him intermittently. After the Hendrix thing, we always had the same women, one way or another. Sometimes I got there before he did and got one over, but only infrequently. In the early days he wasn't the most outstanding musician I'd seen, but he did pull himself together and managed to be . . . he's almost an icon, Lemmy, and it's funny. It's not necessarily because of his music. There was a period in the mid- or the late '70s where he was known to hang out with debutantes in London. Now you know Lemmy, you know what he looks like, we all know the features. And none of us could understand why there was constantly, almost weekly, photographs of him in the leading London newspapers hanging out with debutantes. But that's what he did. And he became an icon."

"I lived with him for some time," muses Hawkwind saxophonist Nik Turner, answering Lemmy's drug question. "I thought Lemmy was a lovely guy, actually. We got on very well. He was a bit difficult to live with in some ways, because he would be sort of on a different time scale to other people in the band. He went his own way very much. I mean, the band were leaning towards a psychedelic sort of influence, really, and Lemmy wasn't particularly into psychedelics. He was more into speed, you might say."

Plus, he wasn't much of a hippie. More like a biker, says Dave Brock. "Yeah, we used to know a lot of the Hells Angels in the early days and all that. But Lemmy was always more so buddies with them. I mean Motörhead had more of a problem with them than we did. Lemmy used to always put down on his guest list, 'Hells Angels England.' And sometimes you wouldn't know who the fuck was turning up there. You'd go to his dressing room, and all the food and drink would be gone and you'd walk in, 'What the fuck?! We don't know anybody here.' A bit problematic sometimes, you know. But we still do the odd bikers thing. We get along well with them actually. I mean, a lot of them are our age now. Their festivals are always well organized, well together. You very rarely get any trouble."

With respect to Lemmy's burgeoning recording career, following up his three singles with the Rocking Vickers, in 1969 Lemmy appeared on his first full-length record, *Escalator*, by Malaysian percussionist Sam Gopal. Lemmy is credited as Ian Willis, as he had been considering changing his last name to that of his stepfather, George Willis. Already long known informally as Lemmy, for years it was assumed the nickname came from young Ian's frequent attempts to borrow money, as in "Lemme a fiver." However, Lemmy later confessed that he made up the story and had been paying for it ever since.

"It was very convoluted, because we had no songs," recalls Lemmy, when asked about those Sam Gopal days. "And then I stayed up all night on methamphetamine and wrote all the songs on the fucking album in one night. I was playing guitar then. But we never really could play live shows too well back then because they didn't have contact mics for the tablas and things, which are very odd to amplify, because they rely on boom inside to get the sound; you can't really record that. I mean you couldn't microphone that; you couldn't then anyway. That was 1968."

*Lemmy, built for speed with white Rickenback-
er and early use of the bullet belt, accompanied
by Larry Wallis on guitar and Lucas Fox on
drums at this short cover-heavy gig in 1975.*
| © Paul Apperly

Lemmy's next gig, after a brief situation with Simon King as Opal Butterfly, was to provide a breeding ground for Lemmy's nasty sound, as it rumbled from both his bass and his face.

"After Hendrix, I became a dope dealer for a while and that was a natural apprenticeship for Hawkwind," laughs Lem. "The guy that played the audio generator in Hawkwind ran out of money and went back to the band. He took me with him because he wanted one of his mates in the band. I had never played bass in my life. The idiot that was there before me left his bass there. It was like he said, 'Please steal my gig' so I stole his gig. So me being a bass player was an accident. I went to get a job as a guitar player with Hawkwind, and they decided they weren't going to have another guitar player. The guy doing rhythm was going to do lead, so they said, 'Who plays bass?' And Dik Mik said, 'He does.' Bastard; I'd never even picked one up in my life. And I get up on stage with the fucking thing, because the bass player left his guitar in the gear truck. And Nik Turner was very helpful. He came over and said, 'Make some noises in E. This song is called 'You Shouldn't Do That.' And walked away from me."

The "audio generator" Lemmy refers to is in fact Dik Mik, and it is said that a mutual fondness for amphetamines cemented Lemmy's entry into the ranks of the notorious space rockers, through the recommendation of Dik Mik. Ironically, Lemmy's behavior on speed would also be the reason he'd be thumped from the band later on.

"You've got to remember, Lemmy was a guitarist to start with," notes Hawkwind guitarist and leader Dave Brock, spiritual twin to the original, pre-Motörhead Lemmy. "I mean, what happened was when Dik Mik brought Lemmy along, he didn't have a bass. We had to go and buy him a second-hand bass. And of course Lemmy's bass playing is very similar to guitar playing, in a sense, by playing block chords and stuff like that. So it was a different technique. Lemmy's fantastic, obviously, now, but you have to think that at the time, the way he played, it was just different. So consequently, that's why me and him used to play really well together, because I used to play similar lines to Lemmy. So that's why we were able to play together very well. And now when I do a solo album, my bass playing is a bit like Lemmy's. I play chords on the bass quite often. It's a style of playing, really. Instead of picking it and playing note by note, quite often . . . it's hard to explain without playing the bass. But when you're playing, it's quite easy, and Lemmy and I used to be able to do that together."

"I don't use distortion," clarifies Lem. "I don't use any pedals. No effects, just plug it straight into the amp. Just a basic Marshall, but it's turned up very loud, and I hit the guitar very hard. That helps, too. But you've got to know how to hit it very hard. A lot of people hit it very hard and it don't happen. Yeah, I'm doing the old-school version, no mechanics for me. Actually I don't play bass. I play rhythm guitar and a bit of cockamamie lead guitar on a bass— that's what I do. It's a unique style but it's not one that people have copied, if you've noticed, so I don't think it's that popular, but it works for me. I always hated it when you get a band playing that was really good, and then the riff drops out because the guitar player has to do a solo, and it sounds wimpy as shit with just the bass player behind him. So I always swore I'd never let that happen."

Nik Turner drills down further to posit a source for the churning bass sound Lemmy would make famous. "The idea came from the fact that the previous bass player had been Dave Anderson, and Dave Anderson had a Rickenbacker. And Lemmy was a friend of Dik Mik's, and he turned up at a rehearsal, and he said, 'Oh, we need a bass player,' and Lemmy said, 'Well, I don't play bass. I play guitar.' He'd previously been a road manager for Jimi Hendrix. And we said, 'Well, you know, there's a bass here,' which was Dave Anderson's bass. And we gave the bass to Lemmy to play in that situation at that time. I'm not saying we gave him the bass. We gave him the bass to play. And then I think that's where he started, really. Because he was an advocate of the Rickenbacker bass from then on, and he quickly gave it a great popularity, really. But Dave Anderson had played with Amon Duul II and I think he played the Rickenbacker then too. And so Lemmy had the Rickenbacker, but he had a guitar technique, and he played the Rickenbacker bass like a guitar—chords and stuff like that, rather than just notes. So he created his own sort of musical genre, really, with what he had at hand, and the situation he was in."

Below proper chords there are bar (or barre) chords and then double stops, which generally refers to two strings being played at once but normally on a bowed instrument. Lemmy would go on to use mostly double stops, switching from fourths to fifths, plus single notes, as well as his turgid and toppy bass sound: lacking in low-end warmth and high on distortion through mid-range and high-end frequencies. His chosen weapon was a Rickenbacker 4001 bass which naturally lacks in low end, even more so when played through a stack and with acceptance of distortion and volume. This general philosophy when it comes to bass puts Lemmy in a club with the likes of Rush's Geddy Lee and Chris Squire from Yes. The difference is that those two guys want their individual notes, their playing, to be heard whereas Lemmy just wanted to be heard.

"The bass and treble are all the way off and the mid-range is all the way up," Lemmy told Jeb Wright of *Classic Rock Revisited*. "I came up with that by just fucking with the sound. I like that sound; it is kind of brutal but that is what we were looking for. I had a Rickenbacker with a Thunderbird pickup on it back in the old days. It was a horrible monster but it wore out eventually. I love the shape of Rickenbackers. I buy guitars for how they look. You can always fuck with the sound once you have them. You always had to change the pickups on the old Rickenbackers because they were crap. Now they have really good pickups. I have a signature bass with them that I designed."

And as for his propensity to play more than one string at a time, having started on guitar is a piece of the story, continued Lem. "Partly it is, but it's also because I am the only back end for the guitar player. I always hated bands where when the guitar player stopped playing the riff and started playing the solo, the whole back end falls out. I always made sure there was plenty behind them."

Lemmy quickly became a beloved member of the Hawkwind clan. Appearing first on the band's third studio album *Doremi Fasol Latido* (1972), plus *Hall of the Mountain Grill* (1974), *Warrior on the Edge of Time* (1975) and seminal 1973 double live album *Space Ritual*. Toward the end of his time with the band, Lemmy gave us signature rock songs soon to become Motörhead staples, namely "Lost Johnny" and "Motörhead."

"Lost Johnny" is a co-write between Lemmy and the Deviants' Mick Farren, but "Motörhead" (existing in versions with Lemmy singing and with Dave Brock singing) is a rare sole-Kilmister credit and his last for Hawkwind before his firing. The set piece for the band and life philosophy to come would be written at the Hyatt House hotel on the Sunset Strip in Los Angeles, ironic for the fact that Hollywood, and specifically the Strip, would become Lemmy's home for the last decades of his life. "Did you know I wrote 'Motörhead' just down the street from here?" Lemmy told Jon Sutherland in 1982. "I was on the seventh floor of the Hyatt House, stoned out of my mind, playing Roy Wood's guitar. Cars would keep stopping and cops would get out and get back in the car thinking, 'I'm not going up there.'"

Reflects Brock on that *Warrior on the Edge of Time* era, "That [album has] got the 'Motörhead' with Lemmy singing it, and me singing it. Basically, it's the last record that Lemmy did with us, and after that, we changed quite a bit, because of Lemmy, or because Lemmy went. Lemmy was a great influence."

Lemmy's firing from Hawkwind in May 1975 is the stuff of legends, almost amusing for the fact that he was already proving to be such an outlaw with substances that he could be fired from this notoriously drug-addled band for going too far.

"I was fired from Hawkwind," explains Lemmy, in his curiously matter-of-fact manner indicative of the man's view of an unjust world—in fact one in which he called his ex-mates fascists, rather than hippies. "I got busted going into Canada. My last gig with them was in Toronto. It was thrown out of court anyway, because it wasn't what they said it was. So there was no criminal record attached to it. Hawkwind just threw me out because they were trying to throw me out for ages." The border agents thought the white substance was heroin, but it was speed, not yet banned.

Asked about how these stories take on lives of their own over the years, Lemmy agrees, adding, "You know, I tell you, it's a funny thing. If you go back as long as I do, there are a lot of people in bands. Bands don't remember that well apparently. Take any four members of Hawkwind and me, you will find five different recollections of the same incident and it runs all the way through your time with the band. You think, is that really what happened? Am I right and they fucked up? Hang on, what drugs were we doing that day? Was I out of it? Was there something that pissed me off? You try explain it and there is no explanation. You remember it different, because you're standing in a different part of the room and somebody else spoke to you at the same time the incident went on. It's funny. That's why I really don't rely on eyewitnesses anymore, man. If I was the cops, I'd throw that category out."

Concerning Lemmy's ousting from the Hawkwind ranks, Nik Turner recalls that "the conditions in which he left were sad, really.

We were playing in Detroit and were going to Toronto. We were in the United States still, and I think we stopped at a service station, and Lemmy went to the toilet and fell asleep in the toilet or something and we couldn't find him. We were ready to go to travel on, and we looked everywhere for him. We couldn't find him. We thought he'd probably hooked up with some people that he may have met and gone off with them, because he did spontaneous things like that, quite frequently. Not on a regular basis, but it wasn't out of the question in our minds that he might've done that. And so consequently we traveled on without him. And apparently he did; he'd fallen asleep in the toilet."

Not so, says Lemmy, who has said that he wandered off with his camera to take some pictures and was knocked out and mugged of his camera, only to awaken and begin his odyssey.

"And then coming through customs," continues Turner, "he'd been searched and they found what they thought was cocaine in his possession, and they arrested him for supposedly possession of cocaine. But when they analyzed it, they found out it was amphetamines, and they didn't take such a dim view of amphetamines, so they let him go. But by this time, certain things had happened that had made him rather difficult to work with. And so we had a meeting and it was decided that he should leave the band. And then everybody was saying, 'Well, who's going to tell him?' And nobody wanted to. But I just took the bull by the horns and said, 'Well, I'll tell him.' I had the very unpleasant job of breaking the news to him. And by this time we'd flown another bass player out from England. We had another guitarist, actually. We had Paul Rudolph from the Pink Fairies and he wasn't a bass player either. He was a guitarist. But we knew he could play bass, and we asked him to come and play with us, and Lemmy was sort of sent back to Britain. I mean, it was all very sad, and Lemmy sort of held it against me, because I was the one who told him. Although now having explained it to him, it's not something he still really holds against me. But it was all a bit of a problem, even though he did make it through the border."

Notes Hawkwind expert Rob Godwin, "Apparently they flew Paul Rudolph in from England because he was Canadian, and he could actually get into Canada without a work permit at the last minute. As for Lemmy's bust, I've heard two stories on why he was let go. One was that he was released because they charged him with possession of the wrong thing, and under Canadian law you can't charge somebody twice with the same crime. The other story was that they released him because amphetamine was considered a foodstuff in Canada and was not illegal."

To clarify, the band had played Detroit on a Saturday and traveled separately, stranding a temporarily lost Lemmy on the Sunday, as Nik explains, with most of the guys arriving in Toronto on that day. Lemmy, having had to hitchhike on the U.S. side and then having been flown from Windsor, Ontario, shows up on the Monday and the gig that night at Massey Hall is to be his last with Hawkwind. It is decided on Tuesday that Lemmy be sent home, and Paul Rudolph's first gig with the band turns out to be Cleveland the following Friday, with an interim gig in Dayton, Ohio, having been canceled.

Further explaining the firing, Nik says, "Because we didn't know where he was, and because we were told he'd been busted for hard drugs, it was very inconvenient. We didn't know how long he was going to be in custody. We just had to make other arrangements, basically. So I think he played one gig and then we dispensed with him. And I mean, he was still on bail for supposed possession of hard drugs. It was all too complicated, really. It's not the sort of thing you want in the band. All you want to do is get to the next gig and play. You're on a tour, you're committed, and you don't really need those sorts of complications. You just want to get on with it and not deal with the side issues of people's personal problems within the band."

"The story as it goes is that he was using different drugs to the rest of them," says Godwin. "They were mostly into hallucinogenics—LSD and stuff like that—and pot, and he was taking speed. Him and Dik Mik, who was ostensibly the synthesizer player, they were speed freaks, and the problem—I don't think was a personality clash as much as it was a case of that the speed guys would stay up for 24 hours and sleep for 24 hours, and frequently Lemmy would be late or barely show up to get in the bus or get on the truck or show up on stage. And the bust at the border was the straw that broke the camel's back. If you look at the interviews he gave, he's said he'd still be in the band if they hadn't fired him. He loved being in that band. Dave loved playing with him. And that period of Hawkwind, if you actually listen to what they were playing when he was in the band, which is from January '72 to May '75, it's the stuff that particularly stands out."

"He was not at all in the limelight," answers Rob, when asked what Lemmy's stage presence was like during his run with Hawkwind. "He was quite content to stand in the shadows as the rest of them were. They all stood in the shadows. In '72, when I saw them, the house lights went down and all you can see onstage was red lights on the amps. And then Nik Turner walks out and starts throwing joss sticks into the audience—lit. You can imagine the fire marshal letting them do that now. And you cannot see the band at all. And then they start playing and the psychedelic lights and smoke take over and you never saw them. If you look at photos from that period, you will see that Lemmy is standing in the back lineup, along with Dave, and the only people who step forward to the microphone were Nik and Bob Calvert, when they were alternating doing narrations. And then Dave would step up to sing. But Lemmy was always singing backing vocals for the most part. And he'd stand in the back, right in front of his amps stacked up, virtually further back than the drummer—Simon King was further forward than Lemmy was. And Dave too."

"So Dave and Lemmy more or less stood side by side, back, almost behind the drummer," continues Godwin. "And both of them said over the years that they had this telepathic sort of empathy when they were playing together. And Lemmy, right up to just before he died, said he'd never had that before or since with anybody else. Him and Dave were totally lockstep. You only have to listen to *Space Ritual* to hear it. It's a live album, and you're going, fucking hell, how are these guys doing this?!"

Cleaved from his space-rock soul brother, Lemmy managed to wrestle home from Canada three bass guitars and a suitcase on the plane. Licking his wounds in England, he would have to plot his next move, forever saddened by the loss of his Hawkwind family. His first plan of action back in London would be to abscond with what was on the band premises of his leftover Hawkwind gear and promptly paint it all black.

CHAPTER 2

"A bullet belt in one hand and a leather jacket in the other."

And so Lemmy is fired for the last time, deposited back in London, his ideas for rock 'n' roll nastiness suddenly potent and palpable now that he is forced into being his own boss. He would soon create a blast of a band, first under the name Bastard—"Our manager pointed out that we would have a hard time getting on TV with that name; I have to agree with him, you know"—and then, more prudently, Motörhead, named for his old song, named for being a speeder, up all night, up all day, up the next night too. Says Lem, "The name comes from the last song I ever wrote for Hawkwind. I thought it just sounded like a good name. When you name a band, it is really tedious. We just thought Motörhead sounded good and I think it worked out for us. We were very lucky to get that great logo."

Summarizing the series of events so far, Rob Godwin says, "So, '75 comes along, and Hawkwind have put out a single: 'Motörhead,' with Lemmy singing. The song ended up as the B-side of the single 'Kings of Speed,' to promote *Warrior on the Edge of Time*. But they had also recorded a version in the studio with Dave Brock singing it, a little bit earlier. They had recorded a version with just the power trio: Lemmy, Dave and Simon King, with Dave singing it first. Incidentally, the roots of the song 'Motörhead' go deeper than that. Right after they did *Doremi Fasol Latido*, Bob Calvert, who was Hawkwind's vocalist and narrator, did a solo album called *Captain Lockheed and the Starfighters* [1974] and Lemmy is on that. This is something that every Lemmy fan should go listen to. Calvert was not famous enough to be able to pull in lots of big names, so he does a solo album, and he essentially brought in Hawkwind as a backing band. And the first track on that is called 'The Aerospaceage Inferno,' and if you listen to the bass on that, it's the song 'Motörhead.' And this is two years before he supposedly wrote the song 'Motörhead.'

"And the roots of Motörhead are in the *Space Ritual* album as well, which is also 1973," adds Rob. "Lemmy joins in January '72, and he plays on *Greasy Truckers Party* [an album by various artists], which is where the recording of 'Silver Machine' comes from, and is released in the spring and goes up to like No. 2 or No. 3. That is when I first saw them; I saw them in August 1972. And immediately after that, the first studio album that Lemmy did with them was *Doremi*. And then the tour for that is what produced the *Space Ritual* album. And if you listen to those two records, particularly *Space Ritual*, which is the one everybody raves about, you know, it's a power trio. It's Dave, Lemmy and Simon King. I mean, it's like a power trio with special effects. Somebody once said it's as though Hendrix, Black Sabbath and Pink Floyd had an orgy on the bridge of the Starship Enterprise, which I kind of liked. In *Star Trek*, all those sort of weird sound effects that they used to have going on the bridge, I've actually seen bloopers where none of that is on there and it's dead flat. It's only when they edit in all those sound effects that it actually comes to life. I always thought of Hawkwind as being like that, when Lemmy was in the band particularly. It was like this kick-ass power trio—with a bunch of sound effects.

"Anyway, Hawkwind put out the album, and Lemmy gets fired at the end of the North American tour. Hawkwind goes back to England and headlines Reading Festival in August, and the album was doing really well at that point—and Lemmy is out on the skids. I was at Reading, and I remember being really disappointed that he wasn't there. Although, I think Paul Rudolph was a really good bass player and guitar player and did a good job. But it was just the fact that Lemmy wasn't there that was very sad. But what Doug Smith—who was Hawkwind's manager and soon to be Motörhead's manager—told me is that when they got back, Lemmy was really, really upset. And by all accounts he actually cried when he was told he was out of the band. Doug said, 'Lemmy came to me and said, "What are we going to do?"' And Doug said, 'Well, I'll sort something out.' And the next thing Lemmy is told is, 'You've got a gig this weekend.' Lemmy was like, 'What the fuck are you talking about? I don't have a band.' And he said, 'Well, put a band together, because you've got a gig.' So he made some phone calls and found Larry Wallis and Lucas Fox. Larry Wallis was another Pink Fairies guy. Larry Wallis was a Pink Fairies guy, and Paul Rudolph, who had replaced [Lemmy] in Hawkwind, was a Pink Fairies guy, and quite often Pink Fairies and Hawkwind used to play a lot of songs together. They were called Pinkwind. Not long after that, they would play opening shows for Hawkwind, as Doug would double bill them together."

✷

"Lemmy and I were involved from 1970 through to, I think, 1989," recalls Doug Smith, who was the manager of Hawkwind and Motörhead and would later have great success with Chumbawumba. "And of course he came through Hawkwind and into Motörhead, having been dispersed on the Canadian border for something that, quite honestly, I won't even get into at this point, but it was a very manipulative situation that took place. And for a period of about six months after his sacking, which quite honestly shouldn't have happened, he sort of tried to put Motörhead together, although there wasn't really a name of the band. He had my support, and obviously financial support, to try to form a band. And he went through the likes of Lucas Fox, Larry Wallis, and I think even Luther Grosvenor [of Mott the Hoople] for a short while was being considered, if the thing was going to become a four-piece. And he sort of settled on those three: Larry, Lucas and Lemmy."

"Went over to Chelsea," recalls Larry Wallis of that first meeting, speaking with *Forced Exposure* magazine, "went in there, plugged into an amplifier, said, 'One, two, three, go!' and the three of us made the most horrible racket you've ever heard. We did that for 15 minutes. When we were finished, we all said, 'Great! Aren't we wonderful? Let's all be in a band.' Then Lemmy put out a big line of white stuff and said, 'Do you want some of that?' I asked the dreaded question, 'What is it?' He said, 'Amphetamine sulphate.' I stayed awake for the next three years. I didn't even blink for three years."

Larry Wallis, ex–Pink Fairies, not looking the part at this early Motörhead gig at Barbarella's on Cumberland Street in Birmingham, August 12, 1975. | © Paul Apperly

But as Doug explains, Motörhead didn't happen as quickly as lore would have it. "No, not at all. What basically happened was Lemmy went into a major depression after that. Because as far as he was concerned, he just wanted to rejoin Hawkwind. He didn't think that Blackie [Paul Rudolph], who was the replacement bass player, would last the tenure, and sooner or later Dave Brock would give in. It was just Dave, really, that manipulated the situation. And, you know, Lemmy could be a complete pain in the ass sometimes, as far as being reliable. And I think that his two days of disappearance prior to the crossing of the Canadian border had a lot to do with the band finally just getting rid of him. And it hadn't been the first time. It'd probably been about the 50th time. I'm exaggerating; it must've been at least the 10th time, there's no doubt about it.

"So he was happy to hang out for that initial period, in the hope that the band would change its mind and he would rejoin and life would carry on. Because in actual fact, at that particular point, Hawkwind was very successful. That's where he wanted to be. And starting a new career and a new life for himself was going to be hard. What basically happened then was that we suggested to him that he should try to put an act together. And it became a rather long-winded situation, because he was in a rehearsal studio, and, you know, he wanted to rejoin Hawkwind. So he took his time. They took a while before they played their first date."

Lemmy, Larry and Lucas played their first gig ever at the Roundhouse in London,

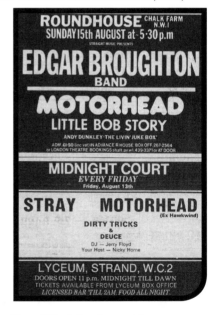

Note the lack of umlauts and the ex-Hawkwind designation. Little Bob Story was France's semi-famous answer to the U.K. pub rock sensation. Edgar Broughton Band was closely aligned with Hawkwind in the freak community.

opening for Greenslade, on July 20, 1975, taking the stage to a recording of a Hitler speech and the sound of marching soldiers— quite the effect. The set list was a loveably lazy one that could only be played by a band that barely existed at this juncture. Covers all, the most cover-y were "Leaving Here," "Good Morning Little Schoolgirl" and "I'm Waiting for the Man"—the first two demonstrative of Lemmy's pride in old rock 'n' roll schooling, the latter apropos of nothing. But the balance pointed the crooked finger way for Lemmy's concept. There was Hawkwind classic "Silver Machine" and from Larry's old band, Pink Fairies, "City Kids," the opening track from that band's final album, 1973's *Kings of Oblivion*. Codifying and underscoring Lemmy's unsteady idea were his couple of penned and co-penned Hawkwind signatures "Lost Johnny" and "Motörhead," the latter used as opener and soon to become the band's "Black Sabbath" and "Iron Maiden."

Wrote Geoff Barton in his review of the gig for *Sounds*, surely the band's first notice, "Given the short amount of time M'head have had to rehearse and forgetting (if at all possible) about the utterly disastrous version of 'Silver Machine' that they played, it was a promising showing. If the band can tighten up (both musically and physically) then there'll be little to touch them in the bulldozer music league and numbers like 'Lost Johnny' and 'City Kids' could well develop into show-stoppers. 'This will be the dirtiest band in the world,' announced Lemmy, upon forming this new band. At the moment Motörhead are just slightly grubby, but they're well on their way."

Added Nick Kent in the *NME*, addressing a gig weeks later when Motörhead opened for Blue Öyster Cult, "The fact that Lemmy's consortium raging through the likes of 'Bye Bye Johnny' and 'I'm Waiting for the Man' ultimately comes on like nothing so much as Budgie on methedrine can't exactly gladden the soul of the more discerning metal aficionado. Forced exile camping it up at the Roundhouse should keep them from harm until such time as they see their way to approaching their craft with something other than all the panache of a butcher stripping meat from an overripe carcass."

"The early audiences were 'amused'—all these blank people standing with their mouths hanging open," scoffed Lemmy, speaking with Chuck Eddy. "People call us heavy metal because we have long hair. If we had short hair, they would've called us punk. We're a *rock* band. I *am* rock 'n' roll. I've seen the whole thing. I remember Elvis's first record. I think we have more in common with the Band. When we first started, we were playing 'Good Morning Little Schoolgirl' and all these Yardbirds-style songs. I wanted to be the MC5. We 'bend' like dance music. Except it's too fast to dance to."

Doug remembers one of the band's earliest dates at the Greyhound club in Croydon. In fact, he is adamant that this "semi" gig took place on July 17, 1975, making this, in fact, Motörhead's first show, not the commonly referred to July 20 show at the Roundhouse—well, sort of. "It was quite a large club, in actual fact, a ballroom above a pub," relates Smith. "The poster for the show read 'Lemmy's Motörhead.' Everybody assumed there would be a lot of people; in fact, it was probably about 65, 75 percent filled. Halfway or 20 minutes into the gig, Lemmy stopped playing and said he couldn't play anymore, and went off. His fingers stopped working basically. He said they froze. And so I had to actually stand at the

Lucas Fox, sporting a bit of a rocker/Teddy Boy look and an odd tom-tom configuration, 1975.
| © Paul Apperly

Exploitative release On Parole *was further delegitimized by being made part of a series of records with similar graphics under* The Rock File *banner.*

venue entrance and hand back the ticket money to all the punters who'd come in. The promoter, Steve Mason, made me do it. And strangely enough, Steve ended up being the managing director of Windsong, one of the largest independent music distribution companies in the U.K. But the Greyhound was a very important venue, and they didn't want their reputation damaged, so they made me pay the ticket money back to the punters."

This first incarnation of Motörhead signed to United Artists, as Lemmy was still contractually bound to Hawkwind's longtime label: Lemmy, as mentioned, using drummer Lucas Fox and guitarist Larry Wallis to make his vision real. A dodgy, uneven album was recorded in 1975, which the label didn't enjoy, preferring not to release it, that is, until the band had moved on to Bronze Records and become famous. *On Parole* would be issued in 1980, and it's obvious why the label passed the first time—the sessions revealed a wobbly band unsure of where they were going.

Recalls Smith on the aborted record with United Artists, "You have to remember this is all going on through the lens of four,

four and a half sackings by the band, because every time Lemmy ran out of money, I'd get sacked. Anyway, we'd reached a point where my partner Richard Ogden and myself formed Western Productions, to put Motörhead's albums out through United Artists. And we had been able to get a substantial advance for him to record and work with Dave Edmunds. Lemmy wanted to work with Dave Edmunds because Dave Edmunds was Lemmy's favorite, favorite artist. So Dave Edmunds went down to Rockfield, and they started the production, and eventually they spent all the money. So United Artists went, 'We're not giving them any more money until we get some tracks.' So when I told Lemmy that, he sacked me. And he said, oh, I'll get a manager who'll give us some money. So then they had a guy called English Frank, who became very well known in Los Angeles for his free newspaper. His brother had a small photographic business, and he, I think, banked off his dad and put his money into Motörhead."

"And then I helped him on tours and so on, because Frank wasn't that knowledgeable about touring. So I made sure they always did tours. I always remember, they'd hand the accounts in—because Frank didn't do the accounts; we did them for him—and there would be something called plumbing in the accounts. And I'll leave that to your imagination, okay? And so eventually Frank and they parted company and they came back and asked us for more help."

"And then there was a Belgian promoter who wanted to be in the music business. And in fact, he was running away from National Service in Belgium, and hanging out in England. He was a promoter in Belgium; that's how I met him. So I rented one of my floors in my office to him and nothing happened, and Motörhead suddenly reappeared and said they wanted some help, and I said, 'Well you know, there's Ludo downstairs who's got some money; why don't you go and talk to him. Maybe he can help?' I got pissed off. I'd been sacked a couple of times and didn't really need it again. So they went downstairs, they did a bit of a short time with Ludo. And that didn't go anywhere, and back upstairs they came."

"But with respect to the actual record, it fell apart with Dave Edmunds's production and their complete abuse of whatever substances they were taking at the time. And what happened from that would be the sort of bolting-on of Eddie and Phil, one after another. Because one knew the other and needed a lift down to the studio to get Lemmy out of the shit, the other joined. It was a very organic moment, to the point of becoming what I consider, and always will consider, the original Motörhead."

Nonetheless, the roots of Motörhead are there within the *On Parole* album. But the band's ragtag first lineup was to implode, in a sense, like Altamont, with the outlaw spirit trouncing and denouncing the values of the hippie generation for something more cynical and biting. Ironically, the shedding of Lucas Fox in particular would evoke reverberations of Lemmy's bouncing out of Hawkwind: in that band, Lemmy's speed-taking was out of sync with what Lemmy called the "drug snobbery" of the other guys with their organic drugs. In Motörhead, Lucas tried to keep up with Lemmy on the ol' amphetamines with embarrassing results; he was trying to take the right drugs but he couldn't. And so Lemmy, now running Larry, Lucas and even himself around the bend, would have to take his sour worldview elsewhere and with new bodies along for the wild ride.

Doug Smith sheds further light on the exits of both Lucas and Larry from the ranks. "I think Lucas left himself. Larry on the other hand, I don't know, Larry had a lot of issues anyway. He had a marriage that was going strangely wrong, and in actual fact, the girl that he was married to, she became Sire Records' Seymour Stein's personal assistant, until she died of cancer about 15 years ago. I mean, it's a bizarre story of connections. So I think Larry was the first to leave—he had had enough. And I suppose he just wanted a band that was already successful. And Lucas, well, he didn't really have a background of anything. He hadn't played, really, majorly for anything. He was just Lemmy's and Larry's friend. And now Lucas is a rather successful entertainment organizer, which is quite surprising. He used to work at Midem on a regular basis, although I don't think he does anymore."

''

Phil Taylor first met Lemmy in a pub on Portobello Road. The relationship developed, says Lemmy, when Phil came 'round the house to buy some drugs and wound up arrested after OD'ing on Tuinal. Later, with Phil convincing Lemmy that he played the drums, the partnership was solidified when Phil also said he had a car—crucial because Lemmy didn't own one, nor did he drive— which came in handy at that very moment because now it was Lemmy that was trying to buy some drugs, and he was in need of chauffeuring, which would become a theme throughout his life. Phil Taylor rose to the challenge of replacing Fox's drums on *On Parole*, an admirable feat in Lemmy's estimation, although Lem was less impressed with Phil's horrid attempts at singing "City Kids." Phil came in partway through and performed this exacting task on all tracks but "Lost Johnny," which retains Fox's parts (Phil was otherwise predisposed, briefly in custody for drunk and disorderly). Ergo, Lucas holds the distinction of being Motörhead's drummer for roughly the first six months of the band's existence, after which he moved on to punk act Warsaw Pakt, in business about London for one year and one record.

"Why did I take up the drums?" reflects Taylor, in conversation with Sam Dunn. "It was less of an inspiration than a command by my dad, because I was getting in trouble with the law, being like a skinhead. I was fighting at that rebellious age, so my dad had to come and get me at the Leeds police station one too many times, and gave me a good hiding. And about a couple days later, he turned up with a battered old snare drum and said, 'Here, here you bastard, and if you've got to hit something, you can hit this.'

And he booked me like two whole weeks of lessons, one a week, at Leeds Music College, and so I dutifully went along, being really pissed-off, because I always banged on my mom's pots and pans when I was a kid. So I went along, and the teacher that I had was an incredible guy—that's another story. But he was 90 years old, and he was a World War I drummer, and after the second lesson he said, 'Well, Philip, I think you've got a natural talent for playing the drums. You should really take more lessons.' And I thought all right. And so I decided to go to him. So really it was my dad that got me into it. But I thought, yeah, I've got him to thank. But not, in a way, because it wasn't done out of love or anything like that. But I realized I had a natural aptitude for the drums and I enjoyed playing them.

Recent hire Phil Taylor circa 1976.
| © Paul Apperly

"Angst—that's a good word, yeah?" continues Taylor. "I guess there was lots of angst, because that's how I started to play the drums. Because I was getting into too many fights. I was getting to be really violent, so that's why I started playing the drums. I mean, that was another great thing that my drum teacher taught. Because at the time, I wanted to be a boxer more than I wanted to be a drummer. And I was training at a gym, and in my first fight, I got knocked out and I had two black eyes. And I went to the drum lesson, and my drum teacher said to me, 'Bloody 'ell, look at the state of your face! You know what, Philip? Do yourself a favor. Stick to playing drums. It's better than boxing.' 'Why's that?' 'Drums don't hit you back, lad. You can hit them as hard as you like, and they don't hit you back.' And suddenly a light bulb went on. Oh yeah. That's just a little side thing, but I suppose great angst was involved. Mucho angst. And yes, a great deal of ardent fervour. And lots of angriness within me. I felt this strange desire to grab myself and rip myself into small tiny pieces, or any small animals that crossed my path."

And so it wasn't a sort of predictable pop or even fully musical inspiration that guided Phil to his future as a musician, versus the somewhat predictable rock 'n' roll influences impressed upon say Lemmy or Eddie. If Lemmy was his own force of nature, a beacon to independence, making music nothing like that of his influences, and Eddie was much the same, Phil Taylor was your virtual tabula rasa, arriving at a similar place with very few influences whatsoever.

"I've never been like a fan of any particular one person, whether they be a drummer or movie star or anything like that. But I've always listened to music as a whole, the whole song. And if there happened to be a fine drummer in the band, it usually stood out. But maybe not. Some of the best drumming I used to like was the Motown stuff, from the '60s, late '60s, '70s, and there was a session drummer called Bernard Purdie, who played on, I believe, a lot of those sessions, and he was really great. That's where I picked up the high-hat thing from. Oh yeah, ol' Bernard was the master of the 'bad-atz, bad-atz'; there are a couple of those, and a couple of those, holding high hats. I learned that from Bernard Purdie. That was great, because he's very good, with good punctuation marks. And some people say it doesn't really fit in metal, but I think it does. Or doesn't fit in rock. It fits in my cupboard at home, I know that. Very nicely."

"But yeah, I listened to a lot of drummers, really. I mean, my dad was a big jazz fan, and so what jazz records he had, I listened to, not out of choice, but I played them. But since I started taking up the drums, and just a snare drum for about a year or 18 months, and then he bought me a bass drum and stuff like that, and so I listened to my dad's old jazz records. And my sister was five years older than me and she was listening to the Beatles and stuff from America, so I listened to her records. So I was getting an extra. Nothing off the radio, of course. There was nothing on English radio, unless you listened to Radio Caroline or Radio Luxembourg, which I did occasionally, upon pain of death from my dad. 'Turn that bloody radio off!' 'Yes Dad.'"

Pressed by Sam about the influence of those jazz records, Phil agrees that, "Guess it must've done, really, subconsciously. I can't see how it didn't. There was a guy that my dad really liked called Lionel Hampton who played xylophone and drums, and I remember he had a record of his drum solo, and I was listening back to it many, many years later, and I wasn't that impressed by it. But I was impressed at the time. And he had the Gene Krupa big band record, and actually, when I first thought to myself, 'Well, I'd really like to do that,' it was one Sunday afternoon when I was watching a movie on British television, an old black-and-white, *The Gene Krupa Story*, Sal Mineo as Gene Krupa. It was really good, because I think actually Sal played drums, because he was really good, and so after seeing that, I never thought that a drummer would be like a big fuss like that, like a big star. But I thought oh, like a lot of things, I thought they can only be like that in America. But I really enjoyed that movie, and that made me want to be a drummer. I just wanted to be the best drummer that I could be. But I never thought I would be."

As for Gene Krupa, "I think it was the intensity of his drumming, like when he played drums, that was the whole thing. I know that a lot of the movie was based on his life, and he was a heroin addict, but I didn't understand any of that at the time. I just liked the fact that he was a great drummer. I just really liked the feel of the movie. It was the first movie I've ever seen where the drummer was the hero, so to speak. Not that I hadn't seen any other movies, apart from the Glenn Miller story, great, playing a purple clarinet. But what movies were there around then, what, when I was 14? That would be 1968, a long time ago. The only other heroes I had were like gunfighters I suppose, John Wayne, 'Get on your horse and drink your milk, pilgrim,' all that shit. After seeing that, yeah, he was quite a hero. He was to me, anyway."

So to recap, for Phil, drumming was a punishment enforced by his dad, and then made glamourous through drummers being depicted in film . . . like John Wayne. And where might we see the link to pop music, let alone rock, let alone nasty, brutish heavy metal?

"Well, I can say, I would say, you would call it inspired, but at the time I couldn't afford to buy my own records, and I was just getting into playing the drums. And I didn't really know anything about music, because I hadn't been a music fan at all, until I was forced into playing these drums. And my drum teacher, the old guy I told you about, he was a total military man, and being a First World War drummer boy, he didn't want to—'I hope you're not listening to that bloody rock music that they play. It's all rubbish. Stick to your military beats.' So that's all I did. The only reason I listened to jazz is because that's what my dad listened to at home, and as I said, on the radio, there wasn't much . . . there was a lot of pop, but the stuff they played on the radio back then certainly wasn't inspiring to a drummer anyway, or to a guitar player, I don't think, for that matter. It was all like Radio One. It would be the Top 20 hits, the Beatles, blah blah blah. That was easy, as far as I was concerned."

"I mean, I liked all the stuff that the Beatles did, and actually at the time, I went out and bought a Chicago album, because they had a hit, '25 or 6 to 4.' Do you remember that song? No, you probably don't. Good song. So I went out and spent all my hard-earned money on this album—it was fucking shit. The whole album was fucking shit. Back then the price of an album was about a week's pocket money, so I just used to listen to my sister's records. And I never really thought of becoming a drummer professionally, not at all, not for one instant. I mean, I didn't even let any of my friends know that I played drums for about two and a half years or three years that I was playing. Because I didn't want anybody saying, 'Well, come on,' because I knew my friends at school had little bands going. Anyway, blah blah."

,,

Soon to be Lemmy's new best mate, Fast Eddie Clarke picks up the story of the great meeting of grind minds. "I knew Lemmy a little bit before. He's one of those characters you would bump into every now and again, because he was always everywhere. He didn't sleep at all and he was always around. I was doing my solo project after I had left Curtis Knight, and then I did this thing called Blue Goose, which was on this label called Anchor Records, and finally, nothing came of that either. And to make a living, I started to do some regular work; I was a laborer on a building site sort of thing, and that's where I met Phil Taylor. Phil was working alongside me, so we got chatting, one thing and another, and after about two months, we parted. I didn't see him much. We had a little jam once, and then he disappeared. As Phil does."

"And then I got a phone call," continues Eddie, "out of the blue, and he said, 'Hey man, I'm in Motörhead now and we're looking for another guitarist.' And because the then-guitarist, Larry Wallis, had done so many overdubs in the studio, they felt they needed a rhythm player. Someone to sort of fill in all the gaps. So Phil said I would be a good choice."

In fact it was Phil who would give Clarke the name Fast Eddie, as Eddie told *Classic Rock Revisited*: "Yes, later we were playing a gig at the Electric Ballroom in Manchester and much to my surprise Lemmy introduced Philthy Animal, and I guess for something to say, Phil introduced me as Fast Eddie. I was not too keen at first, but from then on it stuck like glue. I think it made life easier for Lem when he introduced the band."

The first session took place at the Furniture Cave, which Eddie describes to Jeb Wright in 2014 as "a rehearsal room in New Kings

Road, Chelsea, that I first used with Curtis Knight. In fact, we rehearsed down there a lot. It was in the basement of a big warehouse-type building and had three rooms, small, medium and medium. I also used it for odd jam sessions using my wages from the boat, and yes, my first session with Lemmy and Phil was down there in the small room. I am surprised we are not all deaf; it was the sort of place we could not do without."

"But I was the only one who had any money—funny, really—so after that session, I said, 'Book the rehearsal room,' and I'd go pick Phil and Lemmy up in my old Mercedes. So I set up a rehearsal for my audition—that's the way it was with Motörhead. Phil had taken me over to meet Larry a couple of weeks before so I thought it would be fine. Lemmy, Phil and I started jamming about 3 p.m. but Larry had not showed up. Lemmy called every half hour and Larry kept saying he was on his way. The three of us were having a really good time playing together but at 6:30 the room was booked out to someone else. Fortunately, there was another rehearsal place upstairs, so we moved up there and Larry promised he was on his way. Around 7:30 p.m. Larry showed up. He had a roadie who set up his Fender Twin amp. I only had an AC30 so I couldn't hear shit. He said hardly anything to anyone, plugged in and started playing a tune off their album, which I fortunately had learned."

"The vibe in the room was awful and it got worse but, no lie, we must have played the same song for 30 minutes. Lemmy was getting pissed. Lemmy suggested we do something else and the same thing happened. I am thinking, 'I haven't got this job.' Lemmy then took Larry outside and they were gone awhile. I packed up my stuff. Phil was totally bemused by all this, so we talked about other things. When Larry and Lem returned, I said my farewells, paid for the rehearsal room on my way out and that was that. I am thinking, 'That didn't go very well.'

"They obviously weren't getting on," continues Eddie, "and I felt a little bit in the way. But we had been jamming for three or four hours and we had actually made quite a bit of headway, the three of us. So I left them to it and I went home. I had no idea what was happening. I heard nothing over the next few days. Phil and Lemmy didn't have phones, so I figured no gig. And then 8 o'clock on a Saturday morning, three days later, there's this banging on my door, and I drag myself out of bed in my underpants, open the door, and there's Lemmy. He had been up all night, because of the speed and everything. He knocked on my door at eight in the morning, and I said, 'Who the fuckin' 'ell is this?!' And there's Lemmy standing there. He's got a bullet belt in one hand and a leather jacket in the other, and he hands them to me and says, 'You've got the gig' and then he turned around and off he went. I didn't know what to think but I was over the moon. It's always nice to be wanted. Fucking brilliant, eh? How fucking great, man? Only Lemmy can pull one of those out."

Lemmy's now combat-ready new guitarist Edward Allan Clarke was five years Lemmy's junior, born in London, and had not got serious about guitar until he was 15. Having moved on from early band the Bitter End, Clarke indeed wrote and recorded with Curtis Knight and his band Zeus, on *The Second Coming* (1974) and *Sea of Time* (1974), the latter experience leading to the deal for the Knight side-band, Blue Goose, which issued an album in 1974, sans Eddie.

"I had already left Curtis and gone to Blue Goose," explained Eddie, filling in the backstory with Jeb Wright. "It was a loose arrangement. Nick and Chris then wanted to come to Blue Goose and it was them who were threatened by Curtis. After Blue Goose, who I never recorded with, I was jamming with Charlie Tumahai from Be-Bop Deluxe. He was a Maori from New Zealand and a great guy and bass player. We had an Aussie called Jim on drums and the singer was an American girl called Annie. I nearly secured a deal with Anchor Records but they said they were not sure about the girl singer. Charlie had an offer from Be-Bop Deluxe, which he could not turn down, and things just dissolved sadly. I do have a few old recordings somewhere.

"In my early 20s, I had kind of stopped playing. I used to jam with people and that was about it. Like I say, I had some trouble with the law and that is when people told me that I needed to get serious about music and change things around. Up until Curtis Knight, I was not that serious about music. Once I got in that band, I started to take things more serious. When I got out of Curtis Knight I did the thing that was on Anchor Records but I never finished it, as I fell out with the guys.

"That was when I did the solo thing and, at the same time, I was working on a houseboat; I was building it."

Going nowhere fast, Eddie nonetheless told Wright, "I had not given up on the music biz. I was working on the boat to raise money to pay for my solo project called *Continuous Performance*. I had already laid down the four tracks for the album, and once again, I found myself singing. The money I was making on that boat is what I was using to make my solo album but, once again, I couldn't find a singer, so I sang it myself. I am not a singer so it never went any further. I met Phil Taylor because he came and applied for a job on the houseboat. He needed a job and I gave him one on the boat where I was, by then, a foreman. This was a long project and I was the only one still standing. The boat is still there today on the River Thames in Chelsea. I pass it quite often and always have a brief reminisce. Phil was crazy, but a really good guy and we got along. Fate? I definitely think so!"

Phil recalls about how Eddie looked the mellow hippie with the long hair, but really cracked the whip, not too much of a problem, really, because Taylor got a lot of work done, arriving in the morning still speeding from the night before and maybe the night before that. A Scottish friend had told Phil that his foreman boss was also a guitarist and the stage was set.

An odd way to look at it, but in essence, Eddie found himself in Motörhead because of the *On Parole* record. "Yes, that's right, because it had all come about because the original band had made an album—I wasn't in the band then—with Larry Wallis. He had done so many overdubs in the studio, he felt that he couldn't do it live. So that's when they started—he told Phil that he would like to try a second guitarist to help out. So that's where Phil made that original contact with me, to become Larry Wallis's second guitar player. But obviously, like I said, when the rehearsals happened, Larry had already left Motörhead in his head, you know? I don't even know why he had come to rehearsal, really. I mean, that was the last time he ever played with Lemmy. He already had enough of it, for various reasons. He got me in the band so he could exit the band. I mean, Motörhead is not an easy band to be in. It's not like a piece of cake; it was very difficult. Lemmy was difficult, and the three of us, it could be intense. What can I say? It was intense."

With Fast Eddie, Lemmy had found in a partner another out-sider, another misfit, and something of an enigma, given his tradi-tional rock upbringing contrasted against the abrasive, incendiary music he was about to craft, clang and kerrang.

"My first hero was Eric Clapton with the Yardbirds," Eddie told *Classic Rock Revisited* about his staid rock roots. "They used to play down the road so I was able to see them regularly. *Five Live Yardbirds* was like my bible and I played the whole album with my

first band, the Bitter End, mostly in my dad's garage. Then, Eric went with John Mayall, and I played all of that album with my next band, Umble Blues. Then, along came Hendrix, the Cream and Jeff Beck's *Truth*, and that was kind of the foundation of my music. I always thought of myself as third-generation blues, as I followed the above. They, of course, followed the original American blues players. I guess these were the influences that helped shape a lot of my life experience. My roots are definitely in the blues, but, as I said, I am third-generation. I think that's why Lemmy and I got on so well when we were writing. We both had similar musical roots. We wrote some great songs together and there are definitely some of our early influences in there."

As for Lemmy's claim to fame, Hawkwind, Eddie figures, "I was never a big Hawkwind fan because they didn't have a lead guitar player. I think that kept me away from them. When I would listen to them I would wonder where the lead guitar was. Meeting Lemmy for the first time, I was surprised how friendly he was and keen to have the rehearsal for my audition. I have to say I liked him from the start and was looking forward to a jam together. Having been with Hawkwind, he had toured the States and had all that experience to pass on to Phil and myself. I always thought of him as a big brother."

And so the improbable trio that would become the classic Motörhead lineup was born. We have the "big brother" outlaw and the somewhat dispirited outsider on bass and guitar, respectively. They are, in Eddie's estimation, one rock 'n' roll generation apart. But also by Eddie's math, so is the band's drummer, Phil Taylor, one generation fresher than the two plyers of stringed instruments within Motörhead. Phil Taylor was born in September 1954, injecting roughly five years of youth atop Eddie, and 10 years to the biggest brother in the band, Lemmy.

CHAPTER 3

Motörhead: "Like a fucking train going through your head."

Gigging, poverty, more poverty, and then some more gigging eventually led Lemmy, Eddie and Phil to an attempt at a single for seat-of-the-pants Stiff Records. The single indeed got recorded, the band strumming up "White Line Fever" backed with "City Kids" in December '76, roughly a year after their first gig together, when they blew headliners Blue Öyster Cult off the stage. But the record had to be withdrawn before it ever saw the light of day, when United Artists, who wouldn't release their own sessions with the band, screamed breach of contract. Soon Motörhead found themselves legally able to sign themselves over to Chiswick, but again, comically, only for a single.

"Yeah, I went to shows," recalls BÖC manager Sandy Pearlman. "I saw [Motörhead], not at the Roundhouse, but opening for Blue Öyster Cult, the first show that the three of them did together, for better or worse. They had opened for Blue Öyster Cult at the . . . I think we did five days or something at the Hammersmith;

that's when I first saw Motörhead, and two years later they were a really big band. It was interesting. I was on a panel with Lemmy a few years back. I was like, 'Lemmy, I saw you guys open for Blue Öyster Cult on all those shows,' and then I think I saw them at some big outdoor show in France, and then I saw them next again in France, with Shakin' Street opening for them. And I said, 'It had become so loud by this time that you and Blue Cheer share the distinction of bands that were best enjoyed from outside of the hall.' He liked that! That was cool! And I guess it *was* cool. It was really true. Even for me, it was like OTT. And I have abnormal tolerances for volume, so you can only imagine how loud this was. But they had some pretty good shows. You saw the opening act inside the hall and then you went outside and left the door open and listened to Motörhead if you could find a protective surface."

"We got offered opening for Blue Öyster Cult at Hammersmith Odeon," recalls Doug Smith, "and of course we took it. And the sound engineer, who went on to engineer Sutherland Brothers and Quiver, and then ended up being the managing director and chairman of one of the largest cabling companies in music, who cabled most of China's auditoriums, nowadays, anyway, he mixed the band. And every time Lemmy sort of leaned forward and put his ear out and looked at the audience and said, 'Can you hear us?' the audience was like, 'No,' and he shouted to him to turn it up. And it went so high that eventually it was painful. Motörhead probably did blow them off the stage, but they blew them off the stage with the sound, the volume. And that's where they got this reputation as the loudest band in the world. But they didn't do so well as far as the media were concerned. Because the next week, the headlines in *Sounds* or *NME* were in effect calling them the worst band in the world."

But soon after that, it was time to get serious, and not just seriously loud. "I can picture it in my head just now!" enthuses Fast Eddie, when asked about getting to record an album with

Motörhead, the next step in what was so far looking like a dire career ladder.

"Speedy Keen from Thunderclap Newman, he was a producer, and he was sort of a mate of mine. I'd met him in Ealing years ago, and we used to see each other occasionally and have a jam together and all that. And he was obviously quite successful and a lovely bloke. And I had this nice . . . well, it wasn't a nice flat, it was a squat sort of thing, around in West Kent. It wasn't a squat, but it was sort of a tumble-down shack, with very cheap rent. And people used to come around there and hang out, and it became quite a place. And Speedy would come and hang around, and I was talking to Speedy because we were going to break up at that gig, at the Marquee gig. Phil had kind of had enough. He said, 'Listen, we're not going anywhere,' and we had a few disappointments with Stiff Records with that single we had done, so there was disappointment.

"But there was nobody in the business like Motörhead," continues Eddie. "They were scared stiff of us, because we looked so

Lemmy and Phil, April 5, 1979, at the Empire Theatre in Liverpool.
| © Alan Perry / IconicPix

fucking angry. The Hells Angels and the bikers used to come to our shows. And of course, we just didn't stick with regular people too well, like promoters and the business. So we always felt that they were all dead against us, and we were fucking soldiering on against all that. But it was getting difficult. Phil was intimating that maybe we should knock it on its head, because it's not getting anywhere. And I said, well let's fucking . . . let's get the last gig at the Marquee recorded, and at least we'll have something, for history's sake, you know? This was a Friday night in April of 1977. I was really quite serious. So of course we didn't know anybody. We didn't have any fucking money so there was nothing we could do, and Lemmy had come in contact with Ted Carroll from Chiswick Records. I'd said, 'Why don't you give him a phone, and see if he'll be into bringing down a mobile and recording it?' So that's how that came about. And he said, 'We can't use the Marquee, because they want five hundred quid for you to record there.' And that's even before you start. Money was tight in the '70s. He said we couldn't pay that kind of money to record there.

"So at that point, [Carroll] said, 'Look, I'll pay for you to do a single.' So after the Marquee gig . . . Speedy had this big old Mercedes—it was fucking great, an old banger, but it was fantastic—we all jumped in that, and he drove us down to this studio in Kent that night, and we set up that night at about 2 a.m. and played all that night and all the next day, and just laid down all the tracks as we played them onstage, did the overdubs and all that.

"I had done an album with Curtis Knight in 24 hours. I told the guys this, and as we had been playing the tunes over and over, it made sense. So we started recording about 4 a.m. on Saturday and finished everything at about 6 a.m. Sunday morning. We crashed out and left Speedy and John [Burns], the engineer, to do the mixing and they had anything that was left to keep them awake."

"So come sort of Sunday, we were sleeping, we passed out sometime, I don't know, Saturday night or Sunday about 6 o'clock in the morning. And when we woke up, Speedy and Johnny were still mixing the track 'Motörhead,' and they were mixing it when we had left them. They were mixing it all night and they had 32 mixes of this fucking thing. A pile of boxes . . . because we were all fucking speeding, you know? And the only reason we fell asleep is because we just ran out of fucking . . . we just ran out. We'd had enough."

But when Eddie and the guys woke up and heard Speedy and Johnny working on "Motörhead," what they didn't know was that in the interim, the producers had mixed the rest of the album.

"And then of course Ted came down about 6 o'clock Sunday evening, and instead of saying we had a single, we said, proudly, 'Here Ted, we've actually made a little surprise for you. We've done an album.' And we played it for him and he fucking loved it. He was bowled over by this. Because he was a really genuine . . . he loved the music; he was into it. And the rest, really after that, was history. He wanted us to remix the 'Motörhead' track because it was going to be a single, but we went to Olympic to do that. So basically it was all done in those 36 hours."

Eddie told Jeb Wright of *Classic Rock Revisited*, "Once we had an album the whole landscape changed. We had hope again and there was interest from promoters thanks to Ted and our part-time managers Doug Smith and Frank Kennington. They had something to work with so it was game on."

"Doing the rest of the album was easy," says Clarke. "Just that they got stuck on 'Motörhead,' because it was going to be the flagship song. And because we were all out of our fucking tree— Speedy and John particularly—because they were sitting there engineering, they got right carried away. But that was our thing— drinking and speed. I didn't drink before I joined Motörhead, but after I started taking the speed, I needed something to calm me down a bit. Because before that I was a bit of a hippie; I used to smoke dope and stuff, so of course, I was quite laid-back. But once I started taking the speed, the fucking dope didn't work or nothing. And of course, it was one of those things that was cheap.

Speed was cheap, you know? And Special Brew, the beer we drank, was cheap. Because there was no money, we just had to get by on what we could. That changed later, but that's another story.

"So yeah, they were doing speed before I came along. Because I never used to drink. I was a dope man, you know, a hippie. A long-haired hippie. But I could fend for myself, that's what I did, but I would take a little bit now again, because when I was working, it used to help. But whenever I was with them, Phil and Lemmy, suddenly it was all the time, and then of course I had to start drinking, to calm me down a bit. And that's how my drinking started, because like I say, I didn't really drink before I joined Motörhead.

"Because I was a late starter, that's maybe why I couldn't handle the drink as well as they could, you know. It caused a few problems, but not too many. But it caused one or two. But no, it really was three people who were thrown together through weird circumstances. And the first time we played, it was probably not good, but after a while you work it in, you know? Between the three of you, you work it out. And the one thing we had going for us, we *wanted* to work it out, and we could work together and we were friends, enough. And we really did sort this thing out, and in the end we really had a great band. And we were writing great tunes, and rocking on."

But the drugs and booze, Eddie remarks, "It's kind of what made the world go 'round back then. I was not particularly into speed but I soon got the hang of it. I wasn't a big drinker, but after six months with Motörhead it seemed a natural progression. Of course when we started we did not have a pot to piss in. That always keeps you pretty healthy."

One doesn't think of Speedy Keen as a producer who would churn out a gruff and rough album such as *Motörhead*, even if he had just worked with the notorious Johnny Thunders the previous month. I mean, words have failed critics for years to describe the sound of this middle finger of a record. One could argue that sonically it was approaching putrid, halfway to what Venom would willfully cough up like phlegm three years later and pretty much alone as a predecessor to the toxic works of that notorious band from Newcastle.

"It was just the way we were, really," shrugs Eddie, by way of explanation. "It was quite a weird sound we had. Okay, there's Lemmy's bass obviously, which has always been the same, that grinding . . . like a fucking train going through your head. Phil was a complete nutter on the drums; he was all over the place. And I was kind of . . . I was struggling to keep up, but I was like the newest member, so I was just cutting my teeth. And of course we didn't have great equipment in those days, or guitars. I had a Gibson, but it only had one pickup, an SG, an old 1960, '62. It wasn't that old then, but it is now. And I've still got it somewhere. I keep it in its original case with all the Motörhead stickers on it. It's something I sort of treasure. And so we did have a bit of trouble with our sound. And nobody really tried to record Motörhead in this way before, and it was really quite difficult, I think, for Speedy and everyone else, to get a grip of it.

"I had to work into it, without a doubt," said Eddie to Jeb Wright. "It was very difficult at first. Phil was having trouble as well. It was a difficult situation as Lemmy set the stage by the way he plays rhythm bass. He really plays the bass like a rhythm guitar so there was no real bass parts in that band. There was just this god-awful noise coming from the other side of the stage. Of course, that is what made us unique. I was really a blues player as I loved bands like Led Zeppelin. I had to adjust to work with Lemmy. I actually switched from my Les Paul to a Stratocaster as I found that the Strat cut through the sound better. I needed to cut through Lemmy's sound rather than to try to get louder than Lemmy. The Strat sound is a bit thin but it does cut through and when you run that through a distortion box it sounds rather nice. I really did have to adjust my sound to fit Motörhead's sound. It took a while to get it right. When we started out we had headlines saying that we were the worst band in the world. After about 12 months we began to come to grips with it and that is when things started to happen. It really did take a year or so to get settled in, but once we were in the saddle then we were off and running.

"But Speedy was a nutter as well," continues Clarke, back to the band's improbable first knob-twiddler. "After Thunderclap Newman, he was a pretty rock 'n' roll guy himself, underneath the veil of 'Something in the Air.' After that he was really a rocker. But Johnny Burns . . . he did a lot of Genesis production, engineering. So they knew what they were doing, but once again I think it was the fact that we were doing it all so quickly and partly because nobody had really recorded Motörhead before. It would be one of those things where they would say, 'Okay, boys, play me something' and they probably looked at each other and said, 'What the fuckin' 'ell's that?!' You see what I mean? There'd be a lot of confusion. And with the short amount of time that we had, they had to just do what they could. But in a way it's kind of nice because it does show the reality of it all. It's a real record, you know?"

"Well, we wanted it to sound better than it did," laughs Phil. "I mean, that album was recorded in a haze of speed down in Jeff Beck's studio in the countryside, and I don't think any of us got any sleep. And it was just a little mill house that had been built by this guy, and we literally recorded it all live. And instead of being overdubbed, if somebody made a mistake we just stopped and started again. And Speedy was doing as much speed as everybody else was, so at the time, when everybody is in the same space, it sounds great. And unfortunately there were no outside influences dropping by and saying, 'Oh, it sounds a bit like this or a bit like that.' But we thought it sounded great, and at the time, it seemed to fit in with what a lot of other bands were sounding like, punk bands anyway. It certainly wasn't as sophisticated as, say, Deep Purple or anything like that, but it was the best we could do at the time, I think. We all liked it, and of course, when it eventually came out, it did sound a bit . . . 'Oh, could we remix it?' 'No.' I mean, I would love to go back and remix some of those early albums myself. Because I'm sure they could sound a lot better."

One could argue that it barely mattered what the band was playing. With production nastiness like that, Motörhead were destined to be called heavy metal. Just don't say that to Lemmy. "I've never called ourselves a heavy metal band," spits Kilmister. "In every interview I've done I've just said we were a rock 'n' roll band. I don't have a relationship to heavy metal. I have a relationship to Motörhead. It's the only one I'm interested in. I don't give a fuck about the others. If we had short hair in 1976 we would have been called a punk band. And a lot of stuff we play is very closely related to the blues, electric blues. They're blues tunes, just played very loud and very fast. They've certainly got nothing to do with heavy metal as far as I understand it. Heavy metal to me is Judas Priest.

"I suppose I have a problem with it because I come from way before metal," continues Lemmy. "I'm playing rock 'n' roll and I think rock 'n' roll should be sacred—it is to me. I don't see why it should not be for everybody else. I would guess metal came in with Deep Purple. They were the first one with the wall of sound. Deep Purple did it when they played songs like 'Speed King.' Sabbath came along and slowed it down a lot. I used to call it dirge. It was their thing but I never liked Sabbath. I would much rather have Ozzy on his own. I mean, some of the songs are okay, like 'Iron Man,' but I never liked the slow ones like 'Black Sabbath,' the song. We kind of bridged the gap with the punk crowd. Let's face it, the only reason we were called heavy metal is because we had long hair. If it wasn't for the long hair, we would be in the punk rack. It was a punk audience. I mean, it's because they heard us before they saw us, you see? So they liked the music, and then they saw we had long hair, but it was too late, because they like the music. We sounded more like a punk band than a metal band, didn't we? We were always too fast for heavy metal. I always thought we had more in common with the Damned than we did with Black Sabbath or Judas Priest. I always thought metal was Sabbath's first album and Judas Priest's first couple of albums. Sort of slower, you know? And we were never very slow."

And so, there it was, *Motörhead*, opening with its title track, first a rumble from Lemmy's bass, then a bunch of cardboard drums, and eventually that voice. Lem's surely correct about this one—it's total punk rock, if you didn't know the goodly brand it was issued under. In fact, it was almost outsider music, which is a term equally applicable to many of the shockingly casual songs and albums generated by Hawkwind, original thumpers of this very title track.

"Motörhead," backed with "City Kids," would become the band's first single, issued in early June 1977, ahead of the launch of the album proper. Admits Doug Smith on the "success" of the single, "I would hate to say it, because behind the scenes, we bought it in. Well, we didn't exactly buy it in. We had hundreds of fans go buy records all over London, and we knew that . . . it's before they sussed out that you can do that. Anyway, we

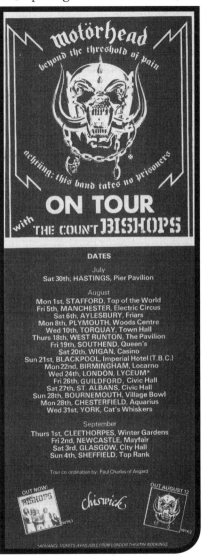

The Count Bishops were top representatives of the rocker movement— an army of traditionalists after Lemmy's own heart.

charted it. But it was very low, in the '60s, right? So that charted, and the situation was that we all got very excited about it, and then the next day they walked into my office and said their current roadie 'Bobs needs some new shoes. Fucking buy them for him.' And I said, 'No, I'm not buying Bobs's shoes.' And they said, 'Tony Secunda offered us a deal, so we're going, bye.' And they did, but of course they were soon back again.''

Clarifying the stratagem on the single, Doug adds, "No, we didn't have fans buy the single into the charts. Having said that, there were a few fans that did help our staff. In those days most labels had a list of chart-reporting shops. We got hold of that list and focused on those shops around the London area. You had to be careful because if the charts spotted an unusual buying pattern, the single would be weighted. However, it would have been difficult for the charts to spot that for the Motörhead single, as the band had never released anything previously. We were able to get a chart position in the 60s; however, I am sure that was also helped by enthusiastic fans around the country, who bought the single anyway. It hung around in the charts at that level for a couple weeks or so."

The second song on the album is "Vibrator," and this one proves Lemmy's above assertion on two counts—it's both punk and sped-up blues, or more accurately, the boogie-woogie end of the blues made famous by Status Quo.

Motörhead was, in fact, notes Eddie, bringing forward and knocking around songs from the shelved United Artists *On Parole* sessions to make *Motörhead* a viable chunk of full-length product. "Yes, they weren't my songs, but of course, I hadn't had a very prolific career at that stage, and I loved playing, so I was really just happy to play. So I didn't really mind what we played. I realized we had to play something, so the fact you could sort of learn 10 songs that were already just there, and they were already Motörhead songs . . . it was the best thing to do to get us going as soon as possible. Because with Curtis Knight, I had written a couple riffs—on the album we did I was only credited with two songs—and they were just two riffs that I came up with. 'Hey man, why don't we do this?' It was a similar sort of situation, but the other eight or nine songs on the album, they came from other people. So in those days it was kind of more the norm. Everybody wasn't running around writing their own tunes. It was more, you kind of played whatever you could get your hands on."

That's what happened, so to speak, with "Lost Johnny," Motörhead pulling forward the old Hawkwind chestnut most associated with Lemmy. Given the bash and crash of the album, one could still say we were still squarely within spitting—or splitting headache—distance of punk, but there was a palpable biker rock and heavy metal to the album by the time we get to this track.

"Punk was fine with us," Clarke admits, the band proving as much by gigging with the likes of the Adverts and the Damned in 1977. "Yeah, we loved it all. But we were independent. We just did our own thing. And the punks, I mean, God bless them, I always admired them for having a go and getting up there. But I was never that taken with punk music. I liked the attitude and everything, but me and Lemmy had been playing since, I don't know, me since I was 11 or 12, so playing was a bit of an art form to me. Whereas the punk guys they were just picking up and thrashing around. The singers were singing out of tune, guitars weren't in tune. I admit, we had our spells of that, but I never felt like a punk band. I always felt that we were Motörhead, know what I mean? We felt we were something different. Even in the early years when we were establishing our identity as a three-piece, I didn't feel particularly related to the punks. Because we had fucking long hair, and we were kind of different. They had the spiky hair and all of that and we were coming from a different angle. But it was a good time for us, and it was nice to be involved at that time. In a way, punk made it possible for us to get a foot in the door. Because without that going, if it had all still been fucking Black Sabbath and Caravan and Pink Floyd and Deep Purple, all of that stuff from the early '70s, we never would've gotten a foot in the fucking door playing what we were playing. So if it hadn't been for punk, we definitely would have struggled. So God bless them all. I still see a few of the boys here and again. It was just a good time, you know?

"But sure, we used to hang out with them," reminisces Clarke. "We were all kind of in it together at the time. We were kind of accepted because of Lemmy; there was just this acceptance of Motörhead. But then of course, we did look pretty mean and nasty. And the punks, well, they looked mean and nasty, but we looked meaner and more nasty, you know what I mean? And I think they just accepted us as on the same page as them. But as I say, we had history. I started playing when I was 12 and all that. And punks would've just been born. But in the '70s, there was nothing. Nobody had a pot to piss in; it was a very poor time. So you all ended up involved, and you knew you were all there scratching around for a pint, a bottle of beer or something. You just all got on."

And the Damned—a hard lot to please—they've definitely said they liked Motörhead.

"Well, they never told me they liked us," laughs Eddie, which says something about Dave, Rat, Brian and the good Captain (i.e., their stinginess with compliments), but also about Motörhead's exiled place within the industry, where it just wasn't okay to like this band. "But we were good friends. We used to play together a bit and we made a couple of records with them and we always got on like a house on fire. So we were just really good friends. It was more about the personal stuff; we didn't go into the music. You know, you can like someone, but you don't have to like the music, particularly. I didn't dislike their music, but we were friends. So you don't say, 'Oh, we're good friends, but I hate your music. So fuck off.' You don't say that, do you? You're my mate. And it's like, if the guy's got a girlfriend, you don't comment on it, you know what I mean?"

Adds Lemmy, more in response to the band's association with the New Wave of British Heavy Metal—in other words, the first post-punk uprising of metal in the U.K.—"We saw ourselves as the fucking . . . *the* guys. I mean, Motörhead was it, really. Not us particularly, but the whole Motörhead thing. We were kind of like the front-runner. That's how I see it. I saw Motörhead as the front-runners and everybody else, sure, [there were] some good bands, but nobody sounded like Motörhead. Because I tell you what, you have to earn that. And you earn that by fucking freaking out because of the weird sounds you got. So tensions were high."

Fast Eddie looking somewhat unscarred, 1978. | © George Bodnar Archive / IconicPix

Start talking about the band in terms of punk or heavy metal, and Phil Taylor quickly gets exasperated as well. "It wasn't us that gave it that name," says Phil, in response to the idea of Motörhead as a metal band. "It was the media, that comes up with these names. I mean, Lemmy came up with the name Motörhead, and that was the name of the band, and the title that one is given, or the pigeonhole that you're put into, that has always been created by the media. So it was a heavy metal band we were, and a heavy metal band we remained. And of course then it became just metal, and then after all, who thought of names like thrash metal, death metal, wooden metal, trouser metal, tripod metal, door metal? I've got a good idea that it was probably the press. So I refuse to answer that question on the grounds that I'm a drummer."

As for his role in uniting the worlds of punk and metal: "I think it was because I didn't really want to be a hippie, like a long-haired hippie, because I was still quite violent. I'd been a skinhead, and I had kind of a Rod Stewart / Ron Wood kind of hairstyle, and I had a leather jacket, but it was like a biker jacket. It was like a punk rocker jacket. And then so kids, the fans, if it was a punk looking at record sleeves, and they saw maybe me with these other two guys, they would think, 'Oh, that's strange—he looks like a punk.' And then maybe the punk would buy that. And then maybe some long-hair would look, 'Hey, two long-haired guys playing with this punk; that might be interesting.' But I think the punks kind of latched onto us because we were playing fast, and that's what most punk rock bands were. That's all they were about really, 'One, two, three, four, dah-dah-dah, the end.' In a way Motörhead was like that, but a bit longer. And I think the punks just got off on the energy, and the fact that from a fan's point of view, it was kind of weird to like a band that had two sort of hippies in it and one punk on the drums."

"Iron Horse" / "Born to Lose," appearing fourth on the album and co-written with roadie Dez Brown, cemented the band's image as "kind of different," as a band for the bikers, an image enforced by the patch / colors / rocker look of the front cover, Motörhead spelled out in gothic, war-mongering font, and the band's skull mascot, later called Snaggletooth, baring its fangs at all those who denigrate the grating in the den.

"No one did it before us that I know of," says Lem, examining the confluence of text and mascot that has become iconic. "Well, before we did it, the Moody Blues and the Yardbirds did it. It has since kind of faded away. You used to have your name spelled a special way with special lettering. It sticks with people that way. It's a trademark."

Snaggletooth, or War-Pig (or Iron Boar, Bastard or Little Bastard) was designed by Joe Petagno, who had worked for the famed Hipgnosis design company and was responsible also for Led Zeppelin's rich and elegant Swan Song logo. Designer Phil Smee reversed the black for white, turning it negative, and there we had it, a record jacket that looked like a biker jacket. Staring out from its inky soul was a concoction collaborated on—or armed—by Lemmy and Joe, who were both going for the same thing—mean—which is also Lemmy's motivation for the iconic umlauts over the logo's second "o," namely that it just looked ornery.

Joe told *Steel Mill*'s Pete Alander and Kassu Kortelainen that he'd first met Lem in 1975. "I had just finished the Swan Song logo for Led Zep, and I was working on some sketches for their formula car that I was to paint. He had just fallen out with Hawkwind, whom I had worked with earlier that year, and [Lemmy] asked me if I would help him out with cover art for his solo project, *Bastard*. I genuinely sympathized with him; he was down and out. This was back in another universe, on another planet, in another dimension. I have a lot of good memories from those days. Times change—unfortunately some people do too."

"Well, Joe had been chasing for years to do a Hawkwind cover," explains Doug Smith. "But what he produced I didn't like, because it looked very much like those fantasy and science fiction books. And Hawkwind wasn't really science fiction. They were mind-bending, basically; they were acid. Initially they were great dopers, but nothing hard. Never anything of any serious consequence passed their lips. But they certainly played around with acid an awful a lot, and a few downers, Mandies, Mandrax, that sort of stuff, and dope, obviously. So really, his covers were too science fiction for us; he never sort of got it right. But he really wanted to do something for Hawkwind.

"At that particular point, Motörhead was starting and we needed to get some sort of logo or image sorted out for them. And Joe came to a gig at Twickenham and met the band. He's an American, Joe Petagno. He comes from San Francisco. And he lives in Denmark nowadays, married to a Danish lady. Joe had an amazing look about him. He had the most outrageous afro you'd ever seen, and his girlfriend did as well. And he turned up at the gig, and of course Motörhead were a rock band, even a metal band. Metal hadn't really become a relative term then at that particular point—we didn't call it heavy metal; we called it rock.

"And so Joe eventually was asked for something, and he turned up with this character, this sort of science fiction image, but it had this head to it. It wasn't quite the way it looks now. It was a bit smoother than that. It was more refined in its face and the rest of it. And I didn't like it. I thought, oh my God, it's too Hawkwind, it's not Motörhead, it's not Lemmy. And I'm going to sound really silly here, but I think the first *Star Wars* had just happened, and I had been quite impressed with Luke Skywalker's spaceship. Because it was the beaten-up and battered one, if you remember. So I said to Joe, 'I like the face; take it back and shoot a machine gun at it.' And that's what came back.

"However, not quite," continues Smith. "Because then they did a short deal with Ace Records, Ted Carroll, very close friend of mine. And Ted took the image and reversed it in negative, and that's why it looks like it does. Now the logo, the Motörhead lettering, Petagno had drawn really thinned-out Germanic lettering. And of course, Germanic lettering can be very powerful if it's in the right form and has the right point to it. And John Curd, when he first promoted them, had fattened the lettering. So the lettering grew organically as well, which is quite the same as the band, really. And I remember when Dave Betteridge and Howard Thompson signed them to Bronze, they turned up at a gig at High Wycombe Town Hall on September 29th, 1978, and 75 percent of the audience were wearing Motörhead T-shirts. Howard and I had been friends when he was at Island Records and originally meeting him during Hawkwind recordings at Trident Studios where Howard had been tape boy. But it was quite a big gig, and so they thought, we'll sign them. The music at that point, I don't think was quite as relevant. T-shirts did the deal. Their decision was made right there and then because so many people in the audience were wearing the T-shirt."

O'er to side two of the album and another couple of riding songs underscore the bitter, weather-blasted, leather-faced theme: "White Line Fever" and "Keep Us on the Road" were a couple of new ones for our desperate and sleep-deprived trio of heroes.

"For 'White Line Fever,'" recalls Eddie, "I think it was, 'We've got to write something, guys.' We were all saying that: we've got to write something. So I just came up with that riff, and the rest of it, of course we just all came in on E. We were very keen in those days, playing-wise. We loved playing together and making fucking noise. So we just kept jamming on it, and Lemmy is actually a very good vocalist, I think; I really like Lemmy's voice. And he would just start singing on it and so of course we knocked it into shape. It was quite a simple song; it didn't really go far. It was basically on a 12-bar framework, but riffing, so it's sort of disguised. And 'Keep Us on the Road' was another one where I was just coming up with a riff. I had all these riffs going on in my head, it seems. So as I threw the riffs out, Phil and Lemmy would pick up on them, and between us, we would knock them into a song. And that was really how we wrote all the time, the whole way through, a little bit out of the ordinary."

There were also covers on the album, such as "Train Kept a-Rollin'." Explains Eddie, "We used all the songs off of *On Parole*, basically; we left a couple off. But we did about eight of them, I think. But we needed more material. We managed to write two. But 'Train Kept a-Rollin'' and things like 'I'm Your Witchdoctor' were just numbers we thought of that we could do, to give us an hour's worth of material to do a few shows, you see? Because it was all sort of hand-to-mouth in those days. It wasn't the glory days; it was tough, in the '70s. We didn't have fuck-all, and it was just one of those situations. So we just had to make do with the material."

Continues Eddie, "Lemmy and I of course, we were sort of Yardbirds fans, back in the '60s—we had a lot in common on that front. And 'Witchdoctor' was done by John Mayall; that was another '60s thing. So it was going back to our roots. The Yardbirds did 'Train Kept a-Rollin',' and Aerosmith did it in the '70s. Though we were actually taking it from the Yardbirds version, with Jeff Beck, after Eric had left."

"Oh yeah, Lemmy knew a lot of that stuff, definitely," adds Phil, expressing an interesting view on the recording of covers. "Because in his formative years, he was first and foremost a fan of all those bands, and he used to play all the 45s. [Lemmy] was totally into the American sound, because that's where it all came from. I mean, did you ever see a movie called *Stardust*, back in the '70s, with David Essex? It was about English guys in the late '50s, and they would form a band, and Keith Moon was in it as well— he was the actual drummer. And there is this one scene where they're rehearsing in a little town hall, and they're all playing, and they're playing an original song David Essex has written, and the guy walks in and says, 'Oi, what the fuck are you playing?!' And they said, 'Well, it's one of our songs.' And then Ringo Starr says, 'What are you talking about?! You've got to be an American to play your own songs.' So it was like that. People thought that only Americans could write original songs."

In total, the band chose to include versions of every song first generated at the spurned *On Parole* sessions save for "Fools," "Leaving Here," "On Parole" and "City Kids." The new ones were "Train Kept a-Rollin'," "White Line Fever" and "Keep Us on the Road." Old friend, deviant and co-writer of "Lost Johnny" with Lemmy in Hawkwind, Mick Farren, was back and in the credits for "Keep Us on the Road."

"Yes, he did that one and 'Damage Case' for us," recalls Eddie. "But I knew him before I knew Lemmy. I happened to run into him many years before. We used to jam together. We had a little setup in Cornwall where we used to go down, set up and jam. I went to see some friends and I met him through these friends. It was him, actually, that when I got into a bit of trouble and I was going to be sent to jail—I was about 23—he said to me, 'Look, man, we've got to get you working. You're too good a guitarist not to be playing.' And so he got me some auditions, I started auditioning and I didn't go to jail.

"Because I got the job with Curtis Knight, when I was in court, Curtis turned up in court," recalls Eddie, on avoiding time. "And so I've got this big black dude sitting there in the courtroom. Very funny. But, it must've helped because I didn't go to jail in the end. This was to do with smokes. You know; back in the day, back in the '70s, having a bit of cannabis was like a hanging offense. Of course, now it doesn't even raise an eyebrow anymore. But back then it was quite serious. Anyway, it was all thanks to Micky Farren, really. So I owed him a big one. He lived in L.A., but he came back here briefly, I think, about two years ago, and I was hoping to go and see him, but he lived down by the sea in Brighton, and I never got to see him. And the next thing I hear he's died on stage. Lemmy and I had a conversation about it, in Birmingham; we sat down and had a little chat about Micky. And we sort of talked in admiration of him dying with his boots on. And that's really what Lemmy would have dearly loved to happen. To be up onstage, thumping it out and then just . . . gone. Which is perfect. I mean, I would certainly love to have the same thing, but of course, I'm not onstage at the moment. You know, I'd have to do a guest appearance with someone and then die."

"The first Motörhead album has *three* Hawkwind tracks on it, which gives you some idea how unprepared Lemmy was to start a band," notes Rob Godwin, whose label Griffin Music later issued a Motörhead compilation. "There was 'The Watcher,' 'Lost Johnny' and 'Motörhead.' The dust jacket has a picture of Dave Brock, and Lemmy thanks 'All Hawkpersons.' He and Phil also thank Doug Smith. Regarding the punk acceptance of Motörhead, yes, Mick Farren co-wrote 'Lost Johnny.' He was a hell of a character.

Farren, Michael Moorcock, Felix Dennis and an assortment of other anarchists drove the counterculture in London. They were constantly in trouble with the police. Farren formed the Deviants, which were like Britain's earliest 'punk' band. Sort of like the Stooges. The Deviants shared billing with Led Zeppelin during

A rare daytime sighting, 1981. | © Wolfgang Guerster

the last few months of 1968 in pubs around England. Farren told me that Plant's voice was totally shot from recording *Led Zeppelin* between gigs so he got him gargling dental anesthetic!"

"Farren went on to write more songs with Motörhead and is pictured on the dust jacket of Motörhead's first album," continues Godwin. "I'm not sure, but there is another guy pictured on there who *might* be Tom Robinson. Farren was also completely nuts about the leather biker culture. He ended up writing the definitive book on the subject, which may have influenced Lemmy. He also wrote *The Titanic Sails at Dawn* in 1976, which some people think predicted—or even precipitated—punk. So it appears that right from the start Motörhead came with legit 'punk' credentials. Spawned by *the* people's countercultural band, Hawkwind, embraced by the founder of the Deviants and then signed to Chiswick—it's punk all the way."

Despite the band's varied influences and their ability to transcend classification, on the buried but rich literary side of Motörhead's debut record, it was pretty apparent that Lemmy could paint graphic, passion-filled pictures with words, irrespective of the clanging music enclosed.

"There are a lot of good lyricists," muses Lemmy, when asked about wordsmiths he admires. "The new wave of bands are pretty good lyricists, except for this heavy metal thing which is atrocious of course. And the rap thing has turned up a lot of good lyricists, but I don't like the musical genre as such, although there are a few good lyrics in there. But there's a lot of complaining as well. But the best lyricists ever I thought were the Beatles, probably, and Bob Dylan. I mean, people dismiss him now, and it's right in a way that he should be dismissed, because he went completely off the fucking track. But in the early days he was a consummate lyricist. Skunk Anansie are good too, for someone more recent. Chuck Berry of course, when I was growing up. Little Richard because he was outrageous. You couldn't tell what he said, but it was great."

Asked by Sam Dunn what his favorite punk acts were, Lemmy says, "You can't be a fan of a whole movement. You have to differentiate. Because you never mention a movement; you should just ask about individuals. If you asked me about individual punk bands, I will tell you what I thought. But the whole thing went from the Damned to Elvis Costello—sorry, I can't like or dislike all that. I wasn't into the Clash. Everybody seems to think they were the only punk band in the world. I was into the Pistols and the Damned, and a band called the Cortinas from Bristol. They were all about seven years old, but they were great. There were all kinds of good bands. Johnny Thunders and the Heartbreakers was great for a while, until the smack came back."

"A lot of people liked The Clash, but not me," Lemmy told me a couple years previous. "They just didn't seem to have a direction apart from *Sandinista!* There's that funny picture of them all wearing that shit behind the walls in Northern Ireland, hiding from the freedom fighters. Joe was kind of mixed-up. He died mixed-up. He didn't really know what he wanted to do and he could be talked into stuff. Nice enough guy. But I play rock 'n' roll and punk was very close to rock 'n' roll. You listen to 'The Chase is Better than the Catch' and it's not metal. It's rock 'n' roll. It's very blues-oriented."

With respect to Eddie's guitar heroes, that's another linkage back to the '60s. "For sure, I'd have to go back to Jimi Hendrix. 'Purple Haze' for me, when he first did that, it fucking blew me away, took me head off. These are the people I look up to, Jimi, Jeff Beck and Eric Clapton. The first Cream album . . . there were some great solos on that. So I was a '60s guy really. I had come up on John Mayall, Eric Clapton, Jimi Hendrix, early the Purple, '69, '70, Led Zeppelin, that was my diet. Lemmy's was a tad earlier, because he's a bit older than me. He had a little bit more of the rock 'n' roll thing—Buddy Holly—whereas where I came into it, I was listening to the Stones and the Yardbirds, Jeff Beck and Clapton. Now Phil was a little later. He was listening to stuff from

'68, '69, '70 and he tended to like a bit of everything. He was really into drummers."

Eddie continues, "Phil's a bit younger—but my roots go back to *Five Live Yardbirds*, and Hendrix and Cream and John Mayall, and Lemmy, he was a bit earlier. Like I say, he was Little Richard and all that because he had the extra five years on me. So he went back even further. So we had these three tiers, really, like Lemmy going back to Little Richard, me starting at the Yardbirds, and then you had Phil starting five years later. So it was probably quite nice, because you had these three eras—that might've been one of the secrets. Three sets of eras in one. Nowadays, it wouldn't matter so much, but this was all happening so fast back then. You know, five years back in the late '50s and '60s was a long time. A lot happened musically."

As for articulating what kind of bands might have been inspiration for Lemmy, Clarke dismisses the idea that at one point Lemmy wanted, for example, a five-piece with a lead singer (actually affirmed by Lemmy in interviews) and that down this road, MC5 were touted as some sort of blueprint.

"Nope. I mean, he liked MC5, but no, all he wanted was a band that could play and do gigs," Eddie says. "And he was gonna play what he was gonna play, and as long as he could do that, that's all he wanted. Because Lemmy never wanted to sound like anybody. Lemmy wanted to sound like Lemmy. He plays a particular sort of bass head, and he had a particular sort of sound, with a lead guitar amp with all the bass off it, so it cuts your head off. So, I'm gonna play like this, and of course we all had to fit around it and make it work. Which was not a bad place to be. Because it makes you unique, you see."

With *Motörhead* now staining record collections up and down England, it fell to the rock press to frame for the punters just what was lurking in the grooves of their latest preposterous purchase.

Wrote Ira Robbins in the respected *Trouser Press*, "Formed around that demented Hawkwind fragment, Ian 'Lemmy the

Lurch' Kilmister, and fueled by the legends of such minimalist superstars as the Pink Fairies and Deviants, Motörhead is the nightmare band of the British motorways. Unbearably loud and heavy, these three outlaws have added another dimension to the darker side of heavy metal—sort of Steppenwolf meets Sabbaff and beyond. Aided by the outrageously inappropriate Speedy Keen as producer, Motörhead has translated to plastic eight of the loudest songs in their repertoire in an album destined to become a metal monster classic."

Kris Needs in *ZigZag* deemed the band the "sound of speed. Raw power incarnate, like the villain says in the comics. But this ain't no baddy's bullshitting. Motörhead hit you right between the eyes with one of the most lethal combinations since they invented dynamite. They make you wanna scale walls and bash holes in the ceiling with your head. Motörhead make you feel like you can do anything. The Superman syndrome which comes from the best high-energy rock 'n' roll which transcends mere notes and chords and becomes the raging wall of exploding, devastating noise. Rampant energy as unleashed by the MC5 on 'Kick Out the Jams.'"

Other than the unnecessarily dated Steppenwolf-meets-Sabbath descriptive, both reviews articulate accurately what is going on inside of this plainly weird, wonderfully and willfully bad-to-the-bone record. It's heartening to see that writers were understanding the concept right from the start, and not simply dismissing the band as inept.

Much of the rest of 1977 would find the band still trying to beat people over the heads with a record that wrinkled the nose like a bad smell 'round back of the pub. Motörhead looked dangerous and sounded dangerous. In fact, the band sounded beyond indignant or defiant into the realm of disdainful—disdainful of the business and maybe even any possible fan base. The ultimate and instant effect was that, sure, girls want the bad boy, but guys were on board too, attracted to the leather, the chrome, the biker menace of the entire drunk and drugged package. As Eddie would attest, Motörhead was the gathering of three misfits into an incubator, a pressure cooker, an experiment in audio terrorism that better work out or no one was gonna eat tonight.

motörhead

Captured for the first time on long playing vinyl

SIDE 1
MOTORHEAD
VIBRATOR
LOST JOHNNY
IRON HORSE/
  BORN TO LOSE

SIDE 2
WHITE LINE
  FEVER
KEEP US ON THE
  ROAD
THE WATCHER
TRAIN KEPT
  A ROLLIN'

NOW
AVAILABLE

THE ALBUM NO OTHER
COMPANY DARED TO RECORD!

Chiswick WIK.2.

ONLY £3.89

A fair claim by the good folks at Chiswick.

And as far as motivation went, was this a band taking the piss, or were they truly *this* ragged, bloody and bedraggled? Fact is, it would become a moot point, as Lemmy, Fast Eddie and Philthy Phil would soon take on a scorched earth policy, cranking in quick succession *Overkill*, *Bomber* and *Ace of Spades*, proving that at least the flaming core premise of the *Motörhead* album—if not its final tally of points on merit—was a particulate bundle worth accelerating and exploding. In other words, *Motörhead*, as weird and hapless and as outsider as it is, would not be a one-off, but rather a sturdy frame to be built upon until the machine that was Motörhead would snarl its way to a No. 1 album, unfathomable by the white-knuckled band as it existed in 1977.

CHAPTER 4

Overkill: "He was a bit of a lad, old Jimmy."

All one had to do was stare into *Overkill*'s front cover—one of the greatest metal flak jackets of all time—and one could visually and viscerally read that Motörhead had wizarded up a massive improvement on their two false starts at a debut, namely *On Parole* and *Motörhead* (who but Motörhead would screw up and make two first albums?). Essentially, as far as guitarist Fast Eddie was concerned, *Overkill*, which was released on March 24, 1979, was the debut of the classic lineup, featuring all new songs written by two beset-upon warriors kicked and punched by the business for years and one drummer who fell into Motörhead like he fell out of bed.

But one can't overestimate the intoxicating effect of moving from the crude black-and-white cover of the debut to Joe Petagno's power-packed sleeve cooked for *Overkill*.

"I didn't know Joe that well," explains Eddie. "Obviously we met a few times, but it was something that Lemmy had already

Full page U.K. music weekly ad featuring cover with added eyeballs.

had done when I joined the band. My contribution for *Overkill* was I said, if we're gonna call it *Overkill*, let's blow up the death's head. And so as you see, that's what they did."

Joe, in fact, was none too pleased with the final result, having felt rushed at having to do the job in about 10 days. He points to his work on the band's 2004 album *Inferno* as a better rendition of the complexity he was going for.

O'er to the back, and any metalhead standing in the shop worrying about his prospective purchase would be transfixed at the promised heaviness of the scene. Eddie looked like some sort of revenge of the hippies time-traveler, Phil promised a wall of percussive death rained down upon as he powered two bass drums, and Lemmy establishes his look for all time, his caustic caw thrust up at the mic, bass as accompanying weapon, and more bullets in the belt just in case his first attack runs into trouble.

But back to the business of the music itself in 1978 and the electric path ahead toward infamy: the deal with United Artists was a disaster, the deal with Stiff was a mercifully brief bust, and the deal with Chiswick at least kept them on the road—it was the band that left Chiswick, prompted by a dispute they had with manager Tony Secunda, with Secuda himself leaving shortly thereafter and moving to California. But now Motörhead had mid-sized Bronze to give them a little substance in their lives. The guys would not take the opportunity lightly, crafting the most brutally rocking album the world had seen to date (please, try name another).

Eddie explains, "Nobody wanted to sign us. But what happened with Bronze was, they'd heard the band and they'd see the audience. They thought, fuckin' 'ell, we've got to sign this band. The crowds are going mad. And then they said, well, we'll put a single out and see how it goes. And then we'll decide whether we will sign you or not. So we had been mucking about with 'Louie Louie' before for this other manager guy, and we said, well, let's do 'Louie Louie' again. It's easy, straightforward, and it will seem not too extreme. Because otherwise if we wrote a song for it, we'd be getting into the realms of the extreme. We were trying to get some fucking . . . some sort of normality to our lives, so we did 'Louie Louie.' Fortunately it got in the charts at No. 75. And then we did *Top of the Pops*. Because the guy, the record company,

Lemmy was always one to celebrate original rock 'n' roll.

he had a friend. And the record company decided to give us a three-album deal or something."

"Louie Louie" is a charming, laid-back rendition of an old rock chestnut that the band would record and issue. The mere fact that between albums, Motörhead was constantly giving their fans a cheap purchase in the form of a street-ready 7" further endeared the original band to their base. All the better when the song was non-LP, like "Louie Louie."

"It's just an old classic and Lemmy liked it," notes Eddie, even as Lemmy, preferring "Bye Bye Johnny," says "Louie Louie" was Phil's idea. "And plus it was a simple tune. And we did it originally, when we had this manager, Tony Secunda, and we did it as a possible demo. What we were trying to do was place ourselves a little bit—or the manager was trying to place us a little bit—not so over the top, you know? So that maybe we could get a record deal."

"So when Bronze Records said, 'We might sign you if your single does well,'—which was 'Louie Louie'—we were actually on the verge of breaking up. Because we just couldn't get any further. Nobody would touch us. The promoters were scared of us, the record company didn't like leather jackets—that was Hells Angels, you know what I mean? General attitude was we were not liked. They tried to fucking kill us off. It was only our determination that kept us going so long. And then fortunately, Bronze Records came along and gave us the opportunity. And that's why we grabbed it with both hands and did *Overkill*. We didn't question anything. They say they wanna use Jimmy Miller? We said fine; we weren't gonna argue. And we got in, did our job the best as we could, got out again, delivered our album, and said thank you very much."

Gerry Bron of Bronze Records actually hated the band's incendiary, almost sullen rendition of "Louie, Louie," but was pleasantly surprised when it charted. The B-side, a new song called "Tear Ya Down," showed much promise, and off to the side, Chiswick, witnessing the band essentially touring in support of the single, issued a version of the first album in white vinyl, pretty much the last color fit for that dark and murky tangle of distorted sounds.

Laughs Doug Smith on helping the band get their Bronze deal, "My contribution was, after being sacked four and a half times, they ambushed me at a friend of mine's flat, Karen, who Lemmy was staying with. Lem wanted to play me the track that they had recorded during Tony's tenure, produced by Leo Lyons, and that was 'Louie Louie.' After listening to the track, the bedroom door burst open and Phil and Eddie appeared. After a short chat they asked if I would manage them again! I said okay, and I got them the Bronze deal and that was it. I finally went back and said, okay, let's have a go. And from that point on, they got Bronze Records, and they got Lilian and Gerry's support, 100 percent. Dave Betteridge and Howard Thompson actually signed them, but the reality was that it was short-lived with those two and we ended up with Gerry and Lilian. And Bronze created Motörhead. You know, between me and Bronze, we worked on it, and people like Roger Lemmon and dozens of people in the record company, very specifically, in fact, worked very closely with the band. Bronze Records was the only record company in the United Kingdom that was connected computer-wise throughout the whole of their building. And one floor of their building was rented out at night time to banks to do their computing. No, Gerry Bron was quite an ingenious guy. Apart from an airline, he also had a studio, Roundhouse Studio, that was amazingly successful. And he was also the manager in a record company and the publisher of Uriah Heep and a few others."

••

With *Overkill*, the key dab of motion potion was that the band was in a room together, writing for the first time. In fact, they were so pumped that they really couldn't wait for a new album to show off their new fangs. In tandem, singles and EPs started to become part of Motörhead's fabric, as they did for many pimply participants of the magical New Wave of British Heavy Metal (NWOBHM), and the effect was that the band was gathering an engaged fan base.

"Oh yeah, by the time we got past doing *Motörhead*, we'd written about four new songs," begins Fast Eddie, "between the first and second album, where we only had two on the first one—I think there was a bit of an EP from Chiswick. It's a bit weird all that; we had a funny relationship, because our management was a bit strange. But we had about a year where nothing was happening. We weren't actually getting many shows and it was all getting to be difficult even though our first album had done relatively well. But then we wrote four tunes. The first four tunes we had included were 'I'll Be Your Sister,' 'Damage Case' and 'Keep Us on the Road'—you see, we did a live radio show in between—and possibly 'Pay Your Price.' But yeah, the writing by then, we would go into rehearsal and we were really flying and champing at the bit because we weren't playing every night. So when we got to rehearsing we were writing songs and they were coming really easy. We had sort of a gold spell where everything sort of falls into place."

Before a gig at the Mayfair Ballroom, in Newcastle, England, on October 30, 1980, during the Ace up Your Sleeve tour. | © George Bodnar Archive/IconicPix

And the celebration of the band's new embarrassment of riches would go off like a bomb, the opening title track on *Overkill* being the most relentless example within a new genre loosely called speed metal, one that Motörhead were unwittingly inventing without much help from other bands.

"When 'Overkill' was written, it was, 'Man, try this!'" exclaims Eddie. "I remember Phil got a new double drum kit, and we were sitting in rehearsals, and he would go in early and set it all up and we'd come 'round from the pub. And he said, 'All right, man,' and we started playing, and he stops after . . . we played for, I don't know, half an hour or something. And he says, 'Hey man, why can't we do a song like this?' and that's when he decided to do the double bass drums of 'Overkill.' So he's sitting there going da-da-da-da-da-da, thundering away with the double bass drums. Because he was always speeding; he was kind of a bit like that. So he's thumping away at this beat and we're sitting there looking at him, so Lemmy starts playing that high bass part, 'grrrrr,' and then I started making a bit of noise, 'grrrrr,' and then we all crashed in on E, and that was the making of 'Overkill.' Once again, we did our usual thing. We rocked on with it for a while and then we started to give it a bit of shape. I said, 'Here, let's do that there, and let's do that here.' And then Lemmy stuck the lyrics on it. Lemmy always did the lyrics—it was his department. He was a very good songwriter. And I always believed the singer's got to write his own lyrics because he's got to sing them. But yeah, to me, 'Overkill' is one of our finest tracks."

"It's funny," adds the drum tornado himself, Phil Taylor, "because it's only in the last few years that I've met a lot of younger musicians who were coming up, and one guy in particular said to me, 'Man, you realize, you are the first drummer ever in history to play two bass drums all the way through a song, and like with the song, not as a solo?' And I just looked at him and said, 'No. What? What are you talking about?' 'Man, you're the only person; you're the first person who did it. You should be in the *Guinness Book of Records.*' And I thought, is that right, really?! And I'm sure it was, come to think of it. A lot of drummers play double bass drums, but it's always during solos. And so I guess I got that, and maybe I should get into the *Guinness Book of Records.*

"I mean, I always liked the look of double bass drum set

ups. The double bass drum setup always looks very impressive on stage, but being the sort of person I am, I couldn't be that pretentious, because Lemmy and Eddie were always, 'Aw man, when ya gonna get a double kit?' I said, 'Well, I'm not going to be an asshole; there's not going to be any drums or cymbals on my stage that I don't actually use.' It's just so pretentious. And there are just so many drummers who do that. I think it's stupid. But I was just at rehearsal at the time, doing a few gigs here and there, not making any money. Well, not making any money at all, really. But our manager at the time had a share in this rehearsal place, so I was just rehearsing. And so every time, I would get there a few hours early, and I was just practicing basically with the basics, just a mommy/daddy, one-two-three-four, with each foot, and that's all I was doing one day, and Eddie and Lemmy came and happened to stop and listen outside the door, and when they came in, they went, 'Hey, don't stop! Don't stop!' And we kept going, and that's how 'Overkill' was born. And it was like the backbone of the song."

With respect to direct double bass influence, Phil figures, "To be honest, there wasn't really any, apart from Keith Moon. You know, Keith Moon was probably the only one who played double bass drums during a song, but even then it was just more or less like when he did a fill, his foot would go from the high hat to his left kick and he would just keep time just for the duration of the drum fill, and then he would go back. I think it was more of a nervous twitch than anything else. And the only other person I would really have to say that I listened to, but not intentionally to learn anything from him, was Louie Bellson, but I didn't even know he had two bass drums. It's just that my dad was into jazz and he had one record by this big band where it featured a Louie Belson drum solo and I thought it was great. But I didn't know it was two bass drums. But I've always admired, actually, Brian Downey. Basically drummers only use two kick drums during solos, but I was always impressed with Brian Downey for double kick drums, but the master of them all without two kick drums is, by far and beyond, Ian Paice—he's the man. He can play one kick drum like some people can't even play two. So there wasn't really anybody that I particularly copied. I mean, put it this way, I'm not the sort of person . . . I've never been a fan of anybody. I like music, but when I listen to something I listen to the whole thing. I don't just dissect it, you know what I mean? And I've never been particularly focused on any one person or any one band. I'm like, if it pleases my ear, then I like it. I don't care what genre it falls into, no matter what it might be. If they're playing two forks and a spoon, then I like it.

"But that's how it turned out," continues Phil. "I was really just practicing. I didn't really know how to use two bass drums. I had ideas in my head, but I wanted to be proficient onstage. But that's okay; even if I used it only in one number, that was good. Two bass drums going sounds kind of like an engine, or a Harley Davidson kicking over, something like that. But it just sounded . . . I mean, especially through the PA, at the volume we had. But of course, new numbers came about, and I brought in the bass drum during rolls in other numbers like 'Bomber' and 'Shoot You in the Back,' quite a few numbers, actually."

Moving on and settling in with a kerrang and a clang, "Stay Clean" is all gristle and yet groove, while "(I Won't) Pay Your Price" is even more primal, stomping about the place on any rodents that might skitter into range.

"Stay Clean" is Lemmy's warning to the world about the evils of heroin. "I hate that shit," begins Lem. "It killed off a lot of my generation. It killed off a lot of my friends. Now this generation is getting killed off again. I can't believe it. How many dead bodies do we need to have piled up? You have to remember that before rock 'n' roll, there were a bunch of jazz musicians all doing heroin. That shit has been around a long time. Every generation thinks they are stronger than the generation before. They think, it can't happen to me. In the past people have died making that same mistake. Maybe you should take note. People lose their lives in the drug wars and you don't have to prove it to yourself because others have proved it for you."

Asked if there was a positive to drugs vis-a-vis the creative process, Lemmy figures, "It was both, you know. Eric Clapton wrote 'Layla' when he was coked out of his mind. Later on, it nearly killed him. You've got to try to figure out which is the bigger benefit and which is the bigger loser. It nearly killed him; he was in a very, very bad way for a long time, but he came through it. Most people don't come through it because they don't have the money to buy the people to look after them. Most people die miserable and lonely deaths because they don't have the people to nurse them and get them through it all. The '60s was probably the best era because there were hardly any rules and heroin hadn't shown up. So people hadn't started dying. It was incredibly upbeat and we almost did change the world."

"'Stay Clean' was written about an old girlfriend of Lemmy's he was very much into, and she couldn't stay off the heroin," explains Philthy, who goes on to provide an assessment of Lemmy as lyricist. "That's what that was about. Just songs about life. 'City Kids' and stuff like that . . . not necessarily all about fucking war. But he is a great lyricist, because he could come up with anything. And he just seems to write songs on the spot. Maybe he would have an idea, like we're actually in the studio, but then it will come to fruition and he'll finish the actual lyrics while we're in the studio. So he's very good, and he's a very prolific writer. He writes them usually on an old brown paper bag or any scrap of paper he finds lying around the studio. And whatever comes into his head."

"I'll Be Your Sister" was always the personal favorite of this writer, for its bright upswing smashes and above average note densities in the riff compared to the rest of the album. "I don't know what Lemmy was doing with that," says Clarke, when asked about the strange title—in fact Lemmy later dreamed about Tina Turner performing this song, part of a wider penchant for wishing to write songs for women. "A lot of times he would pass me lyrics and say, 'What do you think?' I don't recall ever seeing that one. That's one we had before we started the album. It's one we had early on."

The album switches gears for the hazy desert daze of "Capricorn"—reclined, yes, but still a heavy partner on a shockingly heavy side of music for a record circa 1979. Mused Lemmy over whether being a Capricorn says anything about his psyche, "Take a look; the characteristics are many and varied, dark and shrouded, cynical. I'm on the cusp of Sagittarius, but I couldn't think of how to fit that into the lyrics. Not many words faze me, but Sagittarius is a tough one."

"I must admit, I'm very fond of that album," muses Eddie, mulling over the track list and sequence. "'Stay Clean,' 'Pay Your Price,' 'Damage Case.' 'Metropolis,' you know what? I did a solo for 'Metropolis' for Girlschool in 2008. And Motörhead still do 'Metropolis' in their set, so whenever I see Lemmy and the boys . . . yeah, and 'Capricorn,' fuckin' 'ell.

"In fact, all the tracks are fucking brilliant," continues Clarke. "'Tear Ya Down' was the one we did with 'I'll Be Your Sister' and 'Damage Case'—those ones we did on the John Peel radio show, BBC Radio One. It might have been 'Limb from Limb' as well. 'Capricorn,' when I was doing the solo, I had done it as a runthrough, and our producer, Jimmy Miller at the time, he put all this echo on it. So I'm out in the studio playing, and I just got carried away. And he put this repeat on it, and of course, when we went to listen to it, it was fucking brilliant. And then it was like, well, let's do it again. Because it wasn't, you know . . . nobody was really that ready for it. But we couldn't fucking top it. So we had to use the original take of that, because it was just so good. And 'Metropolis,' I remember 'Metropolis,' this is a funny one, because when we were doing it, I think it was a Friday night and they were having a party. Because it was over Christmas, this. And they were having a party at Bronze Records and it was also the Bronze studio, and we were doing the album. And I know that

Phil was sick all over the fucking ceiling. They had this corridor, where this beam must've come across, and they had these little two stairs going down and they went up the other side. And he was of course sick all over this fucking beam; it was ever so funny. And that was the night I did this solo on 'Metropolis,' and I have to admit I was fucking crusted. We were completely all fucking gone that night. And yet I often listen to it and think, 'Ooh.' And over the years, when I listened to it I wasn't sure. And then I kept listening to it and I still wasn't sure, but around the mid-'90s I listened to it and I fucking loved it. I'm glad I didn't change that. Because it had a certain something."

"I think I definitely like *Overkill* as a favorite because it was the first one, the first album that we did proper, under real conditions, with a real producer," says Phil, summing up the qualities of the band's ambitious and bold second record. "And we had some time to do it as opposed to the first album, that didn't come out until much later, you know, the black-and-white one, *On Parole*, the very first one that was supposed to come out on United Artists, and actually did, in fact. But *Overkill* always sticks in my mind because it was the first one we did for Bronze with a proper record deal, and we had time to do it how we wanted to do it, and it was the first album that was all original material, and nothing by anyone else. The other one had like 'Train Kept a-Rollin'' and a couple of songs written by Mick Farren and people from the Pink Fairies. But 'Overkill' also, you see, I like because of the double bass drum, and my other favorite song which was 'Stay Clean.' I like it for that. But yeah, by then of course, we really got rolling. It was everything everybody was expecting, and more than what we were expecting."

"Damage Case" combined smoke-choked verse riffing with, come chorus time, reminders of the boogie-woogie that was dear to the hearts of these old warhorses. And then it's on into the inky night with "Tear Ya Down," toward a stone-cold epic of the catalog, "Metropolis." But before we move on, it's interesting to note that "Tear Ya Down" is from a different session from the rest of the album, laid down by Neil Richmond at Wessex when they recorded "Louie, Louie" before signing to Bronze.

Explains Eddie, "We couldn't get a deal for love nor money. But [Bronze] had an A&R guy there called Howard Thompson, a lovely man, great bloke, and I'm still in touch with him. He did a lot after that, went to CBS and Elektra, but he said, 'Well look, I've got to try get you on a label,' so he spoke to Gerry Bron, the owner, and Gerry would only let us do a single. He would pay for a single, and then see how it went. And so that's when we did 'Louie Louie.' So we went up to Wessex Castle Studios. You've got to remember, Wessex was a big studio in those days where all the punk bands went to, Sex Pistols, *Never Mind the Bollocks*; Chrissy Hynde worked up there. So Neil Richmond was of that ilk, sort of like a punk producer. He was called in to do the production on it. So he took us up to Wessex, and we did 'Louie Louie' on the A-side and stuck 'Tear Ya Down' on the B-side, and so instead of re-recording it, we just used the one we had, and remixed it."

But the rest of the album was caged at Roundhouse Studios, which was (I sense a theme here) "fucking brilliant. Camden Town, right next to the Roundhouse, Camden now is very fancy. Them days it was more of a shithole. It was a lovely brand new building, had all the best desks, two Harrison desks, all the equipment you can think of. Carpets, fucking everything. It was a huge space, the room was fantastic, and it was just brilliant; it really was. It wasn't the Olympic, don't get me wrong, but it was a really fine studio. And it was of course our record company's studio, so we felt like we had a right to be there.

"Because with *Bomber*, we did a couple of tracks at Olympic. I think we did 'Step Down' at Olympic and a couple others there. And Olympic by then, the mid-'70s, was actually getting a bit run down. Because Olympic was where Hendrix worked, Clapton, Stones, it was like the Mecca. In fact, I did a few tracks there with Curtis Knight, back in '74. All those people running in and out, when you're starting out like that, it's like real milestones in your career. Just the studio used, and the people you meet there, those are the things that sort of keep you going, as it were."

As mentioned, the band was in full collaboration mode. Maybe they were living too fast to focus and write at "home," wherever that was, but whatever the case, these songs were slammed together on the spot. "All three of us together, yes, for all of them," says Eddie. "All six albums were done like that. You need to have that realism, you know?"

Still, Phil says his role in the writing was quite limited. "Not in the actual music. Because I don't play guitar or anything like that. I mean my contribution was I would help with coming up with suggestions for the arrangement, or maybe we should do a stop here or there. Just little things, but like I said, I don't know an E-flat from an elbow, but occasionally I would have a tune going through my head or whatever, and I would kind of like hum it, but it's not quite the same. Humming it to somebody . . . but Eddie and I wrote a couple of songs like 'Chase is Better than the Catch' from *Ace of Spades*; we wrote that in Eddie's flat, with me playing on a cardboard box. When me and Eddie worked together, Eddie was a lot more understanding than Lemmy, and I would make guitar noises, just make a change or this and that, and Eddie interpreted it very well. So that was, from my point of view, how my input was. And in lots of other ways, but not necessarily musically. We started out as a family, and to be honest, that was the way of keeping the band together, by including everybody, because famously, throughout history or whatever, drummers have never been included in the publishing, just because they don't necessarily play music, but they always have a certain input, and Lemmy and Eddie both insisted that they split the publishing three ways, so that we could stay together as a band. And as I say, I did have input in my own way. I wasn't just a freeloader, put it that way."

One theory concerning Motörhead's lucky streak of fast, fine albums at the turn of the decade is the contact buzz the boys were getting off of the growing crowds at their incendiary live shows. "We did our first Hammersmith Odeon in November '78," figures Clarke, getting the timelines straight, upon being reminded that the credits say *Overkill* was created between December '78 and January of '79. "Yeah, we got the deal with Bronze. When we did shows, hundreds of people would show up. But we didn't have a record deal. Our fans were fucking loyal; they were brilliant. And of course as Lemmy always said, if you go somewhere and play, next time you go back, everybody brings a mate along. And he was right. Because right at this time we were playing the Hammersmith Odeon and we didn't quite sell it out, but I think we did close to three thousand. And that was just on the back of touring and that first album. And I remember we had 'Overkill' written then, we had 'Sister,' we had 'Limb from Limb,' we had 'Damage Case.' I'm not sure about 'No Class.' But then after we did that we went in and did the album. Of course we were really excited because we finally had a record deal. We were over the fucking moon. And we did a tour to follow up the album, which I think started about March that year—if I remember rightly, we got home for Easter."

Moving on, "No Class" was just ZZ Top's "Tush" on a speed jag and living in a squat, yer leather jacket and bullet belt your only friend. Its mention elicits a tale from Eddie: "I remember 'No Class,' I'll tell you the story; this is Jimmy Miller. God bless his soul, he was a fucking lovely guy. And I think he did a really good job; he had done the Rolling Stones and Traffic in the past. He had this long gray hair and he had a beard and he was really this sort of mellow American guy. But he was a bit of a lad, old Jimmy. Remember, we were pretty fucking headstrong in those days. It took someone who could balance the whole thing out. But what happened on 'No Class,' I did the solo, and he is doing the mix of it. So I was doing this solo, it was an all done, and he's doing the mixes, and he played 'No Class,' and I said, 'Fuckin' 'ell Jimmy, what happened to the solo?' It had actually disappeared! Because it just didn't go down on tape very loud. So I said, 'Well, what are you going to do?' He says, 'Don't worry, man, I'll take care of it in the mix.' That's what he said. When we put it down, it didn't go down very loud on the tape, and he said it was all right, he would take care of it in the mix. And then he did the fucking mix, and I said, 'Jimmy, you never turned the fucking guitar solo up.' And he said, 'Don't worry, I'll take care of it in the cut,' you know when they cut the record.

"So we go to the cutting room, and I said right, what's he going to do about this? So when it came to the solo on 'No Class,' when you hear it, he turned the fucking high mids up at the solo. That's all he could do to get the guitar little bit louder. You can hear the solo and it thins out. He struck the high mids up just to get the guitar out of it, which was fucking hilarious. Yeah, so you think, well, fucking 'ell, that's a bit cheap shot. But he was just a little bit . . . he could test you a little bit. In the end, our relationship was pretty much worn out at the end of it all.

"But I'll tell you, Jimmy kept us very amused," continues Clarke. "He used to do things like, he just wouldn't turn up at the studio. He would be three hours late and it's because he fell asleep on the bus; the cab broke down and I had to push the fucking cab. Or we would be in the middle of the session, and he would go out for a piss, and he would disappear and I remember, we used to go looking for him, but we couldn't fucking find him. But we never looked in the ladies' toilet. And I heard later—I mean, you can check this out with Lemmy—but I heard later that he was in the ladies' toilet having a little sleep, as it were. So yes, we used to turn up at the studio, because we were so keen to go, and of course he wouldn't be there for three or four hours, drive us fucking mad!"

"Unfortunately Jimmy was a terrible heroin addict," recalls Phil, back to the making of the *Overkill* record. "And we mainly got him because of the great album that he did, *Sticky Fingers* for the Stones—that was a great album. And unfortunately we didn't know he was a terrible heroin addict when we recruited him. He was actually suggested by Gerry Bron, and I don't think Gerry Bron even knew about his heroin addiction. Jimmy didn't . . . Jimmy really didn't have any influence on direction or sound. He just recorded us as we were, and produced it quite well. And to be honest, a lot of the times, he was very quiet, due to the heroin, I think. And when you thought he was awake, he was actually nodding off to sleep. You had to poke him with a stick. And more often than not he would be like hours and hours late, unfortunately. We would get pissed off at him. So he really didn't have very much of an influence on the band at all. He produced a good album for us, but I don't think he influenced our sound at all."

As illustrated, Clarke wasn't always completely pleased with what Miller had accomplished with the Motörhead sound. Which is understandable, given the polished vibe Eddie would embrace later with his Fastway records. "True, now when I listen to them, they're fine, but I wasn't sure at the time, I mean, I thought he was just there, you know? I didn't really pay much attention to what the producer was doing. He was more like a suit, you know what I mean? It was hard to discuss anything with him. And you wondered if he was really taking on board what you were saying. So in the end you didn't bother saying too much. But the job got done, and when I listen to the albums now, I think they're fucking great and I think he did a really, really good job. Because I tell you what— recording Motörhead is no mean feat. It's very, very . . . it's a difficult sound all around. It's difficult to play in, it's difficult to do live, it's difficult to record, you know? It's Lemmy's extreme bass sound which kind of sets the tone. And you have to work around that. It's just not usual. It's kind of unique. But also exciting, I suppose."

"I've got two Marshall hundred-watt amps," Lemmy told me, years later, on how he gets his signature "drill bit to the head" sound. "Old amps, tube amps, JMP Super Bass II's, right? They're from the '70s, I guess. I've got four cabs, two 4x12s and two 4x15s, one of each on each side. They're next to the drum riser. The settings are presence at about 3 o'clock, bass at about . . . no, bass is off actually, middle is full-on, treble is about 7 o'clock and volume is about 3 o'clock on both of them. And they are joined by the inputs at the front, not at the back."

And if you're playing guitar against that . . . good luck with it live. "We have talked about it, but it doesn't change anything," says Lem. "If I'm going to play with my sound, then it has to be gotten around. I mean, if you can't tell bass from guitar, I don't care what kind of tone

Lemmy at Maple Leaf Gardens, Toronto.
| © Martin Popoff

you're playing, you're in serious trouble. You better get professional help. But you can always tell which is which. That's nonsense. I play rhythm guitar bass. Later Brian Robertson had problems with it because he was always bitching about it. He used to say, 'There is no bass. How can I do this? Can we set up another bass drum? I need bass.' I said, 'What makes you think that I wanted bass?'"

Chuckles Eddie, "I mean, Lemmy'd probably be the first to admit that he's not a proper bass player, inasmuch as Stanley Clarke or something, you know what I mean? He's not that kind of bass player. But as bass player goes, he's probably the best bass player there is. I mean, the amount of power he gets on that. The guitar, the way he holds it, he's got hands as strong as fuck, Lemmy—he's like Samson. Nobody can play bass guitar like Lemmy. He's definitely a one-off. And then of course, he sings on top of it. So yeah, he's quite a unique animal."

Articulating the Motörhead sound further, Eddie affirms that, "Lemmy would be playing the rhythm on the bass, you got this 'grrrrr,' so Phil and I would work around that and try to see what we could do within it. We'd sort of do a riff power noise thing and then I'd think afterwards, what can I put on this to make it a bit more interesting? So it wasn't just me playing the same as the bass. It was often really fast so it was quite tricky, and I think that's one of the things that gives it its flavour, that little lick that you get. But with Lemmy, as I was saying, it's like any song that he would do, we'd have to work around Lemmy's bass sound. I was playing obviously with Motörhead all those years and I was struggling all the time to get a really nice guitar sound. It was really hard, on stage especially. And I just sort of fought with it the whole time. Phil had the same problems with his drums. It was hard. It didn't always settle right, you know?

"But Phil was very, very fast," Eddie continues. "I remember later when I was doing some remixes on the *No Sleep 'til Hammersmith* live album, I wanted to add some other shows to it, add some bonus tracks, this is in 2001. So I went to the studio, and I used to sit and listen to Phil's drumming, and he'd take off on a fucking roll around the drums, on a really fast song here, and I'm thinking, fuck me, he's not going to make it. Straight off, he's not going to make it. But every time, he made it. So that always fascinated me. I'm thinking, fucking 'ell, I didn't think he was going to make that one. Oh, and that one! But he always got back in time."

Continues Eddie, on the grinding tones of the band, "When we were in Texas and we were supporting Ozzy, Mountain was supporting us and they were using our gear. So Leslie West was using my amps, right? He used all my gear, and I tell you what I said to my roadie, 'Fuckin' 'ell! Why don't I sound like that?!' And he kind of looked at me as if to say, 'Well, you ain't Leslie West.' But what I realized later was that it was the contrast with the bass. Because Lemmy, on stage, he has a couple of Marshall 100s with all the treble full-on and all the bass off. There's no real bass anywhere. So the guitars are clashing with the bass. The frequencies are the same. And a similar thing for the drums. I mean, we used to always say—and our sound man used to always say—the only real bottom end we had was the bass drum. You know, no disrespect to Lem, because it was our sound and it made life interesting, but it was odd. I always wondered about Brian Robertson when he took over from me, how it must have fucking done him in! Because he's coming from a band with two guitars and a nice fat bass, you know what I mean? You fart on the strings and it sounds great. But with Motörhead, man, you've got to fucking work every second to get some sort of sound and cohesion out of it. It was fucking hard graft man, and really the demise of the original lineup came through that. It was a lot of stress at times."

All of that noise is one of the reasons the band was considered punk rock with long hair.

"Well, kind of . . . yes and no," figures Phil, on the extent that punk influenced the direction of Motörhead's mania. "Eddie couldn't stand it at all. Lemmy and I did, you know, just because of the energy, I guess. And I kind of liked it for the energy and the people. The people, really. Because I was more of a punk than heavy metal guy, by the way I dressed and my attitude, but I didn't particularly like playing the music, because to me it was just too simple. It wasn't anything special. It was just a lot of kids—at the time I was probably like 24, 25, and a lot of the punk bands were in their teens or early 20s. But even the ones who were the same age as me weren't particularly good musicians. And I'm not wishing to boast or anything, but they weren't into the same music; they didn't have the same musical tastes as me. I quite liked the energy, and as I say, I liked the people, so that's why we kind of crossed over mainly—because of our personalities. Not necessarily the music. I think the punks liked Motörhead music more than we liked their music. Because we were these long-haired people who played loud, energetic music, and we weren't what most punks thought the hippies would be like when they met us. Because when they met us, we were just as rough and ready as they were, but we had long hair."

,,

Back to *Overkill*, what about engineers Ashley Howe and Trevor Hallesy—what did Eddie figure their place was in the scheme of things?

"I don't remember a lot about Ashley," says Eddie, "but he was obviously, for us, he was the guy, with Jimmy Miller, getting this album together. But he was quite sought after at that time, and unfortunately he married an American bird and disappeared off the scene forever. And Trevor, we used Trevor on *Bomber*. Halfway through *Overkill*, I think Ashley went off and wasn't there anymore. Because we always thought Ashley was fucking great, and then when he wasn't there it made us think he was even greater, because he's not available. But for *Bomber* it was only Trevor. In fact, we tried to do something with Trevor; we did the *Golden Years* EP. I think that was Motörhead and Trevor. I don't think Jimmy Miller was on that because he was back in the States then."

In regard to label head Gerry Bron, forever remembered for his turmoil-enhanced relationship with the Uriah Heep guys, Eddie says, "He was like a fucking headmaster, wasn't he? When you spoke to Gerry, it was like your granddad or something. Not his age, but in the way of respect. We had the deepest respect for him because he was the guy who made it possible for us to do what we did. And plus, he had all the fucking power. If he says fuck off, we would have to fuck off, you know what I mean? When he was about, we were actually quite well behaved. It wasn't until much later Phil got out of his head once or twice with his wife, screaming at her, threatened to kill her, I think. That was in '81, so that was toward my end of the stay in the band anyway."

"I signed Motörhead because there is something unique about Motörhead," mused Gerry Bron, speaking with Dmitry Epstein

Motörhead

FROM THEIR 'BOMBER' TOUR · UK WINTER '79

SIDE ONE
LEAVING HERE
STONE DEAD FOREVER

SIDE TWO
DEADMEN TELL NO TALES
TOO LATE, TOO LATE

'the golden years'
LIVE EP
RRP £1.15
12" ALSO AVAILABLE (LIMITED EDITION ONLY)

BRO 92
(12"-12 BRO 92)

BRONZE RECORDS
AVAILABLE FROM EMI

in 2004. "There isn't another Motörhead—they have a fantastic following! Some of what they do, things like 'Ace of Spades,' are not my cup of tea, and I can't say that Motörhead is something that I play all the time. But it's good in its own area, no question about that. You've got to remember that when we reached our height, when we were very successful, we had Motörhead, Uriah Heep, Manfred Mann, Sally Oldfield. They're all completely different, but everyone thought we were a rock label. And I said, 'Listen to what they're doing, they're not the same at all, they're not like each other.'

"I don't think we would have signed Hawkwind if it weren't for Motörhead," continues Bron, divulging a spot of irony, given Lemmy's firing. "I can't say I was that interested. When you have a record label, you get to a point where you have Motörhead, the manager of Motörhead manages Hawkwind, you know they are—and you hear it—quite good and you can't put them down. When you get to that level, you haven't the same passion for every artist, because it becomes commercial. Although we never lost any money on Hawkwind, we never made any money, so it was okay. It was okay. Once you run a record label and you're employing people, you have to make good commercial decisions. You can't turn away business, even if the business isn't what you particularly want to do. You can't always find many people that you like. You've got to move on. The fun of the business for me is to find somebody who isn't well known and create somebody who deserves that success over a period of time. Most of the things I've signed were not successful before I signed them. I don't think Motörhead would have got anywhere if we hadn't signed them to Bronze. I mean, nobody wanted to sign them. They tried to get a deal, to get a single out, and they never got anywhere. But I wouldn't sign Motörhead again, or Uriah Heep, because I want to do new things."

Respected NWOBHMers Angel Witch were also on Bronze, which bassist Kevin Riddles characterizes as a productive home for diversity. "Yes, well, first off Motörhead were—and still are—absolutely unique. They were, in my eyes, the first punk band. Before people like the Ramones or Iggy Pop or anything like that. But they were a European version of those punk bands, if you can understand what I mean: basic, hard-driving, incredibly loud rock. And, I'm trying to think of how to . . . I wouldn't say that we felt in any way superior, but we certainly felt different from Motörhead. And I think that's exactly why the Bronze record label worked so well: it was pretty much all rock stuff, but every band was different. You had Motörhead, Girlschool, Tank, Bernie Tormé, Barón Rojo from Spain. We were all rock bands, but you couldn't say that we were all similar in any way. But as for Motörhead and what they were like, they were just absolutely brilliant."

Onward through the *Overkill* album, "Limb from Limb" features "second guitar solo" by Lemmy. "Well, when I first met Lemmy—this was about '69—he was playing rhythm guitar," reveals Clarke. "Well, rhythm guitar . . . he was playing guitar in Sam Gopal's Dream, which, I think that all fell through. But he came to a party that I was jamming at. Some friends of mine were having this bash, and Lemmy came and guested, and he came up with his bass player and used our drummer, and he played for about half an hour and it was really good—he was playing a Fender Jaguar. And he was a very accomplished guitar player, I remember thinking at the time. I remember saying quite clearly, 'Oh, he's very profesh, isn't he?' I was 19 then and I hadn't really done much, so I just figured I'll get up and do a bit of the noise and play me solos. So what happened was, Lemmy kept that guitar, and he always wanted to fucking use it, so I saw no harm in getting him to do a solo on 'Limb from Limb.'"

"Myself, I'm blues-rooted, and I just go for it, at the time it's happening," continues Eddie, concerning soloing but also underscoring one of the possible/debated/arguable magic points of Motörhead, namely that their metal rises up from the blues. "And normally once I go for it, that is the solo that sticks. I don't sit down and work them out; none of that. We would be at rehearsals, and we would be jamming, and I would be soloing right there in the rehearsal room, and of course be going for it in such a way that, it seems that whatever I go for initially, is where I sort of stay around, that area. Occasionally there were openings. I think of a solo as how you start it and finish it, really. The middle takes care of itself if you kick it off with a good start. So I wouldn't have much say in it—we would just be jamming and whatever I did seemed to stick. And if I wanted to change it, I would have to really think about changing the beginning. It's all about, for me, the opening. But what happens is I won't be able to get over the solo that I already put down. So sometime I've got to find a way to get that out of my head and just do another one."

As for his own favorite solo on the *Overkill* album, Eddie says, "Fuckin' 'ell, mate, that's a difficult one. On side one, 'Overkill,' 'Stay Clean' and 'Capricorn'—those are possibly the three. Don't get me wrong; I love side two, but those are the three that probably stick out in my mind. 'Overkill' was fucking brilliant, playing on the run-down on the end. It was fantastic. We just turned up and we went for it. And then we went for it again. And then we went for it again, which was fucking brilliant. I remember playing it in the office, with our manager, and he said, 'That's a bit over-the-top.' And we said, 'Yes, but that's why it's called fucking "Overkill," man! We can do this; we can get away with this! Because we are Motörhead and it's called "Overkill!"' That's why we can do three false starts at the end. Well, two false starts, you know, three endings. And I remember listening to 'Overkill' in the studio, because Gerry, the owner of the record company, and his wife came to listen to the session, and Jimmy put 'Overkill' on and it fucking rocked. I mean it was a great studio, and it was loud, and you could see that it just blew them away. I don't know whether they liked it or not, but they just look completely overawed by it. It just sounded fantastic. Because nobody had done it until then, on that level. It was just pounding, and it just kept pounding, start to finish. It was fucking awesome. I can still remember being in the studio and looking at their faces to try and get some idea of what they were thinking. I didn't have a clue. I thought they looked shocked."

Indeed "Overkill" is of paramount importance in the invention of what would become thrash metal. Through the blitzkrieg that was this album and the two to follow, Motörhead became chief and potent inspirers of those who would craft nascent thrash: the bands of the big four, namely Metallica, Anthrax, Slayer and Megadeth. Really, its only precedent is "Fireball" from Deep Purple.

"Yes, but Deep Purple, they never kicked in that way," qualifies Clarke. "The drums in those days were still a little bit back in the mix. And to have two bass drums at the center of the song was fucking brilliant. But these things, they come about just by accident. It's like Phil saying, 'Hey, let's do a song like this. It's got two bass drums.' Because he never had two bass drums before. We could never afford them, you see what I mean? It was little things like that that just added that bit of spark to do something a little bit out of the ordinary."

Shifting sights to the road, Clarke comments that "with 'Overkill,' we took Girlschool out on support. We met them at West London Pavilion, I remember, for the first time. And Lemmy said to me, 'Oh, I fancy the guitarist.' I said, 'Oh, I'll have the other one.'" Indeed Motörhead with Girlschool was a union on many levels that bore fruit for years to come, the former inspiring the latter toward a great catalog of their own, and Lemmy going to his grave wistfully commenting that Kelly Johnson had been the one true love of his life, even though the dedication in his autobiography picks otherwise—one Susan Bennett. "I don't want to say too much," notes Eddie. "Kelly, God bless her, died a few years back. All I will say is we had great times together and I have many fond memories. Yes, and they really could play."

"The majority of that all happened in the U.K.," notes Doug Smith, confirming that he was at many of the Motörhead/Girlschool gigs. "We might have done some dates in Europe, but I can't remember exactly how many. When we packaged the band out on the road, we were looking for a band that nobody else had sort of got involved with. And a friend of mine had made a record with these girls, and the record just happened to come to our attention, and I suggested it to Lemmy, and Lemmy said, 'Oh, why not? A bunch of girls on the road? Sure!' And that was it. There was no further planning than that. They did a few gigs and I went and saw them to decide whether they should be doing this, and they were great. And I thought, well, why not? And so they became part of the whole office situation, joined us for management, and we had so many years working with them until the whole thing went belly-up. Well, it didn't go belly-up, it closed gently."

Further with respect to Motörhead on the road, Clarke recalls that, "There were a lot of parties. We used to party all the time, really. Except we didn't like to go on stage out of it. So we would party all night but we would sleep all day and play the gig and start again. It was kind of like that. Except one or two times in the early days we did make the error of getting a bit too gone. And we made a pact that we shouldn't do that."

It's a cliché, starting with Cream and then The Who and later Manowar and the *Guinness Book of World Records* and all that, but Motörhead most definitely had a reputation for being very loud.

"Man, it wasn't our fault," defends Clarke. "I was forever trying to get a fucking . . . to hear myself. So I was forever adding fucking amps over my side, and Lemmy was just adding more and more on his side, and then Phil had bigger monitors, see what I mean? It was one of those. Each one of us, because we never really interfered with each other's stuff. I let Lemmy get on with his and Phil get on with his and vice versa. So I'd be over my side trying to hear what I wanted to by adding more and more stuff. And of course, they'd be doing the same over on their side. It was like, 'Hey guys, why don't we try turning down and starting again?' It was too late for that. You were all trying to hear yourself really. I mean there were times onstage . . . I'll tell you what, man, your ears shut off. And all you got was this ringing and you had to just kind of look around and watch Phil and what his hands were doing just to keep up . . . where are we? I'd watch his hands and know roughly where we were.

"Me and Phil used to fight a lot. We used to have this running thing. And it was usually about the sound. We'd have these differences about the sound. And Phil, being a drummer, he had a very short fuse. So I'd be sort of trying to reason with him and all of a sudden he'd thump me and I'd have to thump him back and a couple of times we ended up rolling around hotel foyers. But because we were such great mates it used to be a right laugh. We used to have a laugh and a drink afterwards. It was nothing real bad. I don't want to tell you something that sounds really ridiculous. We did have some shitty stuff, but you have to imagine that it was pretty much full-on."

And of course no one is wearing earplugs. "No, fuck that! Yeah, you can't do that, man. Ted Nugent did that. He used to say, 'If it's too loud, you're too old,' and then he wore fucking earplugs! I mean if that's not a fucking hypocritical shitbag, you know? Although I did like Ted Nugent; I was a big fan of his. He was always great. He used to do a lot of shows over here in the mid-'70s. This was one of his markets, which was nice.

"We were always struggling for recognition as musicians," adds Eddie, reflecting on how the band's already uncouth songs made double the racket live. It's always been a point of contention, but it's a badge the fans pinned on their heroes proudly, rooting for their beloved underdogs just like the punks did, but with a band that breaks the mold.

"It was very odd in Motörhead. We were just the fucking noise band, the loudest band in the world, you know what I mean? So we never had any real musician friends and we never had any respect from musicians or the business as players. So that doesn't really matter, you think. But it fucking sort of does. It sort of does, when everybody thinks you can't play. And I remember somebody telling me in the Motörhead office, when I left the band, it was some record guy who phoned up and said, 'Well, what's Eddie Clarke going to do now? Because he can't play fucking guitar,' you know what I mean? It's just an indication that we weren't . . . our actual souls, our musical souls, weren't really fed that well with Motörhead. We always felt like second-class musicians. It's a tricky one to actually put into words but it's something we all had to live with, and that put pressure on us because you're inevitably unhappy a lot of the time, disenchanted, disgruntled."

And then, after the success of *Overkill*, Britain's new noise heroes found themselves crashing headlong into another great record called *Bomber*. "Yes, it was straightforward, carry on," muses Fast Eddie. "Because we were so fucking on it. I remember, we went into the studio, and everything we played was a new tune! We had this couple of weeks that were just out of this fucking world, man. And was, 'Fuckin' 'ell, what about this?!' All that sort of thing. I think we ran a little short. We might have run out at about nine tunes, I think, and we might have had to struggle right towards the end a tad. But basically speaking, that's how it felt, 'Stone Dead Forever,' 'Bomber,' 'Lawman' . . . it's fucking brilliant, man. They just flowed. We were flying along and all of a sudden, you run out, you know? But apart from that, *Bomber* was just a continuation of the spirit of *Overkill*."

CHAPTER 5

Bomber: "They saw us as noisy, scary people."

Bomber, issued October 27, 1979, just might be the second heaviest record ever issued in the '70s, after, arguably, the band's own *Overkill*. Rainbow's *Rising*? *Stained Class*? *Sabotage*? *Full Speed at High Level*? (Look it up.) *Portrait of the Artist as a Young Ram*? (Look that one up too.) For all the grief set upon *Bomber* as "lighter" than *Overkill*, it's quite possibly heavier than all comers by bands lacking mutton-chopped bass-abusers.

"It's weird, but to us we were just a band that was playing hard rock," muses Phil, addressing the idea of Motörhead as a heavy metal band—and perhaps the heaviest goddamn ever, as of 1979. "However it came out, it came out. I don't think any of us—or anybody who is in a band that becomes successful—ever sits down and says, 'Right guys, we're going to be the heaviest band in the world!' Well, a lot of them do, but a lot of them that do never make it. Anybody who sits down and tries to make a plan like that, it never works. It has to happen naturally. So really

At the London Zoo, 1980. | © George Bodnar Archive / IconicPix

it just happened naturally, and it's other people who apply these great labels. Or say good things about you. And as the saying goes, people who truly have talent don't need to tell people they have talent. Other people tell them. And so we didn't really intend to be heavy. I mean, we thought we're a heavy rock/hard rock band, but we certainly didn't think, 'Oh, we're going to be the heaviest band in the world.' We wanted to be, but we didn't actually sit down and work on it. It just came out like that.

"But sure, when those two words came out, and were pointed on us—heavy metal—we didn't mind at all. Because we thought, 'Oh, that's quite a good name, heavy metal.' Based on heavy rock. But to us it didn't really matter what you called us; it was what it was, as long as somebody didn't come up with a name like pink metal or nice fluffy pink elephant metal. So we thought heavy metal, oh, that's cool, that's all right."

Jacked up on a diet of crank and booze a mere six months after the incendiary *Overkill*, *Bomber* opens with the gnarly "Dead Men Tell No Tales" and the record's producer has gotten his second warning from Lem's pen about the evils of the narcotics, Miller being a notorious heroin addict, eventually dying of liver failure in 1994 at the age of 52.

"Me and Lemmy particularly, we had an anti-smack thing going on," explains Eddie, "as you can tell from *Overkill*. So we felt very strongly about that. Lem's lyrics sometimes got a little dark, but I always loved Lemmy's lyrics, so I never interfered. He'd do a lyric and he would show it to me, and I'd read it and I'd think, fucking fantastic, man. I never really interfered with it because on *Bomber*, he was cooking as well. I mean, as I was firing out the guitar riffs, Lemmy was firing out the lyrics. And that's why it all worked so well; Lemmy and I were a very, very strong writing team. I don't care what anybody says, we had a fantastic chemistry between the two of us."

"We have tried throwing the police at it for years but there is more heroin on the streets than ever before," Lemmy told Jeb Wright, so exasperated with the scourge of horse that he'd be willing to try legalizing it. "We have tried throwing all the junkies in jail where they get sodomized and turned into real criminals. Before they went to jail they were usually just pretty quiet junkies. The people who kill each other and everybody else are the dealers. If you legalized it then you could ration it out better. It would be trackable and you could cut out the dealer. People are going to buy it, whatever you do. I hate the fucking shit; it killed my old lady. I've never done it myself. If you are going to have it in society—and apparently you are because people want it—you might as well legalize it and control it; that is my take on it."

Kilmister goes on to distinguish heroin from his own banquet of chemicals by saying, "I only saw people die on heroin. I never saw people die on speed or coke. I only saw them die on smack, and hundreds died on that. I hate it because it turns you into an animal and then it kills you. I just never wanted it. I never thought it was a viable proposition because I saw it steal people's lives. They would become heroin. They don't have music anymore and they don't have any goals—all they want is the heroin. Anything that controls you that much and makes you hurt that much when you don't get it is bullshit to me."

Jimmy Miller, of course, had also produced Motörhead's previous album, but this time 'round, the sound would be somewhat brighter and more immediate.

"When we first heard we got Jimmy Miller," recalls Eddie, "we were like, this is something very special. And Jimmy was great. Motörhead was not an easy band to control, because we were a bit out of our heads all the time, and Phil was a very difficult man to deal with. Lemmy would be the cool, calm and collected one. He's very calm. Phil would be the extremely jumpy one and I'd be the really moody one. But we were all kind of moody; Lemmy was moody, I was moody, I was prone to losing me top, and Phil was too—we were all pretty crazy. So Jimmy was actually perfect for the job because he was fairly calm. He just used to sit there."

"Sometimes he was too calm," continues Clarke. "I remember shouting at him once, 'You fucking . . .' giving him a right earful. It might have been the previous album, actually, the solo on 'Capricorn.' I remember doing a solo, looking up, and seeing what they thought of the solo, and fucking Jimmy's reading the paper. You fucking bastard. Of course, I storm in there, fucking ready to have a fight with someone. But he did have a little bit of a problem. He used to like a bit of narcotics. And he used to disappear. He'd disappear for hours on end. And of course, we'd be in the middle of the session, and where the fuck's Jimmy? We could never find him. Like I was saying, we used to look in the toilets, we used to look everywhere for him. We didn't know he was hanging out in the ladies' toilet. And what we've done, he's obviously had a fix or something, and he was having a couple of hours chilling out. And we couldn't find him. And he was often very late for the studio. Some of his stories were fantastic. You know, how he had to help push the cab to the petrol station, how he fell asleep on the bus and went past the stop and then, you know, took the bus back the other way. We'd be sitting there in the studio waiting for him for hours to show up. But we did like Jimmy, because he was sort of like the grand old man. You had a lot of respect for him, just because of what he'd done and everything. And he was American. He had a great demeanour, but he did get a little difficult at times."

Back to *Bomber*, "Lawman" dials it back, offering more of a bluesy heavy metal shuffle—but then again, the boys come from that background, original rock 'n' roll with its limited forms, one being the shuffle.

"Yeah, well not blues blues," corrects Clarke (who, incidentally actually has to his name his own ripping Gary Moore–style blues album called *Make My Day*), "but rhythm and blues, from the Yardbirds and all the local bands in England, really. As I was saying, I think of myself as a third-generation blues player whereas people like the Stones and the Yardbirds are second generation, because they copied the old masters, as it were. I copied the Stones and the Yardbirds, so it's not from the root, you know? Heavy metal came along later. The album *Five Live Yardbirds* was quite rocky and has quite heavy shit going in it, like build-ups and stuff like that. So I was brought up on that, and that was the start of heavy metal, really. Because they were all thrashing out a bit, and the volume was up."

So there's a bluesy riff to "Lawman," but also bluesy soloing, of a sort one might hear from Tony Iommi, arguably the only place you hear blues in Black Sabbath. And, curiously, the boys reprise that vibe for track three, "Sweet Revenge," which takes the blues about as dark and brooding as it can go.

"Yeah, a bit in the soloing, a bit in the riffing," answers Eddie, on where his blues can be located within the context of Motörhead. "Lemmy and I were both brought up on that era. Lemmy was a bit before my time, but only by a few years. He goes back to Little Richard, back to late '50s, whereas I suppose I came around about '62, '63. Lemmy always thought of us as sort of a rock band. I always thought of us as a metal band."

Which is a very important distinction and nuance, really, and possibly one of the reasons the original band is beloved by so many, this balance between crushing, no-compromise heaviness and something familiar and traditional and grounded. What Eddie is implying is that his interpretation of the blues, being second generation, leans more into nascent hard rock than Lemmy's. Add Phil to the mix, his look, his demeanour and that strange manic shuffle he'd articulated, and those of a punk disposition can find common ground as well.

"I knew he did everything different," laughs Clarke, asked about Phil's roiling shuffle signature, especially up there on the high hat. "Lemmy used to shout at him at rehearsals, 'Hey, Phil, why can't you just play straight 4/4?' And I'd look at them and think, 'Well, it sounds all right to me, Lem.' So we'd just carry on. But I know, he did find Phil a little odd. When I describe Phil to another drummer, I always think of Mitch Mitchell, really, or Keith Moon. He was not just laying down the straight 4/4, like John Bonham or even Mikkey Dee in Motörhead now. Phil was creating his own corner. You'd be playing a tune, and he would actually be augmenting the melody with his drums. He would be creating something more than just 'boom, jab, boom, boom, jab.'"

Back inside of *Bomber*, "Sharpshooter" underscores the band's approximation to punk, the band's bashed performance jostling the listener back to the unsafe and urgent sparks-a-flyin' scrapyard metal Motörhead had become cult famous for from their first two records. Plus, the immediacy of the track serves as microcosm for the record as a whole. Everything was immediate this time around—contrasted to the band's experience with the *Overkill* material, *Bomber* featured songs that the band did not get to gig-test in advance of recording.

"We started recording *Overkill* in October/November of '78, I think," explains Eddie, reiterating how quickly the band was working in those days. "It was to get the Bronze deal. And we did the Hammersmith on November 5 that year. We worked over Christmas on *Overkill*, and I think it came out probably March/April '79. So we'd been doing it for quite a while, and we were on tour with it quite early on—that was the Girlschool tour. And then of course, we came back from the tour, and it was probably about Easter. I've got a feeling it was about Easter when the tour was over, because I remember sitting there on Easter Sunday thinking how fucking boring Easter is. Because it's got a Good Friday, Saturday, Sunday and Monday off, you know what I mean? No partying. So I'm thinking, fucking 'ell. I remember sitting there after the tour fucking depressed because I wanted to be on the road. So that tells me it was Easter. And it was a great tour because of Girlschool and all of that. You know, you had . . . anyway, enough of that."

"We did a couple of festivals in the summer, and then they said, 'We want another album,'" continues Clarke. "Well, we were hot to trot then. I mean, once we hit the ground running, once we got Overkill out of the way, we were hot to trot. So Bomber actually came very naturally to us. We went in the rehearsal room and we were just firing off the riffs. We were just on fire, really, at that point. And so we just knocked it out. We wrote songs very quickly, and then we went through the same process with Jimmy Miller, down in Bronze studios, and in fact we had a little stint, as I remember, in Olympic 1, which was fantastic. You know, we did 'Step Down' there, plus one other, I believe.

"To clarify, we started at Roundhouse, but the studio was booked out; I think Uriah Heep was booked in. So rather than lose the momentum, we went to Olympic. We had been into Olympic before—we mixed the first Chiswick record at Olympic. And I'd worked at Olympic with Curtis Knight. Olympic was like Mecca. You've got Zeppelin, Hendrix, Stephen Stills—all that stuff in the '60s was all done at Olympic. At Olympic, as I recall, the Generation X, Billy Idol, he popped in. He was in another studio, and he's a lovely fellow, very funny. Yeah, but not really any other guests per se. I'll tell you what we were. We were a bit scary, Motörhead. And you know, other musicians didn't see us as musicians. They saw us as noisy, scary people. So we were kind of avoided. You wouldn't have Sting putting his head around the

Phil and an army of Motörheadbangers. | © Piergiorgio Brunelli

door and saying, 'Hi guys.' People avoided us. So no, we didn't have many visitors in the studio."

"It didn't scare me," says Phil Taylor, asked about the band's aggressive, leather-and-studs image. "To be honest, we didn't embrace the biker thing. It's more like they embraced us, which is through Lemmy. Because Eddie and I didn't know any bikers at all. But when we joined Motörhead . . . well, actually, Lemmy was living in a squat with the Hells Angels in London, and that connection came through Hawkwind, and all the acid days, and the Hells Angels going to their gigs. So naturally the Hells Angels got into Motörhead, and they seemed to like Motörhead more than Hawkwind, so that's how we got this image. Because we weren't really associated with the Hells Angels, like in having photographs of us with them, and we weren't bikers. None of us ever claimed that we were bikers. But we just kind of looked like bikers, because in those days, if you wore a leather jacket you were a biker or you were affiliated with bikers."

"None of us ever claim that we were bikers." There's much telling in that statement: it would have been easy to, but the

Motörhead guys were so much on their own path, so unconcerned with impressions, that they would have instantly felt like prats trying to play those connections up.

But Doug Smith alludes to the idea that there was a little more to the association than the band lets on. "We had this relationship with the Hells Angels that caused a few problems," recalls Smith. "And I had to put them all in separate hotels so that the Hells Angels couldn't find them all. It was exactly the same time my wife was pregnant, and the majority of my staff in the office was female. So I told the band that we had to sort this out with the Hells Angels and keep them away, keep everybody away from each other until the whole situation cooled down. Because there was a little fracas that went down that I won't go into, between them all. And I had to go to America while my wife was pregnant at the time, and of course she was the main person in the office then. And they could be . . . well, Marco was their official spokesman as far as the business was concerned, and he and the rest would march in and they would tell us what they wanted to do and what they were going to sort out."

"I mean, nothing against the bikers," continues Phil, "but I don't think we had any more kinship with bikers than we did with factory workers, really. None of us ever owned a bike. Well, I owned a Honda 250 for a few years, but that's not really being a biker. But, as we say, we certainly knew a lot of bikers and some of our roadies were bikers, and we knew plenty of Hells Angels, and they were cool, and it's kind of a lifestyle. Our music seemed to fit in with the way they lived their lives. And a lot of them since have said they really related to the lyrics. But I mean, whether you agree or not, I've always thought that, well, any lyrics by anyone, no matter what kind of song it is, lyrics mean all things to all people. It all depends who you are and what you've been through. Every song is something different to different people."

Biker image or not, Phil, speaking to Robbi Millar back in 1981, said Motörhead was shunned nonetheless. "I don't think many musicians come to our gigs in London. I don't know if it's anything to do with the type of people that we attract, but we don't get many megastars mingling with us. We had a big party a while ago and all the people that ever invited us to a party—Lizzy, the Police and that—they didn't turn up! I don't think they're afraid of us anymore so much as the other people who seem to be attracted to our parties, the seedy, heavy-looking characters."

And this wasn't an entirely nonsensical reaction. Especially from the hostile messaging of the debut, it almost felt like Motörhead was threatening to destroy music. Granted, this was sort of the punk proposition as well, but with Motörhead, it looked like they could—and would—carry through, 'cos they had nothing to lose. No one liked them anyway, other than the unwashed and unlearned, and who cares what they think?

"It was the fans," says Eddie, on the band's appeal. "Right place, right time. We really had nothing to lose and a lot of our fans could identify with that as they were in the same boat. We never sold out and we rubbed a lot of people the wrong way, but we were honest about it. I miss those times. Things were much simpler. I think life is more fun when it's a bit of a struggle. They were great years and we made some great music. It was a good time to be in a band. I think we were really lucky. But if you told me then we would still be an item, I probably would have laughed."

"It is my dog-eared determination to ignore the evidence," adds Lemmy, on the band persisting despite the struggle. "If we were in it for the money then we would be gone by now. If we were in it for big record sales then we would be gone by now. But that is not what we are in it for. You know, my only allegiance is having a good time, and fuck everybody else. Rock 'n' roll is supposed to be fun. That's the idea. If it ain't fun, why would you do it?"

Back to *Bomber*'s track list, "Sharpshooter" is more a general tale about a sniper than anything directly war-related. On top of an opening salvo consisting of "Sweet Revenge," "Lawman" and "Dead Men Tell No Tales," what we've been subjected to, by this point, is an oeuvre of menace more or less about the seedy side of life, even though in "Lawman" the biggest nuisance is the police themselves. And yet, Lemmy considers himself one of the good guys. "Yeah, but it's like a joke, isn't it?" muses Lemmy. "Nobody's that bad, are they? It would be a full-time job and cost a lot of money to be that bad, you know." And Lemmy considers himself honorable as well, despite all these tales of deceit he was writing. "Yes I am. Because it's like, the only thing you have that you can take to your grave is your integrity. If you sell out, then you're fucked. I believe so, anyway."

Next up is "Poison," one of the better pure heavy metal classics on the album, slashed with some memorable lyrics from Lemmy, who, says Fast Eddie, lived by the time-honored tradition of gathering up inspiration on the crapper. "Yeah, well, he'd go off and have a shit or something. We'd say, Lem, you go have a shit and maybe write some lyrics, you know? Take a quiet moment. Or he'd go off and have a beer somewhere in another room and just write a few down. He could do it almost instantaneously. He was fantastic like that. So it's a bit like the guitar riffs. I'd say, Lem, why don't we do something on this, say on 'Sharpshooter.' He'd go yeah, fantastic, and he'd be on it and Phil would start playing. That's what I mean, the song is on its way then and it's practically done. So the moment you say, 'What about this?' it's off to the races and because we were all so in tune, it was done. And Lemmy was the same with the lyrics. He'd go off into a room, he'd come out maybe 15, 20 minutes later, and say, 'Here, here's me first draft.' And he'd show it to us, 'Fucking, that's great, Lem.'"

The "Poison" lyrics find Lemmy artfully yet viciously and tragically blaming his absentee father for the poisons in his life. The ex-preacher is poison himself, but there's plenty more toxicity

Dueling banjos. | © Martin Popoff

around to deaden the pain of his life in rock's blackest sheep of a band, a life Lemmy wound up banging together in the absence of advice from a male role model.

"Sometimes I write on the road," says Lemmy, fleshing out the discussion on inspiration. "I'll be on a long bus journey, and you'll be bored shitless and you'll write down a couple words. But they won't always fit the tune when you get into the studio. Sometimes I don't know where the fuck they come from. When I wrote 'Orgasmatron,' I wrote those lyrics in my sleep. I woke up and I had the first verse altogether written in my head. I went over to the notepad and I wrote it down and went back to sleep. You can't just say, 'I am going to sit down and write a song.' It just does not happen like that. But yeah, I do always have a few lying around.

"Normally I'd do them in the studio, under the clock, though," continues Lem. "I do them at the last minute but, believe me, I concentrate on them. I have a pretty good vocabulary. But we always wrote better that way. I don't know why. In the early days it was because we were fucking broke. We had to do it quick because we had to get out of the studio."

What Lemmy means by that is the only way the guys made any money was if they were playing live, and even then it was sometimes only a pittance. Most bands would cite the cost of the studio time as the most onerous part of recording albums. Motörhead was more worried about how making records was taking them away from playing live, their best shot at making any money being Motörhead.

In terms of subject matter, in Lemmy's early songs, there is much about living the life of an outlaw. Later on, war themes creep in and become prevalent, but a perennial theme is, essentially, getting shafted, man against man and neither acting particularly mature or benevolent in the battle, the machinations, the back-stabbing ruses. "I always write about injustice, asshole politicians," laughs Lemmy. "You'll always get couple of those on the album. And the rest is sex and rock 'n' roll, mostly. But there's always plenty of injustice, you know? No problem there. So I write about the usual—war and sex and murder and playing in a band." And what are his best lessons about playing in a band? "Read the small print and never trust a promoter."

Over onto side two of the original *Bomber* vinyl—blue for the U.K. (Eddie: "We never got told anything; they had blue vinyl, they had fucking gold vinyl, they had green vinyl. I mean, Bronze Records would do anything to sell a record.") The first track is a mid-grade Motörhead anthem called "Stone Dead Forever," yet another metal rocker set to Phil's oddly shuffling high-hat work. As for what happens when we're stone dead forever, well, says Lemmy, "I have no idea, but I figure I can wait, you know? People spend their whole lives thinking about avoiding death. I mean, that must be pretty depressing, to think about dying. No, I know about mortality. I know there's no Santa Claus."

Says Eddie, "The riff on 'Stone Dead Forever,' the actual run-down of the chords, is something you do when you first play the guitar. And you do that, and then play a solo over it, because it's easy to solo over. It's got a descending pattern. If I had to put that into context, it's probably similar to an early '60s song called 'Fortune Teller.' But yeah, 'Stone Dead Forever' was a case of 'Let's try and do something on this.' I remember playing it, and then what we would do was set about sorting things out, just concentrate for sort of 15 minutes and put it into shape. Lemmy would start singing on it, and it took a natural shape."

This assembling of songs was taking place in between bouts of getting legless, however—a state of being that soon became manageable—simply because the guys had to get the record done so that they could go back on the road.

"We were all the same," laugh Eddie. "We were all speed freaks and drinkers, so we all pretty much had the same roster, you know? The only thing was, with me and Phil, we used to drink very quickly. So we'd have our speed or whatever, and then of course we'd drink quite heavily. Whereas Lemmy, because he was an old soldier, he could sort of control his drinking; he would pace himself. And so Lemmy was always standing and me and Phil would be in a heap on the floor. Lemmy would still be there doing a vocal, and me and Phil would be fuckin' passed out somewhere. You know, after we'd have a fight. So you get the good periods. But as for sleep patterns, sleep—for me, particularly, and Phil to a point—was passing out. Lemmy used to stay awake all night. So it did give us a slight problem at some shows later on, because Lemmy would stay up for maybe three or four days at a time and then he would suddenly find himself getting very weak. We did Bingley Hall once and he collapsed at the end of the show and we couldn't do the encore because he was just absolutely fucked. So we tried to avoid that in the future. We'd kind of have to look out for each other."

"Well, when I get drunk, I don't fight people," laughs Lemmy, citing this as one of his positive attributes. "So that's one good thing. I can't stand those drunks; three drinks, and they're saying yes, I'll fight anybody in the place. That's really boring. And another good point I suppose I have is that I persevere, and that I believe in the innate goodness of people, although I'm terribly cynical, and I believe that we're all going to hell in a handcart." As for what else it takes to get the job done in the studio, "Ruthless determination," says Lemmy. "And I'm in a job I like, so it's a privilege, isn't it? Most people have to work in jobs they hate all their life."

And so the guys had to figure out how to be productive, when to work and when to fall down, says Eddie. "When were we most productive? Well, we realized after going into *Bomber* that recording until six in the morning was a waste of time. Because after fucking 12 o'clock at night, you know, you go in the next day after working all night, thinking it sounded great, and you listen to what you've done, and say, what the fucking hell's that?! And you'd have to redo it all because you were so out of your fucking head. So we made a thing that we knocked it on the head at midnight, sort of thereabouts, 1 o'clock-ish, in the end. We had kind of a regime going. We'd get in the studio, 4 o'clock, 3 o'clock, after getting up at noon, 1 o'clock, eat breakfast, whatever. Just generally putter about, make your way to the studio, get to the studio for three or four. Of course, typically wait for Jimmy Miller; that would be a bit difficult. We'd have a few beers at the studio, maybe a burger and that, and that's how it would start. Speed, have a few toots, a bit of speed and that. You know, nothing too over the top I'd say—the normal amount, you know. And then you'd be working."

Second track into side two of *Bomber* was "All the Aces," another searing heavy metal number, rendered so by its sinister melodic structure and its sophisticated riff. That title, like so many others throughout *Overkill* and *Bomber*, was setting up Motörhead nicely for the image that would be solidified with *Ace of Spades*, less the outlaw about London town and more the outlaw archetype as it exists outside the shackling rules of space and place. Lyrically, Lemmy picks up a bit of the theme of "Stone Dead Forever," namely the corruption of those running the music business. No threats this time, but it's a scathing denouncement nonetheless.

Next up on *Bomber* is "Step Down," another dirge in the leaden spirit of "Lawman" and "Sweet Revenge," but with a twist.

"We'd done this track, 'Step Down,'" explains Eddie, "and, well, it wasn't called 'Step Down' at the time. We'd done this sort of bluesy thing, thinking we needed something a bit mid-paced. And Lemmy started singing it, and to be honest, I didn't feel it suited Lemmy's vocals well. So I said, 'Should I have a go at this one, Lem?' Because I felt it suited my range a bit better. And he said, sure, sure, sure. So I went out and had a go, and we agreed that it sounded quite all right. And it was good to get me singing, because it broke the album up a bit. I wasn't keen on singing, but it would have been more helpful had I sung more with Motörhead, I think. The original plan, even back when we did *Overkill*, was to have me singing more. There was talk of me doing vocals, but I don't know what it was, I just didn't have the desire for it. It would have been just occasionally, to break it up with Lemmy, just to give him a bit of a break. Lemmy used to work so hard on stage. I mean, he had to do everything."

Then we're onto a punk metal highball called "Talking Head," Phil turning in a frantic shuffle, Lemmy and Eddie scurrying along, trying to keep up. "Lemmy told me once, not long ago, 'That fucking "Talking Head," I never want to do that again,'" laughs Eddie. "And then the song was stuck in my head for about three weeks after that. I couldn't get it out of my head. The thing was, that was the one tune—I'm just remembering now—where we were struggling."

"Talking Head" is charming enough but bordering on filler as we move on to the album's highlight, its closing title track: Lemmy's stun bass sound pervasive, Eddie throwing off melodic licks, the whole thing rumbling along hook-laden and highly memorable, transition to transition to simple chorus. "Bomber" wouldn't have been out of place on the Damned's (also) 1979 album, *Machine Gun Etiquette*, again, underscoring the nasty rule-breaking punk aspect to Motörhead's subversive approach to heavy metal mores.

Bomber's title track, besides its ties to a terrible and romanticized time of war, is also illustrative of this idea that the sound picture for *Bomber* is brighter and—dare say some—lighter, than that of *Overkill*.

"Yes, I think, it was," agrees Eddie. "It was somewhat of a move forward for us, inasmuch as we'd been waiting a long time to do *Overkill*. It's cleaner and sharper. *Overkill* was kind of a dark, although I'm quite fond of *Overkill*. But I suppose it's a bit mushier, and I don't know why that would be. The guitars certainly stand out a lot more on *Bomber*. It's more guitar-oriented, because I was leading the charge with the riffs. I was really firing on all sixes, at that point."

And even though much of the talk around Motörhead's sound focuses on Lemmy's head-drill of a bass tone, Eddie was working hard to get it right as well. "Yes, but I didn't actually change much for *Bomber*. I used to use my Marshalls, and my Les Paul and my Strat—they were my two guitars of choice.

"I used to like using them both for rhythm tracks. So I had two separate guitars, left and right. When you played the double-track, you got a really good, nice sound out of it. So that was how I got me double-tracked-guitar sound, two tracks, a Les Paul and a Strat. Later on, with Fastway, I started to use just the Les Paul for both tracks, and I did notice that it didn't quite have what the Motörhead sound had. It was nice and rich and warm and punchy, but the Motörhead sound was quite unique—raunchy, as opposed to warm and cuddly. I probably used the Les Paul more for solos, although I did use the Strat as well. I couldn't tell you which ones are which. The trouble I had with the Strat was sometimes it would get a bit dirty. I liked it dirty, but I liked it hard as well. And the Strat used to sometimes flatten out a bit, so I found myself going to the Les Paul.

"I didn't really change much, so the cleaner sound of *Bomber* as compared to *Overkill* . . . I wonder if that's to do with the engineer, Trevor Hallesy, or whether that was a directive from Gerry Bron, you know, a directive put down behind our backs."

Ah yes, the legendary Gerry Bron, associated, surely, with Motörhead, but more tied to his monolith of a cash cow, Uriah Heep. Eddie offers an additional vignette on the mild-mannered man back at the office.

"Gerry, well, he was all right, the head honcho," reflects Clarke. "You know, we never had too many dealings with Gerry. He was like the big boss, as it were. And he would come in and have a listen. I remember when we did *Overkill*, for instance, him and his then-wife, Lilian, came into the Bronze studio, which was a great studio. I have to say, the Roundhouse was a great studio, and we were very fortunate to have that, because it was like our home. I remember, when they came in to hear *Overkill* for the first time, and we were loving *Overkill* with the double bass drums. It was cooking like a bastard. And him and his wife came and sat down, and we played it to him, and you could see it just blew his fucking head off. He loved it. I mean, he did love his music, you know. He loved his guitars and heavy music, so fair play to him. But he was a rich businessman and somewhat unapproachable, I would say. You know, he's not the sort of guy to slap on the shoulder and say, 'Oh, let's go have a fucking beer, man, and a fag,' you know what I mean? You wouldn't do that with Gerry. He was like seeing a lawyer or something."

"It was just a natural progression," shrugged Phil, when asked by Sam Dunn about the element of power inherent within the nascent idea of speed metal, represented by the first song on *Overkill*, and then, oddly, the last song on *Bomber*. "Any band that stays together for a while, you progress. I mean, hopefully—obviously, the ones that digress, don't stay together. But the longer you stay together, the better you get, and the more comfortable you feel playing with each other, and it becomes easier, and hopefully

Eddie wearing Oakland Raiders, the Motörhead of the NFL, or, for those of us growing up in the '70s, the Kiss of the NFL. | © Wolfgang Guerster

you come up with better numbers, and hopefully you come up with more, and they're more powerful, if powerful is the correct term to use. But I mean, that's always what it's like with music, for me anyway. If people think that our music is powerful, that's up to you. Because as the saying goes, if you're a great person, other people tell you that you're great. You shouldn't go around ... everybody who goes around saying how great I am, they're not great. If you truly are great or good or fantastic, believe me, other people will tell you. It's the same with music. I don't think anyone ever set out to be called great or powerful, what was it, the god-fathers of heavy metal or whatever, fucking 'ell. But I mean I'm certainly glad we're thought of that way, and as being powerful, powerful, Motörhead powerful."

"I guess because Motörhead was the first, as far as I can remember; we were the first band to play really fast," continues Phil, speaking to his influence on thrash drummers. "But as they say, again, it wasn't intentional at all. But I can see why I would be the influence of a lot of thrash metal kids. Because all the bands that came after us, a lot of them, they intentionally wanted to play that fast, whereas for myself, I never intended to play intensely that fast; that's just how it ended up. So, it's very nice; it's a great compliment to be cited as sort of an influence, and a lot of people say that now and again, and I'm very flattered by that.

"But as Motörhead got faster and faster and faster, I was always wishing that it would slow down," chuckles Taylor, "so that what we were actually playing could maybe be actually heard by people. Because there's an old adage that goes, you know, volume can cover up many mistakes, just sheer volume and speed. And it can. And it would have been nice to have been recognized by other musicians at the time, as being good musicians, but I don't think we were thought of like that. I mean, it's great to be admired by the fans, but at the same time, you kind of want to be acknowledged as a good musician by your contemporaries as well, and I don't think we ever got that, because we just played so fast and so loud. But don't get me wrong, I'm trying to relate to how I felt at the time. And of course now, with hindsight, which always comes too late, it's a great thing. And if we had slowed down, as I used to think about sometimes, then we probably wouldn't have gotten to where we got to at the time. So my way of thinking was obviously wrong."

The song "Bomber" (inspired by the Len Deighton novel of

the same name) is thrown into higher profile not only given its status as title track, but also its ties to the record's highly professional and amusing album jacket, painted, figures Eddie, about two foot square, and damned if he knows where it resides (probably at Gerry's house).

On the album jacket, the band's proud Joe Petagno–penned "Snaggletooth" logo is emblazoned expertly on the side of a bomber plane and all is well with the world. "Well, it's never spoken to me," chuckles Lemmy on the band's monster of a mascot. "Not like, one-on-one, you know? I think it's more a symbol with an attitude. I'm sure if it could talk, it's screaming, 'Fuck you,' if you could hear it. Joe's brilliant. He's got a book out now called *Orgasmatron*; you should pick that up if you can, it's brilliant. He's very odd. Most people who listen to Motörhead for more than two years will become kind of odd, you know? He lives in Denmark. He's American, but he lives in Denmark, and he has for years now. He does advertising stuff for a living, and we are his pressure cooker valve. We let him go nuts for a while, enjoy himself. I usually just ring him up and say, 'Send us a few drawings, Joe.' I mean, he's pretty quick. He's a Capricorn like me, you know; he's paranoid and pretty quick, and he sends them over and we pick one. I've only asked him for one painting. I'm sure he would give me another one if I asked him for one, but he likes to keep them. And that's good, he should keep them; it's his life, you know?"

The back cover says as much about this band as the front does. Lemmy is pictured in a typical "morning after" state of bedraggledness with a bit of the ol' hair of the dog. His youth is still apparent in this oddly Hawkwind-evoking shot. Eddie is shot in low light, fag in hand, looking bewildered at what fresh hell has just shown up. And then there's Phil, who, undermining the seriousness of what looks like a very plush and expensive sleeve, is inexplicably allowed to pose goofed-up like Captain Sensible from the Damned. The effect is . . . well, for this writer

Bomber *tour program, autographed by all three members.*

buying that record as a new release in 1979, I remember looking on mildly irritated, thinking, this band ain't no joke . . . stop it. Disdain bled into an uneasy sense that Motörhead represented anarchy, an upturning of metalhead mores very much like the punks, specifically perhaps the Damned, who were clearly the least serious of the lot.

"I remember we had a lot of fun doing the sleeve. They got the head guy who does the paintings of World War II bombers to come and see us in the studio. He showed us all these pictures and Lemmy was in his element. 'Oh, fucking hell, man. Oh, let's do a bomb there!' We've got Lemmy on the machine guns, Phil underneath. It was fantastic, very enjoyable. We were really at the top of our game at this stage. And we didn't care. We didn't have any money or anything, but we never gave a shit. You didn't need money in the '70s, you know? It wasn't like how it got in the '80s. Everybody was after money. Now it's ridiculous."

"There are a lot of us into this," muses Lemmy, on the subject of his interest in war themes and its logical extension for those serious about it, the collecting of war artefacts. "There's Ozzy, and who's the other one? John Sykes. There's a lot of guys into it, you know? Wars are the more interesting periods in time. I mean, you don't hear about medieval agrarian reform, do you? You hear about fuckin' Attila the Hun. It's much better. Have a few swords and lots of gore and a few maidens carried off into northern regions where they are repeatedly ravaged by huge Viking warriors. You know, much more fun than fucking around with the printing presses."

And that's really the rub when it comes to Lemmy's hobby of collecting Nazi memorabilia. First off, he was a hobbyist and ardent student of the great wars in general—let's not forget his absentee father's role in World War II, nor Lemmy's birthing directly in the rubble-strewn wake of it. It's ludicrous to pen Lemmy as a Nazi sympathizer (as some have tried and then become quickly dissuaded through the sense of Lemmy's words to the contrary). It's more like, as Lemmy says, war is simply interesting, and, deeper than that, the senselessness, waste, cost and atrocities of war affirm Lemmy's world view that man is a brutal beast. It's therefore a huge topic for him to write about simply for color, but it also serves as a platform for Lemmy to espouse his philosophies.

However, Eddie sees Lemmy's hobby as more of an obsession, sometimes to his detriment, "All the time since I've known him until I left the band, this thing with war and Hitler and Nazi Germany was like a healthy sort of hobby sort of thing. It didn't mean anything, but then it kind of got worse and worse, and now, in the last 20 years, it's been almost like an obsession. I mean, if you go to his apartment, there's nothing but wall-to-wall Nazi memorabilia, this, that and the other. And all the songs, virtually all of them that he seems to write, all have to do with war, and I don't think that's his forte. I mean, when I was with the band, he wrote great songs like 'Stay Clean,' 'Capricorn,' 'Dead Men Tell No Tales,' all kinds of stuff. And he'd come up with stuff that wasn't just about war and the futility of man and fighting and killing each other. It gets to be a bit boring after a while when all the songs are about how futile war is, because we all know that. And I do think that he has wandered away from what I thought his forte was, which was writing lyrics that were pertaining to life in general and life experiences."

"Somebody gave me a flag," recalls Kilmister, addressing how his collection of Nazi accoutrements started, one that turned his Hollywood apartment into a cluttered war museum unto his death. "A couple of girls gave it to me back in 1977. Later, somebody gave me an iron cross. I liked the designs. I think the designs were very attractive. I think they got a hold of a lot of people just through skilfull marketing. Hitler's auditory skills were great. Hitler said the same thing for 12 years and people just sucked it up. He was such a good speaker and he was really good with his hands. He rehearsed in front of a mirror for hours before speaking. He didn't have the speech written down; he only had topics. He would get on a topic and just run with it. He was spontaneous. He led the world into hell because he was a good speaker. It is amazing, isn't it? I hold no grief for the man because he was a boring asshole. His secretaries used to wake each other up when he was talking after dinner. He would just say the same shit every night and once he started in, then no one could get a word in the rest of the night. It was all just listening to Adolf. He had theories and he was surrounded by yes men. With no one around to contradict you, then you just go on believing you are right until you turn into an idiot. He fucked up so badly. It was incredible but for a while there—watch out! The Nazis in America used to hold rallies in Madison Square Garden—did you know that? They had a big picture of Washington in the middle and swastikas on each side of it. You can look them up on the internet. They are called the German American Bund."

And prized possession? "I have an air force sword made out of Damascus steel. It is overlaid again and again and again. It was made like the Japanese make swords. It is a beautiful thing. It cost me a couple of months' rent. I gave Keith Emerson some daggers once. He used to throw knives at his keyboards when he was with the Nice. I gave him the daggers and I told him not to throw them at the organ. He told me that he has since stopped doing that.

"So yeah, I collect Nazi German stuff," continues Lemmy. "I've got a couple of good flags, a large swastika flag on the red background with a gold wreath around it. I got it in Arizona. They brought everything home, the GIs. I've got a lot of daggers, a couple of nice daggers, a couple of nice swords. Beautiful things, you know?" Lemmy made sure he read many a book on the topic as well. "Sure, yeah. I mean, if you're going to collect you've got to keep up on your research otherwise you're going to get sold turkeys all the time."

Besides Keith Emerson and John Sykes (Tygers of Pan Tang, Thin Lizzy, Whitesnake), Ozzy Osbourne was also into it, says Thom Panunzio, who produced records for both Motörhead and Sabbath. "Lemmy and Ozzy, incredible historians," notes Thom. "Lemmy can tell you more about history. In fact, the History Channel have consulted him on different issues. Seriously. And when Iggy Pop would come over, when Iggy was sober, he would sit and talk about history, and he was captivating. Lemmy was just about Europe, first of all. Not American history. Berlin, back in the day, things like that, where Lemmy knows everything. Even though Lemmy is a Nazi fanatic, he is not a Nazi in his thoughts, and he's not a racist; actually when I worked with him, he had a black girlfriend."

"I'm sick of fucking collecting it," Lemmy told me in 2006. "If I had known there was this much shit to collect, I wouldn't have started. I can hardly fucking move in my apartment. What an advantage, you know. It's kind of a benign sickness. It's a nice thing to collect stuff. I think most people collect something, even if they don't realize they're doing it. Most people have a thing they will buy if they come across it. A friend of mine used to collect elephants. And another one, it was frogs. I mean, it's much better to have a place full of World War II stuff than a fucking apartment full of frogs, believe me.

"Yeah, I have thought about it," reflects Lemmy, on where it goes after he dies—there's an amusing moment in the *Lemmy* movie where he almost off the cuff reminds his son, Paul Inder, sitting next to him, that's it's getting dropped in his lap once Dad is gone. "Because nobody I know . . . I mean, my son is going to get most of it, anyway, but he's not got any interest in the thing itself. So I think I'll just put him on to a good dealer who can consign or sell it for him. But yeah, I've got a beautiful Luftwaffe sword, a Damascus steel blade, and I just got a dagger which is a Damascus blade with an ivory handle, and a friend of mine in Germany gave me his uncle's old sword, which was pre-war, with a Second World War blade on that. That's a beautiful piece too. They look like they were made yesterday; it's incredible."

◢◢

"Bomber" was issued as a single from the album, reaching No. 34 in the U.K. charts, with the album as whole rising to an impressive No. 12. As was expected and respected within the band's punting class of fans, the B-side to the single, the boogie rockin' "Over the Top," offered value through its non-LP status. The initial 20,000 pressed of the single were blue, before it reverted to black. "Yeah, we used to go out of our way to not put an album track on the B-side," notes Eddie. "Because we felt that the kids, they're buying a single, which is on the album, so to do them justice, we used to stick something different on the B-side. So we used to write them specially for the B-side."

Perhaps lacking the notoriety of *Overkill* and for sure the smash star quality of its follow-up, *Ace of Spades*, *Bomber*'s significance is enhanced in the public consciousness through fond memories of . . . a lighting truss. There had been an *Overkill* backdrop with flashing eyes, plus for the next album, there'd be the short-lived lit-up ace of spades, but it is the band's ersatz "bomber" for *Bomber* that would live on in infamy—forever Motörhead's most remembered prop.

"I seem to remember sitting in the office, and we were all talking about what we could do, there were no good props for previous tours," recalls Eddie, "and it was like, well, why don't we have some sort of wings across the stage? Across the stage, with lights on, amongst the equipment, the back line. We were talking on those terms. We hadn't really got into the flying idea. And then the lighting guy, Pete Barnes, and them started to come up with an idea of why don't we make a lighting truss out of a wing? So that all the front spotlights and everything would be on these sort of wings, in front of a plane.

"And then of course it went from there to a whole plane, and then it was, why don't we fly the fucking thing on chain hoists? Which was actually quite dangerous, really, because there was no safety in them days. We didn't have a safety thing on it. Sometimes they said they did do a safety, but they never did, I don't think. So it was just on four chain hoists, well, three chain hoists, one at each wingtip, and one at the back. And they were hand-operated. The

The bomber lighting rig flying over Stoke-on-Trent, August 1981.
| © Alan Perry / IconicPix

The Rise of Motörhead ♠ 121

fucking . . . you'd be standing under the bomber thinking, fucking 'ell, you know."

"It was a very, very expensive building project, because it had to be built out of aluminum that was highly, highly expensive," recalls Doug. "Otherwise health and safety wouldn't pass it. Not only that, all the motors that controlled it, health and safety had to inspect. So we had to have health and safety in there every gig to make sure those motors were okay. I mean, it worked fantastically; it was my idea but it was designed by Patrick Woodroffe, the guy who has done all the Rolling Stones stuff. He came up with building the bomber, because originally, what we were going to do was build a bomber that wouldn't do what we finally ended up with. It was his suggestion that, why don't we skip that and turn it into a lighting gantry? And that's what we did. And then we were able to mount lights and all the rest of it.

"I remember Eddie's first comment, when we had it all rigged and ready. We erected it in a studio, had it all set up, and Eddie walked in and said, 'It's got nothing covering it! What the fuck is it? It's a fucking skeleton! Fuckin' 'ell. You've got to sort it out, Doug. It's got no sides!' So it took a while to convince him that it would work.

"But yes, it was expensive. It had motors and the whole thing was on safety chains, so that if the motors broke down and the thing collapsed, it would have safety chains to pick it up. This is for insurance. Insurance companies want to know that we are putting in stuff that is safe. But the funny story about that is that the one that they used years later is not the original. The original was stolen by a bunch of didicoys—didicoys are gypsies. Because they saw it in our lighting company's yard, and at night they nicked it. The aluminum was very valuable, and they could get a lot of money from the scrap dealer for it. So that was rebuilt at extraordinary expense. But we did have it insured. In fact, I think the lighting company had it insured and they had to rebuild it."

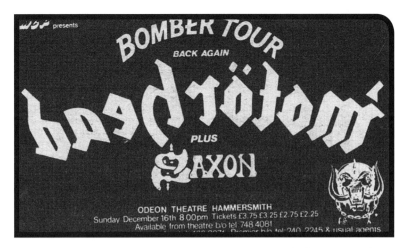

Back again, get it?

"Our first ever tour was with Motörhead in 1979, on the *Bomber* tour," recalls lanky Saxon lead singer Biff Byford in late 2015. "We'd just written *Wheels of Steel*, and we went on tour with them, and it was a long, long tour, actually, a massive tour of England. And from that we jumped straight on Judas Priest. Those first two were our first two major tours, really. So we spent a lot time with Motörhead. We traveled on the same bus, stayed in the same hotel; we were pretty close, and still are, actually. The bomber was cool. I think they're using it on this tour we're starting in a week or two [with the planned Girlschool, Saxon, Motörhead campaign that was sadly not to be]. It's just a mangle of bits, really, the bomber. It's not like our eagle, which is actually a fully assembled eagle. I think the bomber is more . . . they bolt it together at the gig. So I think it's a little bit more sensible than ours. Those images stay with people, don't they? Because they're such huge live effects. They're legendary and people want to see them. We don't use ours every tour and neither does Motörhead. So when we bring it out, it's something special."

Expounding on Motörhead's musical oeuvre, Byford figures, "They were quite heavily influenced, like we were, with the punk thing. They wanted to write fast metal, fast songs, because they were a bit of a speed band, weren't they? Playing fast and taking speed as well. But coming from the Hawkwind thing to Motörhead is a huge jump, and it was a new style that those three guys created."

Asked to assess the personalities of the Motörhead guys, Biff says first of Taylor, "A great guy, to tell the truth, a bit of a cheeky chap and a bit of a Jack the Lad, Phil. Northern boy, really. He lived in London, but he told you how it was if he'd got anything on his mind. But I liked him; we were good friends. And Lemmy, with all people that sing and write lyrics, I think we're quite complex. So I think basically what you see is, it's not all what you get, you know what I'm saying? But Lemmy is a great lyricist, for the style that he writes in. It is a bit like me, really. He tells stories and they're history based, often. So yeah, I think the early Motörhead, with Fast Eddie—who is a great friend as well, actually; I see Fast Eddie quite a lot—they were a force to be reckoned with, and like us, they've been through ups and downs and survived."

"It was the most wonderful thing, I'd have to say," reflects Fast Eddie, putting himself back in the *Bomber* days and underneath that big rig, which Lemmy describes as 40 feet by 40 feet of heavy aluminum tubing. "I think it gave me more pleasure than anything else, was seeing the kids, when that bomber used to start moving. We used to start the show with it. Of course, this is like 1979. Things hadn't really been done like that. You know, this was for our kids. We could get it in Hammersmith Odeon or anywhere. It was just something spectacular. You've got the fucking aircraft lights going at the beginning and the Lancasters flying over, and it added a whole thing to the show."

Asked for more specifics on how it was used through the pacing of the show, Eddie explains that "Basically, in the beginning, before we came on stage, it was nose down, with the aircraft lights and the Lancasters going over. It was in the dark then, and it just had the propellers and aircraft lights spinning. So they were just spinning. So what would happen was, it would be sitting nose down, right on the front of the stage, with its ass in the air. It would slowly rise up at the beginning, and once it was up in the air, we would be onstage in the darkness, and bang, we were off. And then we didn't really use it much after that. It used to tilt side to side a little bit during the show—that was at the lighting guy's discretion. And then of course, in 'Bomber,' at the end of the show, it would come down and start moving.

"I tell you, if the gig wasn't going that well, or you might be in France somewhere and it's snowing badly and you're thinking, oh, fucking 'ell, this ain't going well, you'd think, well, wait for the bomber to come down. And sure enough, the bomber would come down, and it would transform the last 15, 20 minutes. It was absolutely brilliant, mate. What can I tell you?"

CHAPTER 6

Ace of Spades: "It wasn't that it was the best we did; it was that it was the best they heard."

Motörhead greeted 1980 enjoying, apparently, their golden years, if the name of their fetching new rip-roarin' four-track EP, which was released in May, was to be believed (the title was suggested by Lemmy as a joke). Live renditions of "Stone Dead Forever" and "Dead Men Tell No Tales" were set against a crushing non-LP metal number called "Too Late, Too Late" and A-side oldies cover "Leaving Here."

Notes Eddie, "Trevor Hallesy was the engineer at the time. We didn't use Jimmy on that. Trevor did that one, although we kind of did that ourselves, which was fine. It came out okay. 'Leaving Here' had come from Lemmy and was on the original album, *On Parole*. It's a great song by Holland and Dozier, and it worked well."

The effect of this spot of product was to continue to place the band in the minds of fans as aiming to please, in the traditional sense, namely knocking out an old song everybody knows, or could learn between pints. From a management point of view,

Phil and Lem catch wind of the Bingley Hall gig. | © George Bodnar Archive / IconicPix

this sort of thing keeps the band in the papers between albums, and even on TV, in this case, Britain's best show for widespread exposure, *Top of the Pops.*

One memorable gig was the so-called *Heavy Metal Barn Dance*, at Stafford Bingley Hall, on July 26, 1980, featuring, at the bottom, Mythra, Vardis and White Spirit; in the middle, Girlschool and Angel Witch; then second to top, Saxon, headliner being Motörhead. The show stood as the first big gathering of NWOBHM bands.

"Motörhead were just absolutely brilliant," recalls Angel Witch bassist Kevin Riddles. "Bingley Hall, in Stafford, was basically a cattle shed. It's where they used to hold cattle auctions. They used to sell horses out of there and it holds about twelve thousand people when it was empty. Sadly, it took about a week to clean it, to get rid of the smell of horse and bullshit. And so we were due to play there on the Saturday. On the Friday night, we were playing further north in England, and to get there, we had to drive overnight. We walked into this place about 8 o'clock in the morning, and this huge PA was set up, and there's a huge crowd of people at the other end of the hall. And all of a sudden, I saw an arm come out. I don't know if you've ever seen any of the King Arthur or Camelot or Excalibur type films, where the arm comes out of the lake, holding the sword? So that's what this looked like, except he was holding the biggest bottle of Smirnoff blue label vodka I'd ever seen. And this gravelly voice just said, 'Morning Kev, fancy some breakfast?' And, of course it was Lemmy himself, who obviously hadn't been asleep the night before, and he was just surrounded by sort of acolytes and all that. It was just fantastic. And that's exactly what they were like. Philthy Animal was just like that too; he was an animal, just brilliant. And of course Fast Eddie was in the band then and he was the musician out of the band. And we had a great relationship with all of them, I have to say."

And three months later came *Ace of Spades*, the album considered by the widest swath of fans, casual and serious, to be the band's crowning achievement. Still, it's more debatable than common practice would suggest that the music all over Motörhead's penultimate studio album, *Ace of Spades*, was leaps and bounds better than that of *Bomber*. And once we bring *Overkill* into the conversation, then the band's kerranging catalog begins to blur even further into one sonic maelstrom, the fierce selection of songs from all three serving, essentially, as interchangeable.

No doubt, *Ace of Spades* was a hit record, albeit localized to the U.K., and no doubt that it set the stage for an even bigger hit in the live album. But there's something more important to this moment in Motörhead history, in that with *Ace of Spades*, the legend of these three outlaws emboldens and expands, as suggested by the album cover and title, beyond association with bikers and war, toward band as bandit heroes, gamblers in the game of life and all that entails.

Quite simply, the world started to love Motörhead as personalities on this record, and something like that starts innocently enough, by dressing the guys up as Mexican banditos and sticking them front and center on the band's next record jacket. Visuals have always mattered, and here was a bold one.

"I'm not quite sure how we come up with that idea," reflects Eddie. "It might've been a management/band chat thing. We were discussing with management what we were doing for the next album cover, and I think that's when it was mooted that we should dress up as cowboys. And of course, I thought, well, fucking fantastic, I'll be Clint Eastwood. Because I was a big Clint Eastwood fan. And so of course it got exciting, because we were going to dress up. So we really took it seriously. And we went up to this place, a sand quarry in Barnet, North London, and it was a wonderful day. Of course, a lot of people think it was taken in the Arizona desert. But of course, Motörhead's budget wouldn't stretch to that."

The trick worked, partially because the weather cooperated, but by this point, well, Lemmy, Phil and Fast Eddie were known to us, as was Motörhead's plight on this globe, and the band's smart fans all knew there was no way Motörhead was going to ponce about and go to Mexico for a cover shoot. This was the band and Bronze making do, and we were all in on the joke.

"It was about midday, 1 o'clock, as I remember," continues Clarke, on the South Mimms shoot, "and it was all over by about 4 o'clock. And in fact, I think the last one we did was us standing by a door somewhere. And then of course we tried to repeat that with *Iron Fist*. We did a sort of little movie for *Iron Fist*, in the same spot, around the same area, but it never works when you try and follow a path, you know what I mean? We were waning on *Iron Fist*. We should've had more time to ourselves. But *Ace of Spades*, really, why I keep referring to that time so much is because *Ace of Spades* was probably the peak—we were flying up. *Ace of Spades* just had that little cherry on the top."

As for that title, that emblazoned credo, "Well, it just came when we were fucking about writing the tunes. We would say, 'Lemmy, come on, we need some lyrics.' I definitely remember deciding, let's call it *Ace of Spades*, because we had the song 'Ace of Spades,' and we hadn't thought of a title at this stage. And it just seemed to be the right thing to do—and it's the best title in the world as well."

Underscoring the contention that Motörhead's zeitgeist-capturing record was no more particularly inspired than *Bomber*, Eddie explains that, "*Ace of Spades* is the third record in the series, as I call it. And by then, we were starting to struggle. It was becoming more difficult to come up with the riffs. Bands are good for two or three albums and then it gets difficult. And so *Bomber* was really the highlight of just, 'Yeah, here's another one, man! Great!' It was like, 'Oh, and I've got another one here.' It was just like that. We just literally, we were in the rehearsal room, and said, what about this? Yeah, fucking fantastic, let's do it. It was that good. We were so on top of our game during *Bomber*. As I say, *Ace of Spades* wasn't quite so easy. We went to Rockfield to do a sort of demo album first, and wrote most of the material, and then we went and recorded it, changed some of it as we went.

"So that was a longer process," continues Clarke. "*Overkill* had been a build-up as well, of a long period before. We had maybe four or five of the songs we already had written when we got to deal with Bronze. Things like 'Damage Case,' 'Limb from Limb,' 'I'll Be Your Sister'; we'd done them on the John Peel show during that summer. So we have some material for *Overkill* but we had to write extra material to make up the album, as it were. Whereas with *Bomber*, we had to start from scratch. Where we started on, say, September 10, and by October 30, we had an album done. It was brilliant, you know, just brilliant. It just had a huge sense of ease about it. We were excited, and I remember when it came out and went in the charts. I think it got to, I don't know, No. 6 or something, but better than before. We seemed to be going in the right direction, as it were.

"But with *Ace of Spades*, we did that in another studio, Rickmansworth. I hired in a Yamaha drum machine for some rhythms, just to add a little bit of spice onto the thing. And you used to try very hard in those days; that's what people don't get now. You've got your fucking computer and stick it on and you plug in and you've got a great sound and that's the end of it. Back in the day, you were working 24/7 trying to improve your sound. You were cleaning your guitars, you were changing the frets, you were changing different strings, trying different pickups, trying different amps. It was all about getting better all the time. And the recording techniques . . . see, when you're playing live, all of that's gone. And it was full-time trying to get the gigs sounding better. You know, fuck me, how can we get the sound better? It was a real concern to us all the time and I think that's what made it so marvelous."

Ace of Spades, recorded over a five-week period in August and September of 1980, was issued on November 8, hot on the heels of its world-beating title track. Not that this would mean mass success for the band now, soon or ever, but remarkably, *Ace of Spades* would be the first Motörhead album domestically issued in America, through Bronze's longstanding distribution arrangement with Mercury Records. It's simply the case that records could be optioned for the U.S. or not, and now, finally, one of Motörhead's was.

Still, the album would go gold on home turf, and give to the world an artful and intriguingly inscrutable autobiography in its speed metal title track. "Ace of Spades" was a lethal update and improvement on the wall of sound that was "Overkill," improved in terms of the complexity of the riff at hand over both that crude song and over the original "Ace of Spades" demo that Phil and Eddie scratched heads o'er.

The song would become a bit of an albatross, because, let's face it, in the most distilled, simple, abbreviated telling of this band, Motörhead is known for one defiant and abrasive song alone, an anthem nonetheless banished to the fringes so deftly that we can't even call Motörhead one-hit wonders. They are no-hit wonders, because "Ace of Spades" wasn't even a hit. And yet it has barged into the pop culture lexicon and will likely be part of it forever.

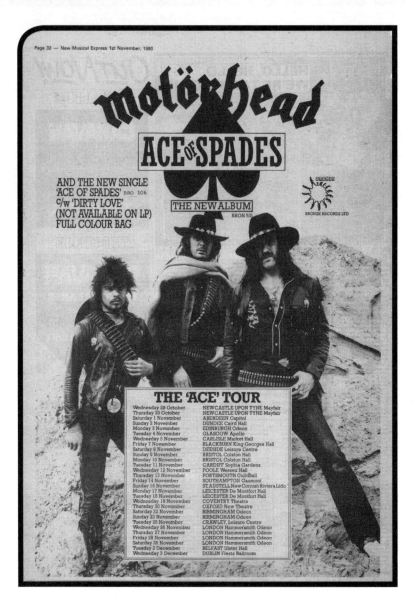

Motörhead

ACE OF SPADES

AND THE NEW SINGLE
'ACE OF SPADES' BRO 106
c/w 'DIRTY LOVE'
(NOT AVAILABLE ON LP)
FULL COLOUR BAG

THE NEW ALBUM
BRON 531

BRONZE RECORDS LTD

THE 'ACE' TOUR

Wednesday 29 October	NEWCASTLE UPON TYNE Mayfair
Thursday 30 October	NEWCASTLE UPON TYNE Mayfair
Saturday 1 November	ABERDEEN Capitol
Sunday 2 November	DUNDEE Caird Hall
Monday 3 November	EDINBURGH Odeon
Tuesday 4 November	GLASGOW Apollo
Wednesday 5 November	CARLISLE Market Hall
Friday 7 November	BLACKBURN King Georges Hall
Saturday 8 November	DEESIDE Leisure Centre
Sunday 9 November	BRISTOL Colston Hall
Monday 10 November	BRISTOL Colston Hall
Tuesday 11 November	CARDIFF Sophia Gardens
Wednesday 12 November	POOLE Wessex Hall
Thursday 13 November	PORTSMOUTH Guildhall
Friday 14 November	SOUTHAMPTON Gaumont
Sunday 16 November	ST AUSTELL New Cornish Riviera Lido
Monday 17 November	LEICESTER De Montfort Hall
Tuesday 18 November	LEICESTER De Montfort Hall
Wednesday 19 November	COVENTRY Theatre
Thursday 20 November	OXFORD New Theatre
Saturday 22 November	BIRMINGHAM Odeon
Sunday 23 November	BIRMINGHAM Odeon
Tuesday 25 November	CRAWLEY, Leisure Centre
Wednesday 26 November	LONDON Hammersmith Odeon
Thursday 27 November	LONDON Hammersmith Odeon
Friday 28 November	LONDON Hammersmith Odeon
Saturday 29 November	LONDON Hammersmith Odeon
Tuesday 2 December	BELFAST Ulster Hall
Wednesday 3 December	DUBLIN Fiesta Ballroom

It's a similar situation to the Ramones, who are represented by "Blitzkrieg Bop" at hockey and football games and yet never had much of a hit with that "Hey ho" anthem or any other of their beloved songs. But "the brudders" sure punch above their weight in T-shirt sales, as does Motörhead. Both acts represent a walk on the wild side for eschewers of hard rock, and in Motörhead's

132　♠　*Beer Drinkers and Hell Raisers*

case, it's because of Lemmy and his three-minute blast of nihilism, "Ace of Spades."

"Well, every band gets that," shrugs Lemmy. "Every band is attached to one song: Lynyrd Skynyrd, 'Free Bird,' Eric Clapton 'Crossroads'—but he's got a few actually—Hendrix, 'Purple Haze.' All these bands with different songs, you have to just grin and bear it. And we were lucky—we got famous from a good song; 'Ace of Spades' is a good song. I don't mind playing 'Ace of Spades' because it's good. But imagine if you are famous for a fucking turkey, and have to play that for the rest of your life."

Playing it is one thing, but being asked about it in interviews all the time is another. "No, I like doing interviews if they're good questions," explains Lem. "If someone has done their homework and they don't want you to do all the work for them . . . because you get some people that say, 'So, tell me about "Ace of Spades."' Oh, fuck off. I mean, there are only a certain amount of things you can say about one fucking song."

I asked Lemmy if it's ever come to a head, where perhaps he's got to go in for some superficial and short TV chat at eight in the morning and it all went pear-shaped. "Well, I won't go there at eight in the morning. I'll probably kill somebody. Especially in TV. No, I usually breeze through it, it's certainly not something new to me. I've never walked out of an interview. Except me and Phil Campbell did once, because this chick was really a pain in the ass, and she insisted on doing an interview in the bathroom for some reason, and it was very echoey. You can imagine all the tiles and all that, and the hallway. And she said, 'Did you ever do anything really funny in an interview?' And Phil said, 'Yeah, well, me and Lem once got up and walked out of an interview and never came back.' And then we got up and walked out and we never went back. And one time we were waiting for a radio guy, Radio Clyde, from Strathclyde, in Glasgow, Scotland, and me and Eddie missed a sound check to go and do this fucking interview because it was so deathly important. And like this guy kept us waiting for half an hour, so we put the fire hose inside the fucking studio, shut the door and turned it on and left."

"Ace of Spades" offers a ruthless peer into Lemmy's carpe diem life credo, which is roughly live fast roughly and play the game for the rush of playing it. Even though you win some, we are all born to lose. It'll be proven in the gambling and all the games that make up our illusory lives, and then, ultimately, as intimated in the last verse, death will play its card, the ace of spades. And therefore, back to the opening sentiments: roll up to the table, ante up and play the game.

Inspiration for the closing sequence, particularly the reference to the dead man's hand, derives from the tale of Wild Bill Hickok holding those cards when he was shot dead. As for wider influence, Lemmy qualifies that he's more of a slot machine gambler than a card shark, but where's the drama in that? Nonetheless, his recent left forearm tattoo of the phrase "Born to lose, live to win" circling a spade might also have played a role in the lyric's birthing.

"If you listen to the lyrics in the song, it kind of sums it up," reflects Eddie. "'I'm born to lose, gambling's for fools,' you know what I mean. 'That's the way I like it, baby.' All that sort of thing. 'I don't wanna live forever.' The lyrics for the song are kind of like a rock anthem in a way. It's like how I don't give a shit and I'm doing what I want to do. And, fuck it—if I lose, I lose, if I win, I win."

And then it's all over, in a scant 2:47 stuffed to the gills. "We used to want to keep our songs punchy," notes Eddie. "Apart from 'Overkill,' generally our songs were quite punchy, aside also from 'Stone Dead Forever.' Lemmy always said three-minute songs. He always loved three-minute songs. He didn't go in for any of this fucking, as he called it, jamming. He said, you know, there'll be no fucking jamming in this band. I said, 'What do you mean, Lem?' He used to say things, I didn't know what he meant. Because we actually did used to jam."

What Lemmy also didn't like was slow or turgid hard rock, what Clarke calls "ploddy, ploddy," and nor did Phil. This is why Lemmy wasn't a big Sabbath fan, it's why he didn't have a wet, warm and fat bass tone, and it's why Phil and his circular, over-active, often near violent approach was a perfect fit for the razor-wired chicken coop of a band that was Motörhead, as exemplified on this track, where indeed everybody seems to be playing above the clef.

"Yeah, and that's why at the beginning it was quite difficult," muses Eddie, "because once you get it under wraps and you start learning to work together, it's creating this unique thing. And Phil was a really major part of that. He never liked the ploddy ploddy much, the power drummers. He always had a slightly jazzier approach.

"Phil and I spent a lot of time writing tunes together, and his drumming just brought something. It filled in holes, where if you didn't have Phil, there would be a big hole there. Like my guitar, I brought a little bit of melody to it. It sounds strange, but there's a lot of melody in what I did, and then Lemmy could sing over my melody. And Phil would fill in the gaps. So we would complement each other all the way around, and it actually worked very well. But of course you take that away, and you've just got ploddy ploddy, really, with some sort of singing on top. Whereas I used to put a little thing underneath, for Lemmy to sing against, which we do in 'Ace of Spades,' where Lemmy sings and I throw in a lick. 'Only way to feel the noise . . .' so what he's doing, he's got somewhere to put his vocal on. And then Phil would keep the bottom end lively and interesting. I mean, you could call him a busy drummer—and he was—but what he did was he filled in the spaces."

And therefore sonically, Lemmy, Eddie and Phil create a seething cauldron of sounds, a veritable wall of sound, Lemmy scraping from his throat and from his bass, Eddie lashing with licks and Phil frantically displaying his effortless energy but also his signature high-hat roll. Everything has its place in the mix, but the situation is uneasy and threatening, each sound grinding against the next.

"But *Ace of Spades* was actually the start of the more difficult period, as it happens," says Eddie, "but it was probably our

pinnacle, inasmuch as it rolled off the tongue relatively easy, but not nearly as easily as *Overkill* and *Bomber*. First we went to a place called Rockfield in Wales. They have a studio, but they also had a rehearsal house, where obviously you could rehearse your band. And then, I guess, the idea was to go to the studio and record. It was a good little place, but I never recorded in the studio. Although the very first Motörhead album, the one I wasn't on, the *On Parole* album, was done at Rockfield, with Dave Edmunds. But that album has nothing to do with me. So we just used the house. We went down there and stayed for a couple of weeks. They had a big room there and we set up, and when we weren't drinking and falling about, we played a little bit. And so we wrote a few tunes. In fact, quite a few tunes. I mean, it was quite difficult, because by then we were on our fourth album, and by then it gets more . . . Every time you write an album—and I'm sure other bands have told you this—they get harder to write, as you go along, because you get restraints, really. Because you've had a couple of relatively successful records, you start to feel a little bit hemmed in. Oh, we can't do one like that because the fans won't like it—that's one of them. So you already put in restrictions on yourself.

"And then of course you play a riff or solo, you go, oh, we did one like that on the last album," laughs Clarke. "So all these little things start coming and *Ace of Spades* was the start of that. But fortunately we got through it. I mean, Phil and I were doing a lot of writing at a time. We were living in a flat in London together for a while, and we wrote things like 'Chase is Better than the Catch,' and Phil and I used to play an awful lot, just jamming the drums and the guitar. So it meant we could develop a couple of riffs. So when Lemmy was around, we could present to him what we had. And then of course he could join in and then stick some lyrics on. Which worked very well at that time. So we did some demos in those Rockfield sessions on an eight-track—a little eight-track mobile turned up. We just recorded everything, and later we put some vocals on those back in London, just for the crack to see how they were sounding. And they weren't sounding too bad. So we had sort of like the makings of a good record. But it wasn't until we went into the studio with Vic Maile that it really started to take shape.

"He was a nice little fellow, he was," continues Eddie, on the subject of producer of choice this time around, Vic Maile, gone from this world nine years later. "Yeah, he was a quiet, little, reserved kind of chap. But he used to come up with these magnificent mixes. And he used to get our sounds down. He used to piss us off. He had this little studio stuck out somewhere. We had to drive out there every day. It was a real pisser, but we used to like working with him because he didn't say a lot but he always got a good result. So when you work with someone, you put up with all that stuff. And he didn't take any shit either, which was quite funny. He was only a little guy but he didn't take any shit. So we didn't bother giving him any in the end. So our work down there was quite productive. We had a good productive working relationship. Whereas with the *Bomber* and the *Overkill* albums, I thought they were great albums, and I thought Jimmy Miller did a great job, but it was a different circumstance. Those two albums, we were putting out stuff that was all kind of balled-up for couple of years; it just kind of poured out. We didn't have to write those, really. They just came. But *Ace of Spades* . . . we had to kind of write it a bit more. So that is why Vic came in very handy."

Vic, nicknamed "Turtle" because of his looks, had served minor roles on some major sessions with the likes of Jimi Hendrix, the Who and Led Zeppelin, but his main connection to the band was that Vic ran the mobile recording unit used for Hawkwind's seminal *Space Ritual* live album, on which the seeds of Motörhead are most graphically scattered, in terms of the Hawkwind canon. "Discussions were taking place regarding producers and that is when we were steered towards Vic Maile," notes Clarke, "who was favored by the record company and management. We didn't really care too much; we just wanted to record the album and get back on the road."

"Vic Maile was one of the most wonderful people I've ever worked with," says Doug Smith. "He was originally the engineer of the only mobile studio in the U.K., Pye Mobile, the only one available, and that's how we met him, right from the very beginning. He recorded a whole bunch of live stuff for Hawkwind. And Lemmy was very much part of Hawkwind, he was the frontman, he was the singer of 'Silver Machine,' etc., so Vic became very close, a great friend, and he was the person that recorded *Ace of Spades*. And as it happens, we did a few things together outside of that, including the joint Girlschool and Motörhead single, 'Please Don't Touch.' And he, sadly, died of cancer. But he had carried on being an engineer for a number of years."

After the *Ace of Spades* demo sessions, it was over to a little-known studio just north of London, where the heavy lifting took place.

"Jackson's was a very nice old little studio out in Rickmansworth, which is out Gerrards Cross way; about halfway to Oxford," explains Clarke. "It was owned by an old DJ called Jack Jackson, who was very famous, and his son took over. But he had a wonderful old Neve desk in there. It was a particularly nice thing and Vic Maile was a little harmless guy. He had diabetes, and he was a small guy, which I think was good. Because in a way, because he had diabetes and everything, we couldn't throw tantrums with him, really. If he was a bit of a big strapping bloke, we would've probably ended up having fights with him, you know? But because he was a bit fragile and that, we always had the utmost respect for him. Never gave him too much stick. So when he came up with an idea and said, 'Hey guys, why don't we go out and stand under a microphone and hit two bits of wood together?' Instead of saying, 'Fuck off, you silly twat,' we'd say, 'Oh, all right, Vic, if that's what you want us to do, we'll give it a shot.' So to hear on 'Ace of Spades,' you know, they got that thing that goes 'tttrrrrrr,' and a couple of bits of wood we'd bang together, you can hear it. So he just brought in a couple of little things into the production that we'd never had before. Because we had Jimmy Miller before, and it was all straight-ahead—you know, put it down and rock on. But *Ace of Spades* was the first time we actually thought about it a bit more. And that was thanks to Vic Maile, really."

Expanding on Vic's role, Eddie affirms that: "He certainly had his own idea. He'd put his little bits in, little bits and bobs, and he would subtly just try and steer you a bit. Like if my guitar was a little too dirty, he wouldn't pull his punches. But he did it in such a way where you didn't want to argue with Vic. You tried to please him if you could. It was a good relationship, really. Especially for a band like Motörhead. And if you listen to the two albums before you hear it—it just seems a little bit more presentable, *Ace of Spades*. Plus we were growing as a band, and like I said, because the material was becoming more difficult, we had to spend more time on it. And so we had it in one form to start with, and then we took that to Rickmansworth with Vic, and then Vic would say, 'Look, why don't you try doing this?'"

"And that's how the 'Ace of Spades' lick changed from what it was on *Dirty Love* to *Ace of Spades*," says Eddie, citing what is a graphic example of this idea where songs were labored over this time 'round, rather than just considered fine, ready to go, from the start. "It was a discussion we had about the riff being a bit ordinary the way it was. And let's try something else. So we came up with that, which isn't a normal kind of riff—it's slightly odd. And remember, the album was as yet untitled. But we had decided to write at Rockfield. Motörhead didn't really do the country thing, so we spent a lot of time drinking and falling over and at first, did very little work. After about a week, we did start to do a bit of playing, surprisingly, and the songs started to take shape. We recorded the songs as they were so far and split back to London.

"Eventually, we decided to go to a studio and put some vocals on the tracks and this was the first time the title 'Ace of Spades' appeared. Lemmy threw down a few lyrics and we moved on to another track. Not much more was said at this time as they were, after all, only demos for the album. We started laying down the backing tracks but when we got to 'Ace of Spades' we decided that the riff needed a makeover. This was unusual for us, as we were always in a hurry. The result was that the main riff was completely changed and wedded to the old part of the song. We all got very excited about the new arrangement and we knew we had a killer track on our hands. This new approach was then applied to some of the other songs and the results were equally impressive. It was only a matter of hours before we agreed the album title would be *Ace of Spades*.

"But that's us thinking about the material," reflects Eddie, again, showing that confidence in the band's writing abilities might have already been slipping in the lead-up to *Ace of Spades*, or, more positively pointed, that the guys were now smart enough to know better—and likely do better. "Yes, and of course the follow-up to that was *Iron Fist*. We were struggling big time for material for *Iron Fist*. The pressure was on from the record company for an album, and in contrast to *Ace of Spades*, we struggled. And unfortunately with *Iron Fist*, Phil and Vic Maile fell out. So Phil wouldn't work with Vic anymore and we had a problem there."

Past the career-making opening track and onto the second selection, "Love Me Like a Reptile" demonstrates Vic's work in pushing Lemmy to sing more, a necessity for this fast yet very melodic track. "Shoot You in the Back" opens with the exhortation "Western movies!" which sets the cinematic scene for a second track on the album, playing up this Mexican or southern U.S. or Wild West banditry theme, as does the punchy riff and drumming from Phil, who also credits Maile with improving his sense of timing. Of note, the original version of the song sported a chorus that was too much of a lift of the band's own "Like a Nightmare"; this was changed, with the tempo increased as well.

"Live to Win" and "Fast and Loose" keep the pedal to the metal, while Lemmy continues to plunk down a philosophy steeped in the Wild West but just as applicable to bikers and the new metalheads showing up at gigs in droves. "Live to Win" is as punky and bass-churned as anything Motörhead had ever done, but is rendered bleak from Eddie's dissonant licks, while "Fast and Loose" demonstrates the band's sophisticated use of circular, Budgie-like riffing over an expert ZZ Top shuffle that comes easy to Phil, who also adds double bass drum accents to his performance.

"We Are the Road Crew" is yet another fast-paced and cantankerous rocker, built on a Taylor rhythm that had him whacking the snare on the one and the three.

"'We Are the Road Crew' was actually a very simple tune we came up with," notes Eddie, "and it never really got finished. We had this riff going, and Lemmy came up with the title when we only had a riff. And what happened was that the title took over the song. But we never really finished the song—you can kind of hear that at the end. We kind of let it be a little bit, because the lyrics were so strong, and we loved the groove of it. But it doesn't have a proper chorus. Just the 'We are the road crew' is the chorus, in a way. So it's kind of a strange tune, because I never felt it was finished, and yet it worked fine. Sometimes you get tunes like that where you really don't have to go far if it's all working. And yet other tunes you think, well, this need something else, and then you struggle around and put a bridge or chorus in or something. But no, that one, we used to laugh about it, but it turned out to be one of our greatest tunes, really."

Nice idea, that, writing a song for your crew. Roadie Ian "Eagle" Dobie was particularly touched by the track, but then again, road crews worldwide have adopted the song as their anthem, Lemmy deftly capturing the repetitive grind of the crew's tough job with little sleep and bad food.

"By the time we got to this stage, *Ace of Spades/No Sleep* era, the road crew had obviously been through thick and thin with us," explains Clarke. "We had been through quite a lot together, Europe and all that. And they had joined up when we weren't doing so well. So they were more like friends, you know what I mean? We were like a team, the whole thing. And they prided themselves on what they did. And they fancied themselves as one of the best road crews around. And there was a lot of talk that they were a good road crew. And just because of that, we just wanted to do something that was a thanks to the road crew. So we bumbled about with a riff for it. Lemmy didn't have too much trouble with the lyrics; the lyrics are quite basic. We just sat down in the rehearsal room and banged out a riff and then tidied it up a bit. We didn't really write our songs in depth. We just kind of jammed them out.

"We had a really great road crew, to be honest," says Eddie. "We had our guy called Mick Murphy. He was kind of our minder. He was a real tough nut; he had to be. There was a time when he first got involved, there was a really big . . . no, I'm not going to go into that—fuck it. I don't want to come off too stupid. But our crew were probably, at the end of the day, on reflection, a little bit too powerful, as it turned out. They almost ran the band, a tad. It gets like that because they were always in competition with other road crews. And of course we always had punishing work schedules and they'd always pull it off, come up trumps. And when we took the *Bomber* out, that was supposed to be beyond the pale, but we got it out there. But the road crew, they used to get in at six in the morning and they had to unload. And once we finished, they had to pack it all up and make it to the next show. So they never got any sleep. So that's where the *No Sleep 'til Hammersmith* thing really started from. Because the road crew never got any sleep. Fortunately, we were speed freaks, so they could keep going on the ol', you know. They were a wonderful crew. I mean, they worked their fucking bollocks off. A couple of them fell by the wayside—it was that punishing, a little bit worse for wear—and had to retire as it were. But hats off to them, you know?"

◢◣

Opening side two of the original vinyl of *Ace of Spades* was "Fire, Fire," another blistering fast track pounded into submission by Phil and interestingly "strafed" by Eddie, oddly, a guitarist in a heavy metal trio that still had to pick his spots. "Jailbait" conversely finds Eddie front and center, lacing in a strident NWOBHM riff atop a fast Taylor pattern with interesting counterpoints, Phil getting to show off his double bass drums as well.

"When *Ace of Spades* came along, it was all a bit of a blur, to be honest," says Phil, already tiring of life in Motörhead. "We were just working so much all the time, and as soon as we came off the road, we had maybe a week off and then we went into rehearsals to write another album, and into the studio, etc. And once you've done the songs and you've recorded them and you're playing them live, it sometimes becomes a bit of a blur, and you don't much think of them as being songs, the way the fans do, anymore. I'm not saying it because it's like a job or work, but to a certain extent, you play them automatically, put it that way. Most of the time. But then every two or three gigs, we'd get one gig where it was really excellent and the old fire would come back. But most of the time we were just trying to get it right, and stay sober."

Along with "trying to get it right," Motörhead would also wind up playing their bounty of fast songs even faster. "I mean shit, we played so fucking fast, it was like, 'Fucking 'ell, quick, stop me,'" says Phil, with a flourish of air drums. "It was just so

The Apollo in Coventry, U.K., November 19, 1980. | © Alan Perry/IconicPix

fast that unfortunately a lot of our playing was not really heard. Lemmy would just speed up and speed up and speed up, and of course he would always accuse me and Eddie of slowing down. It was never him slowing down. It was always me and Eddie slowing down. And I mean, compared to the album versions, most bands speed up when they play live, but not as much as we did. Our songs really went into overdrive, you know, overkill. And I kept noticing that our set was getting shorter and shorter and shorter, but we still had the same amount of numbers in it."

But it was having an impact on making those who were inspired by Motörhead faster as well. "Obviously there was Metallica," recalls Phil, "like when we first saw Metallica was when they supported us. Christ, I think it was 1982 or 1983; I forget where it was now, just a few gigs of a little tour we were doing over here in America. I remember at the time thinking, 'Fucking hell, what kind of music was that?!' Because it was so fast, you couldn't tell what the fuck was going on. And I never thought that Motörhead was like that. And to be honest, I didn't even remember their name until they became famous. And so I did see and hear other bands that just seemed to be playing incredibly fast. But you know what? I don't think any of us ever picked up on the fact that they were doing it intentional, trying to copy us. I don't know if they were or not. Because after all, there were bands like Iron Maiden that were coming up that weren't playing thrash stuff. And there were still bands around like Thin Lizzy and they weren't a thrash band. But Metallica . . . it's a great compliment. Seeing that they are so successful, it is a very great compliment. I can't say anything about that, really, except that I'm very flattered.

"I guess it was unlike anything that had been heard before, but again, we only realized that years and years later, with hindsight," continues Taylor, addressing punks and their aggressive tempos as well. "We just realized that we played a lot faster than most bands that were around. But we didn't do any of that stuff consciously. I mean, at the time, we lived in London, and we all lived along at Chelsea, which was sort of the bit where your Malcolm McLarens and the Pistols were from; that was Chelsea—rich area. You got a better class of pauper, a better class of squat, which was us, and a lot of punks. It was not just the music, I mean, for us, either. We came up with Billy Idol and the Damned, because they're buddies that go to the same boozers. In Chelsea. So I don't know, it was a social thing as well as a music thing. We didn't discriminate between metal or punk or rock or big band or jazz or whatever— or black or white—or anything. It's just like, 'Oh, where's the party, where's the action going on?' As you are, wherever it was happening, that's where you went. And so we mixed and rubbed shoulders with all kinds of people, as one does."

Back on *Ace of Spades*, "Dance" perpetuates the formula of relatively note-dense riff set next to a simplistic and accelerated punked-out churn, which is pretty much all that "Bite the Bullet" is as well. Not that it was designed to be much more.

"Yeah, that was really the front of 'Chase is Better than the Catch,'" says Eddie. "It was like a little flash to introduce 'The Chase.' And so actually, they're part of the same tune. It was the introduction, because we liked 'Chase is Better than the Catch' so much. I mean, Phil and I wrote that, we were in our flat, and he didn't have a drum kit there, and I had me little guitar, and in the old days you had a cassette recorder, a four-track recorder, a little Tascam. I was always into recording. It was one of my things I used to like. And I had this spare room in the flat we were in—it was the junk room—and so we kicked around and got a cardboard box, put a pedal on it, so that he could use it as a bass drum. And I stood in there with a tiny little amp, and we put the recorder on, and we came up with 'Chase is Better than the Catch.' Phil and I were just pissing about. We liked the groove so much, but we felt it was a tad laid-back, hence we put 'Bite the Bullet' on it. And live we always did it that way—it was the intro. So that was why 'Bite the Bullet' seems so small."

"The Chase is Better than the Catch" is of course a Motörhead classic, and one surmises it's gotten that way because it's a nice plodding break from all the breakneck music at any given Motörhead live show. On the lyrical front, it's a lecherous stack of words, but in between the lines, one sees echoes of the credo espoused on "Ace of Spades," namely that the living is in the playing of the game, not the victory, because, as they say, arriving marks the end of the dream—it's the death of hope.

As mentioned, the "Chase is Better than the Catch" was mainly composed by Phil and Eddie, like a lot of the songs on the album were. As Eddie put it, "Yeah, most of them Phil and I'd done at Rockfield [in Wales] together while Lemmy was otherwise engaged. Phil and I would spend a lot of time playing, because we used to get bored. But Lemmy wasn't that kind of guy. You know, he never got bored. He always had a bird with him and a bottle of Jack and a book. Trying to get him to rehearse was difficult at times. Even at Rockfield, he was up in his room, 'Come on, Lemmy,' 'Oh, fuck off, I'm busy.' I remember one time, Phil and I, we had been playing all day, and we were pissed and it was two in the morning. Lemmy turns up, comes down and says, 'I wanna play now.' Of course Phil and I can hardly fucking stand up. 'For fuck sakes, Lem, we're gone.' It wasn't always like wine, women, and song with Motörhead; we did have our ups and downs, as you can imagine. So there were tensions over rehearsals and doing work."

Reinforcing this attitude that Lemmy thought it was sufficient just to be Lemmy, a sort of anti–rock star but some kind of star about town nonetheless, plus the band's scribbler, Eddie's proclamation that it was up to him and Phil to bang together the music was very much a complaint of Phil Campbell and Mikkey Dee up into the modern era as well.

Flash forward through the decades, and not much would change with respect to Lemmy's perception of his role in the band. Noted modern-period Motörhead guitarist Phil Campbell in 2000, "We'll probably be practicing all day and stuff and Lemmy will be working on the pinball machine, and then he'll come in for an hour or so and say, 'Change this around,' this and that. But me and Mikkey start off with the basics of it and most of the guitar riffs are mine. Mikkey, he'll sing riffs in my head. He's quite musical for a drummer. He's got a chromosome missing for a drummer; he's quite good. Lyrics, we leave that to Lem. He's said, 'Boys, go write some lyrics if you want,' but we can't come anywhere near to Lem's lyrics so we just leave it to Lem. He's probably one of the best lyric writers in the heavy metal business. A lot of his songs are sort of love songs, just set to hard music.

"But Lemmy, he likes to have a good time," continues Campbell, guitarist on 16 Motörhead studio albums. "He constantly reads, very well-versed in literature, European history and stuff. None

Lem settling in for a rare studio shoot. | © Piergiorgio Brunelli

of us suffer fools gladly. I don't know about the full psychological profile of him, but there are probably slight traces of megalomania in him, which he will admit as well. I'm not going to go into it too deep, but since he moved to the U.S., he became a lot happier.

He enjoys the sunshine and the girls wearing less clothes. Better quality drugs over here too, I think. He's never been happier."

On the other hand, Phil Taylor's assessment of Lemmy, as told to Ronnie Gurr in 1980, went something like this: "He's a selfish bastard. We all are to a certain extent. He's very level-headed when decisions need to be made. He's a great geezer, fun to be with. He's the best loony I know. He spends money like mad. He can go out with a hundred quid, and it can be gone in ten minutes. I get totally annoyed with him. Me and Eddie fight but I could never hit him. I've never attacked Lemmy, even though sometimes I would like to kill him. Me and him just tend to argue more; we sometimes stay up all night arguing things out."

,'

Ace of Spades ends in a cloud of dust, like the villain blazing out of town on a black horse, crimes committed, with another fast track of menacing proto-thrash called "The Hammer," which is just as long as the opener and just as brutal. It's one of the band's angriest and most threatening tracks yet, which, as Lemmy says, comes naturally. "The British are generally angry because of our climate, and the lack of things to do after 9:30 at night because the police close them all down as soon as we start liking it. It's bloody impossible in England. It's so fucking miserable. The weather there is just going to depress the hell out of you before you get out of bed. Just as soon as you look out the window, 'Oh fuck, I gotta go out in that again?' It rains all the time. You have no idea. And rain is worse than freezing to death. Freezing to death, at least it's quick. But constant rain really beats you down and it ruins your hair, if you've got long hair. Life is a bitch, right? And so are you. You can't get around life being a bastard because it is, and it's not anybody cursing you, it's not the devil getting on your case, it's random shit. And it can happen to you. A piano can fall on you as you walk down the street on a sunny day. And if you're lucky it will."

And with that coda, Motörhead had somehow, by sleight of hand and/or by the goodly senses of Vic Maile, created a record that is somehow more communicative to the band's discerning audience, more punctuated by peaks and valleys, delivering a new batch of anthems in, certainly, the title track, "Shoot You in the Back" and "Chase." But, maybe, just maybe, the appeal of *Ace of Spades* is equally made potent by the presentation of these three guys so boldly on the front cover, all packaged up with the concept of Lemmy's saloon tarot tattoo.

Whatever the reason, Motörhead were now local anti-heroes, certainly in London but also in hotspots like Germany and increasingly among the quickly growing army of metal fans all over North America.

However, there would be limits. "We were not pretty enough for America," says Lemmy. "We also didn't come here on either of the big invasions. We came in between them. Motörhead has impeccable timing—we fucked the whole thing up. The New Wave of British Heavy Metal had not happened and the old wave, with Priest and Sabbath, had gone. We couldn't get a record company to touch us."

"I can only assume it's because we were a little bit ahead of our time," reflects Eddie, on why the band never broke America. "I think the sheer onslaught of our sound put a lot of people off. It was not until a couple of years later that metal was accepted in the U.S.A., although in places like Chicago, Seattle and New York we went down real well, but in places like Omaha, not so good."

As for *Ace of Spades* still enduring, despite not even reaching gold in America, as the band's main achievement after so many more records, years, beers and tears . . . was it a case of the band being so on fire that the album just could not be denied?

"I think the people who bought it were the ones that were more on fire, so they remember it that way," explains Lemmy, 20 years on. "I mean, I think we're just as on fire now, really. And if

Lemmy in Toronto during the Ace of Spades *tour.* | © Martin Popoff

you've seen us, you'll know I'm right. That was a lot of people's turning point, when they were 16 or whatever. That's what you listen to for the rest of your life, what you listened to when you were 16. That determines what music you're really going to be into. So a lot of people just remember it as their personal thing. It wasn't that it was the best we did, it was that it was the best they heard. It's a tricky thing."

CHAPTER 7

No Sleep 'til Hammersmith: "The bomber, the sweat, the noise —it was an event."

aking to stages up and down the U.K. like they were stage-coaches to be hijacked by highwaymen, Motörhead's profile on home soil was something to be celebrated. And what better way to toast Motörhead's unplanned lording over the NWOBHM and the release of their fine fourth record than with some beer drinkers and hell raisers?

There was no better way, in the opinion of Chiswick Records boss Ted Carroll, who raided his vaults for some extra recordings from his 1977 sessions to come up with the *Beer Drinkers* EP set for release on November 22, 1980. Lemmy, for his part, was fine with the idea, indicating that without Ted's interest, Motörhead would not have gotten off the ground, so fair game.

"That was just pure drinking," laughs Eddie, when asked about the band's cover of ZZ Top mid-classic "Beer Drinkers and Hell Raisers," one of that band's heaviest songs and one of the key biker anthems in the catalog of the bearded ones. "We always liked to listen to a little bit of ZZ Top. And my drinking at that time had only really just begun. I was a bit like, 'Oh, the song's got beer drinkers in it,' so Lemmy said, 'You could fucking sing it then.' And I said, 'I don't know about that,' but after another beer I did. It was fun just for the sake of it."

And so Eddie does, singing both parts, where on the original, the vocal is shared by Billy Gibbons and bassist Dusty Hill. Lemmy is added in subtly as a second vocal track, but it is Eddie who we hear prominently. Eddie also sings a raucous version of John Mayall and the Bluesbreakers' "I'm Your Witchdoctor," which contains just enough heavy metal licks and speed to overcome the '60s chorus. All told, it's an intriguing choice, and a track that was part of the band's early sets when they had little of their own material. There's also the instrumental "Intro" and a small, punky version of "On Parole," a charmer of an original that evokes images of pub rockers gone punk, sort of Eddie and the Hot Rods meets Vibrators. All told, an interesting curio, given its prompting of armchair conjecture as to how the Motörhead album could have changed in complexion if some of these tracks were swapped in for others—say "Beer Drinkers and Hell Raisers" or "Witchdoctor" (or another original, but an almost poppy and rock 'n' rollsy one, "On Parole") for the more pedestrian and old-news "Train Kept a-Rollin'," for example.

But Motörhead were not done with the EPs. Like *Beer Drinkers*, the *St. Valentines Day Massacre* EP, issued two and a half months hence, February 1, 1981, served as comic relief of sorts, to the serious business of the Motörhead albums. As touched upon, the idea of the band letting their hair down as it were, for these bits and bobs of new (and affordable) material now and again helped endear Motörhead to the punters while keeping them in the NWOBHM game, one in which the lifeblood was a steady stream of seven-inch singles.

The *St. Valentines Day Massacre* EP was a novel collaboration between Motörhead and impressive NWOBHMers Girlschool (named on the cover as Motor Headgirl School), punk-rocking their way through Johnny Kidd and the Pirates' "Please Don't Touch," while Girlschool covered "Bomber" and Motörhead covered Girlschool's "Emergency." Lemmy says that "Please Don't Touch" was Vic Maile's idea, but originally, the idea was for Girlschool to cover it in the conventional sense, that is on their own. Sealing the deal for the collaboration, Lemmy copped to the fact that it was one of his favorite songs growing up.

It was natural that Lemmy would relish covering a track like "Please Don't Touch." As we've discussed, Lemmy loved the old rock 'n' roll, and indeed his iconic look, as it became honed and focused and quite standardized over the years, was a mixture of biker, Wild West, Civil War and rockabilly or Teddy Boy. Johnny Kidd and "Please Don't Touch" was perfect for Lem, in fact, the most autobiographical or intrinsic choice the band ever collared for a cover.

"I don't want to break out of the genre," Lemmy would say, referring to the type of heavy metal Motörhead played (although that's my shorthand for it, not his). "Because the genre is our music and we must be doing it right because so many people stuck with us. But within our musical form, we still bend the envelope quite a bit. We did a lot of different sound effect things on different albums. I think we've kept pretty well adventurous within what we do. I don't see any reason to stray from what we do because what we did in the beginning and what we do now is good music. And you can't get it anywhere else. I mean, I've listened to everything from Little Richard to Art Blakey; I understand music. I know what I'm fucking doing. I come from a very diverse background. I remember Elvis's first record coming out. And ever since then I've been influenced by him. So I'd like to do a country album, I'd like to do a blues album, and even, given the money, I'd like to do a disco album."

But true to character, there's even a sad side to Lemmy's fandom of the rich nascent rock history he got to experience first-hand. His voice dripping with cynicism, stoicism, and just a sense of "there you are—that's the state of mankind," he once told me, "I had my entire music collection stolen when I was living in London. I had a thousand albums and six hundred singles stolen. And they were all original singles. I had shit like Roy Head doing 'Apple of My Eye' on Back Beat Records, all very exotic. All of them were stolen. I've got a good selection again, but I wouldn't say I'm a collector. I never really got into collecting records again."

Lemmy's tastes even ran towards the original country greats, which would be an influence, along with the rockabilly, on a side project he would have with Slim Jim Phantom of Stray Cats and Danny B. Harvey of the Rockats called Headcat. Note the similarity of nomenclature with "Headgirl," one of the shorthand names of the collaboration with Girlschool.

"I mean, that was a surprise to me," chuckles Phil, remembering the original rock 'n' roll *Lemmy, Slim Jim and Danny B.* album of 2000. "I went to see him when he first played a gig here in L.A. with Slim Jim, and I've never been a country fan, and to be honest, I thought . . . I walked out basically. Because I thought what the fuck is this?! It wasn't Stray Cats and it wasn't Motörhead—I mean Lemmy singing and playing acoustic guitar? I think he was going through this period in his life where, in his own mind, he was thinking, I want to be recognized as a great musician, not just Lemmy, the speed freak. It's that kind of thing. But unfortunately he'd chosen the wrong genre to get that across. Because he doesn't have a powerful voice. He has a very guttural voice but it's not very powerful. It certainly doesn't lend itself to that kind of country and western or whatever you want to call it. Although I don't think he had any vocal influences at all, not really. Maybe John Lennon. I think secretly he always wanted to sound like John Lennon, because he's got that kind of a voice; he always tried to sing in a similar meter that Lennon sang in. Yeah, John Lennon was one of his favorite vocalists."

Motörhead were big metal wear influencers with their bullet belts and studded wristbands. | © Piergiorgio Brunelli`

"I mean, obviously he must like it," continues Phil, back on the roots of rock. "I know that his favorite artist—and not a lot of people know this—has always been Buddy Holly. He always admired Buddy Holly; God knows why. I mean, I could never stand any of that sort of twangy twangy stuff. But Lemmy looks at it from a different point of view. I guess it's because he was a teenager, and him being ten years older than me, he *was* a teenager when all those Buddy Holly–type bands came out. That was the music that was being played on the radio when he was 14, 15 and dating. So I guess it holds a lot of memories for him. I certainly don't think it suits him at all. But he seems happy with it."

It's an interesting point Phil makes about Lemmy and what happens when he tries to "sing." Lemmy, does in fact, sound wheezy and asthmatic when he's not pushing much air, and his ear for staying in tune starts to fail him. The effect points to another reason fans love the guy—although it might be something subconscious, something they don't think about much—there's a vulnerability in his voice, except it's not the emotional vulnerability one usually talks about around vocalists, but rather a physical one, a reminder of all the hard living Lem's packed into his head. The effect is that if he's not screaming full-throttle at the dying of the raging inferno that is his life, his own pilot light is likely to go out.

On the strength of the catchiness of "Please Don't Touch," not to mention the obvious mutual love and admiration and energy in the performance of it, the EP vaulted to No. 5 in the U.K. charts. And no surprise either, given the spirited harmonies laid down wobbly by all these punk metal friends. "You've got to remember," reminds Lemmy, "I was doing all these influences before I did Motörhead, because I was in bands doing harmony songs. And I used to do the high harmonies in Hawkwind, so it's not much of an adaptation, more of a recollection."

"Well, it's one of Lemmy's old songs when he was in the Rocking Vickers, really," notes Eddie on the rollicking flagship track. "So it came from Lem. I'd never heard the song. I mean, I knew 'Shakin' All Over' from Johnny Kidd and the Pirates, but that's about as far as it went with me. But Lemmy came up with that one, and it was kind of like a love duet, because he was very fond of Kelly [Johnson], you know. And of course, the management loved the idea. But of course unfortunately, that little collaboration meant that the management thought collaborations were great, and then later insisted we did the Wendy O. Williams one, which destroyed the band. So, in hindsight, maybe we shouldn't have done the *St. Valentines Day Massacre.*

"Oh, they were fucking great," continues Eddie, remembering the Girlschool gals, good for one classic NWOBHM album by this point and months away from another. "They supported us on the *Overkill* tour. They really were a good little outfit. Kelly was a great guitarist, and, I've got to say, Kim was a great vocalist / rhythm guitarist. In fact, they were just a great little band. Don't get me wrong, in those days, it wasn't that common for girls. Of course there was the Runaways, which I never gave a lot of time for. But Girlschool could kick ass and we really liked them. So when this came up, of course, Lemmy had this thing with Kelly. He was very close to Kelly. He loved her to bits. And of course Lemmy jumped at the idea, and we thought, you know, why not? We were kind of in between things at the time."

"Basically people were fed up with what was going on," figures Girlschool guitarist and vocalist Kim McAuliffe, on how she ended up in the NWOBHM's first all-girl band. "At that point, we were missing heavy metal bands coming out. Obviously you had all your great ones, didn't you? You had all your greats, but there wasn't any more coming out, so we decided to do it ourselves. And obviously Motörhead, really; that's the main influence. Right in the beginning we were just writing our own stuff and it was influenced by Black Sabbath and Deep Purple. Obviously we were into heavy metal when we were young, but then later it was punk and Motörhead.

"As for getting signed to Bronze," continues Kim, "what happened was obviously they had Motörhead at the time. It was Lemmy, basically, that came along and saw us at rehearsal. We were literally touring around ourselves, doing everything ourselves. We got our own little single out, 'Take It All Away,' which, because of the punk era, everybody at that point could actually do what they wanted. What happened was me and Enid, since we were little, we used to play at this little club, and so we started off there and we got to know this guy at the new club and he started his own little record label with a punk band called U.K. Subs, who were fantastic and great mates of ours. So of course we started out with them for the first single. And then Lemmy heard about us, and then they wanted to get out with our band, support them on their very first major tour. And of course they thought, oh yeah, girls, a bit of a laugh, whatever. So he came down to see us play at rehearsal, and we were all really frightened. He looked really scary. Of course he came down and he was lovely."

The idea for the EP came from Vic Maile, who had been with Girlschool in December of '80 into '81 at Jackson's in Rickmansworth recording *Hit and Run*, their second album with him. Vic had produced *Ace of Spades* just before, and Girlschool's debut album *Demolition* just before that.

"Vic was our first producer," answers Kim, offering a profile of Vic. "That was at a time when we were really stubborn and pigheaded and we didn't think we needed a producer. We thought we knew it all, at the tender age of 18 or whatever we were. The first time we met him we didn't get along at all! We thought we were a bunch of God knows what and we didn't like him at all. But when we were going to record 'Emergency,' our very first single for Bronze Records, nonetheless they made us work together, Bronze Records did. Of course, as it turns out, we struck up a great friendship with him and obviously used him quite a bit over the years. And of course, so did Motörhead—he did one of their best albums for them, which went straight to No. 1. So it was so funny that after that first meeting, that we got to be great friends afterwards and really liked his work. He was a lovely bloke as well. He was really funny. He was very quiet and had this really dry sense of humor. At each recording session—we should have twigged, I know, by now—but at each recording session he would be taping us without us realizing, and then he would give us a tape and we obviously sounded like twats at the time arguing and doing what we used to do; it was usually quite hilarious, really. We had some great times, great fun. Sadly, he died in '89, and he was only 40-something."

••

Work on the proposed *St. Valentines Day Massacre* EP didn't go exactly as planned, with Phil Taylor having to settle for an "insults and inspiration" credit due to injury. As well, but not impinging on his being able to perform, during that same month, Phil and girlfriend Motorcycle Irene got caught in a drug sweep of houses associated with the band all across London (deemed the Great Motörhead Police Bust) and were charged with possession; two roadies, Graham Reynolds and Geoffrey Lucas, were also nabbed in the operation, which found cannabis residue, methaqualone and cocaine.

"I know them all in West London," snorted Lem, when asked about the coppers in 1982. "They can't surprise me anymore. It's usually, 'Hi Lemmy. Phil, what have you got on you? It's just a quick search. You aren't doing anything for a few minutes. Are you?'" Added Phil, when asked if he'd ever done time, "I have. Three weeks in a mental and psychiatric ward for getting busted with 1.9 grams of absolutely useless grass. They couldn't find enough to test."

So coppers and jail couldn't stop Phil—he had to do himself in. "That's correct," affirms Eddie, on what would be Phil's most grave physical miscue. "We were in Ireland. We used to go to Northern Ireland. Not many bands would go to Northern Ireland because back in those days it was a trouble spot. Because the IRA, they had sort of a semi-war going on. But we always wanted to go because the fans are starved for music. Because a lot of bands were scared to go there. And of course, we said, we fucking ain't, we'll go. So it was one of our main places we used to love playing.

And of course they treated us like bloody gods over there. We used to stay at the most bombed hotel in Europe, which was the Europa. And it was a wonderful hotel; we used to party all fucking night. It was a wonderful place.

"So we partied all night and Phil, about five in the morning, he's having a weightlifting contest with one of the guys that loaded out the equipment. Not one of our crew, but it was sort of a fan that we had working on setting up the equipment in Belfast. And they were playing pick each other up, hauling each other above their heads. And so Phil picked him up, you know, like a dumbbell and pushed him above his head. And then the guy picks Phil up, and he lost his balance, fell over backward with Phil up in the air, sideways on, like if he was pushing iron, and he's tipped over, and as he's gone down, he's tipped down onto Phil's head. So Phil's head hit the ground, but of course, it shattered his neck.

"So yeah, I didn't know anything about this. At the time I was already in bed shagging or something. I got a phone call in the morning—well in the morning, about lunchtime—and, 'Listen, man, I've got to tell you something.' 'Well, what?' 'We just . . .' 'Well, go on and fucking tell me.' He says, 'Phil's in hospital. He's broken his neck.' I went what?! Because when you hear broken neck, you think end, you know what I mean? And so I thought, fucking hell, off we go, we have to go fucking right through no man's land, which is like bandit country, to get to this fucking hospital, Victorian Hospital, and it's got all sorts of troops and fucking gunmen and all sorts. Every guy in there's got a security officer sitting by the bed with a shooter, you know. And there's Phil being filmed for local telly. His neck in a fucking brace, and he's lying there, and I'm saying, you little cunt, what have you done now?"

As for the guilty party himself, Phil's first-hand explanation was, "I was drunk out of my mind at 6 o'clock in the morning waiting for the slowest elevator in the world. I picked a couple of guys up and fell over. Everyone else got up and I couldn't. I broke my neck."

Fast Eddie contemplating a future with less mania and encumbrances.
| © Wolfgang Guerster

"We had more trouble with Phil on the road," continues Eddie. "We had to cancel two other tours because of Phil. Once because he . . . well, twice, actually, we nearly lost our first break, which was supporting Hawkwind. Only the night before, he punched a bloke. Broke his hand. We got a new drummer in, just to play the gigs, but it was the ex-Hawkwind drummer, Alan Powell. And Hawkwind comes in, and what's his name, the fuckin' guitarist, Dave Brock, he saw the drum kit, and he said, 'If that guy's drumming for you, you ain't on the tour.' Because he had obviously fell out with Alan Powell. So we said, well, what we going to fucking do then? So that's when we gaffer-taped the stick to Phil's hand. Well we had to—it was that or no tour. We were desperate in those days for work. That was our first big break, the Hawklords tour. So anyway, we managed to get away with that one.

"Then we got the first album out and we got this big 40-date tour booked with Girlschool supporting. We took off around the country. Well, after the third show, Phil had a fucking punch-up with the tour manager over a bird, broke his hand, and we had to cancel the fucking tour. So it's all back on the bus, back to London, tour canceled. So fucking, I lost it, you know. And many other occasions when Philip . . . good ol' Philip, I remember we were in the Pyrenees coming over into Spain from France. He lost it on the bus. The coffee machine didn't work or something. We were parked. He got the coffee machine and kicked it all over the car park, right? Of course, by the time we get to Madrid, his foot's swelling up like a fucking football. So of course, we're looking to cancel the show. But there's ten thousand angry kids out there. If we cancel the show, we're not going to get out of there, or our equipment isn't. So they get a hold of the football guys. You know, they've got this magic spray stuff that they put on it and it deadens everything? We got some of that off the trainers from the football team, and they gave us a couple of cans, and the fucking drum roadie had to spray it on his foot every ten minutes. So Phil was an absolute fucking nightmare. So him doing his neck was just another Phil thing. So God bless him. Oh, he was a fucking nightmare, Philip. He was a lot of trouble, Phil.

"But no medical stuff that cost us a lot of money," chuckles Eddie. "There were a couple of moments . . . he's a drummer. You know, he could get a bit uptight. But I can only think of really a couple of occasions when anything got damaged, and it was nothing bad. He might break a chair or something. I think that happened in a hotel once in Italy, and there were a couple of incidents, but they were very few and far between. We cared about, you know, not doing that. A lot of bands went out, 'Oh, let's do this.' Especially Rat Scabies and the boys. They used to go, 'Oh, what can we smash up?' It was sort of on their list of things to do. Our list of things to do was, let's chop one up, roll a joint, open a beer and go to the bar, find a chick. You know, we had a totally separate set of things we wanted to do. And you can't take a chick back to your room if it's completely destroyed, can you?"

Manager Smith confirms that Phil's misdeeds didn't often find the band out of pocket. "No, we were very lucky, because we're British, and we have something called the National Health Service. I mean, he broke his hand and we had to tape the drum stick to his hand, and he often sprained it. And as you know, broke his neck in Belfast. Being an idiot."

So the elders of the band, Eddie and Lem, managed to stay out of much trouble. In fact, one looks back on the history—all of it—and Motörhead, by dint of good luck more than anything, remained quite scandal-free. "No, we were pretty good," muses Eddie. "We were pretty good, I have to say. Lemmy and I managed to sort of get out of there unscathed. We never had to cancel a show because of me or Lemmy. It was only Phil. But Phil's neck was gone, so we couldn't do much else anyway. That's why you look at the cover, he's got the brace on."

Plus an old suit, a stylish hat, and a machine gun in his hand. The *St. Valentines Day Massacre* sleeve was additional fodder, on top of the amusing music enclosed, for those who thought Motörhead was having too much fun away from the menacing main music that the metalheads found manly. As Eddie alluded to, the general concept of the EP would come back to haunt the band two years later when Lemmy befriended Wendy O. Williams. More on that later, but the pattern is one that Lemmy defends with the attitude that you can call him sexist all you want, but he's obviously proven that any time a girl wants to join the lads in this business, she's got his full encouragement. Girlschool, Wendy, Skunk Anansie, Evanescence . . . these names would crop up in conversation with Lem, sometimes shoehorned in as if Lemmy was making a point to put in the good word before your time on the phone with him was up.

"That was Christmas, and I think it was about March, April," figures Eddie, on how long Phil was out of action. "Probably four months. But it was that period there from Christmas to after, obviously, *St. Valentines Day Massacre* came out. They weren't actually sure whether he was ever going to be able to play again at one point, in the beginning. It was, oh we'll have to see when you get back together. I don't know if you know, but Phil, on his neck, he had a lump the size of a golf ball. Maybe slightly bigger now. This lump, over the years had got bigger and bigger and bigger. And it's where his spine had protected itself and created all this stuff. He'd grown all this cartilage, and it was this big ball on his neck. It was really funny. I think on the *Ace of Spades* video, he talks about it and says he's going to have a face tattooed on it. But he never did."

Thinking again about the timelines, Eddie consults his diary entry for me and cites, "Yeah, this is interesting. 'The Ulster Hall, and the Dublin Fiesta, Phil was inadvertently bounced on his head by a friend.' So, no, he was only out of action for three months, well, four months. According to this, December 2nd we played the Ulster Hall and that's when he bounced on his neck. When we came back from Ulster that time, I remember coming through the fucking airport at eight in the morning, because the police busted us on the way in. And then when we came out, they said, 'Oh, come back and see us tomorrow. We'll have a drink.' They were going to bust us but we ended up chatting and having a laugh. But we had to go back and I remember them waiting for us at the airport, eight in the morning. They gave us a glass of potcheen; that's the Irish homemade stuff."

May 7, 1981, Danforth Music Hall, Toronto. | © Bill Baran

Indeed Phil was back for a tour that raised the stakes for the band, an intensive campaign throughout North America supporting Ozzy Osbourne, April 22 to July 15 of 1981, marking Motörhead's first time across the pond, with, really, even their mainland European touring having been not that extensive to this point.

"Oh, fuckin' 'ell, shit," swears Phil, "I think probably the best tour, at least from a music point of view, was the first time we toured America supporting Ozzy, Ozzy's first tour with Randy Rhoads. And it was just great to see Ozzy back, and the band was so awesome, and the audiences were great. It was an electric atmosphere. From that point of view it was great, and to be on that tour was just marvelous, and it was such a shame that poor Randy died. And as regards mischief and mayhem, there are far too many that I can possibly remember. There are way too many—mayhem and madness went on on just about every tour."

"We met when Motörhead opened for him on the *Blizzard of Ozz* tour," says Lemmy, asked when he'd first struck up what was to be a long friendship with the famed Black Sabbath singer. Of note, some of the best money Lemmy made in the business would came from his co-writes with Ozzy and appearances on Ozzy's smash solo albums. "That was a great tour, with Randy Rhoads. I got to know him; he was a nice guy. He was small. He was a little fellow about the size of Ronnie Dio. He couldn't play Asteroids worth a fuck. I beat him right away across America! But he was really a good guy. I never could get over how incredibly little he was. Randy had small hands. Boy, could he play guitar. He became an even better guitar player after he died. It is a well-known mystery that guitar players suddenly get better once they are dead. Buddy Holly was the first. Stevie Ray Vaughan is known by a lot more people than had ever heard of him when he was alive.

"Ozzy's only problem was that he couldn't get any more!" quips Lem, on Ozzy's drug problem, offering a comparison to his own more scientific techniques. "I have a personality that rejects loss of control. Even when I was in my acid days, I was taking ten at a time at the end. We had heard that acid won't work two days in a row but we found out that if you double the dose then it does. Even in those days, I used to always have what I call my window on the world. I could always stop and look out of it to see what was really going on. Ozzy didn't have that. Ozzy was doing a lot of downers, which I never did much of. I have always been a 'Let's be present at the wedding' kind of guy. I didn't want to be outside in the graveyard."

Ozzy, who thinks the world of Lemmy and has called him the ultimate rock 'n' roller, remembers that all Lemmy had with him on the tour was a plaid bag with a notebook in it and three books to read—conspicuously absent was a change of clothes. As for Lemmy's rider, Ozzy remembers it as being nothing but vodka, orange juice and bourbon.

"Randy was a really good guy," adds Eddie, on Ozzy's virtuosic axe prodigy. "He was very quiet and modest for such a great player. We talked a fair bit, as you would over three months, and I watched the shows whenever possible. He was a pleasure to watch. He played the L.A. speed style a bit but he had the ability to make it fit with the tune and he still had bags of feel, whereas a lot of the later speed guitarists were just quick with no real feel. I used to think guitar playing was becoming an Olympic sport all about who is the fastest—not really my idea of guitar playing. But we owe Ozzy a big one for that. His office got in touch and said Ozzy wants you to support him in the U.S.A. Without that, we might never have got there. My memory is a little faulty now, but I can say it was a lot of fun and we were really excited to be in the U.S.A. for the first time. I have to say we did not go down well everywhere, which was a big change from Europe. I think we came back a bit damaged by the experience and should have taken a little longer before our next album, *Iron Fist*."

Preceding the Ozzy dates, however, is where we get the material for what would become the band's first and only U.K. No. 1 album, the live *No Sleep 'til Hammersmith*, issued June 27, 1981. The dates culled for the seminal live stand would come from a short tour with Girlschool called the Short Sharp Pain in the Neck Tour, celebrating Phil's return from near death by misadventure.

Aside from a fall 1980 performance of "Iron Horse" (NWOBHM hopefuls Weapon supporting on the night), the rest of *No Sleep* consisted of selections from shows at the West Runton Pavilion, Norfolk, on March 27, 1981, Queen's Hall, Leeds, the following night, Newcastle City Hall on the 29th and 30th, and then Maysfield Leisure Centre in Belfast, Northern Ireland. The brunt of the album was

Support from Tank, who were, in so many ways, the baby Motörhead.

recorded at Newcastle given the superior sound from those two shows over the other dates.

"We had a full month there, a gig every night," recalls Eddie, accounting for how on fire the band was, playing these songs with an unmistakable authority that ensured that the record would be seen as one of the greatest live albums of all time. "And this was after the layoff, then, which was December, January, February and then Phil was back in the saddle for March. So it wasn't so bad then. And then of course earlier, on the *Ace of Spades*, we played four Hammersmiths, and that took us to the end of November [Note: of which none are featured on the album titled as such]. As it says in my diary, 'The three gigs were recorded by Vic Maile on the Manor Mobile, which was to be the June 1981 live album,' *No Sleep 'til Hammersmith*."

,'

Motörhead's first live album is a frightening document of this most egregiously powerful of power trios at the height of their power trio dominance, despite Phil having just returned from a life of toddling around in a neck brace. In fact it is Phil that ensures the record is high octane from start to finish, exemplified by his amusing two tries and two different tempos of high-hat count-in on the band's landmark song, "Ace of Spades," which opens the album. Chaos is averted for this landmark opener as the traditionally trained Taylor switches to lock-perfect snare and the band is off to the races. By the time we get to track two, "Stay Clean," Phil executes the signature drum roll flourish that opens the song perfectly and then lays down a driving groove that is eclipsed only by his performance on track three, "Metropolis," which Phil elevates eons o'er and above the murky studio version, aided and abetted by Lemmy's gorgeous and top-shelf bass line. Lemmy dedicates the fourth track on the album, "The Hammer," "To Little Philbert," after which comes the older performance,

"Iron Horse." Once more it is Phil that gets—and gives—the most spirited workout, but this one's got probably the best bass sound from Lemmy on the album, making it a huge improvement over the version on the crusty debut.

Concerning the dedication on the last track of side one on the original vinyl, Lemmy quips that, "Because Phil's already had one, this one's for me and Eddie" after which "No Class," the band's NWOBHM update on ZZ Top's "Tush," gives new heavy metal meaning to the term shuffle.

Onto side two and the band absolutely tear it up on "Overkill," injecting new violence and speed, Phil impossibly bashing harder, Eddie hitting his marks aggressively, arguably setting the tempo, pushing Phil harder with every revisitation of the riff. After roadie Ian "Eagle" Dobbie does his scheduled roaring into the mic, Lemmy dedicates "(We Are) The Road Crew" to "a fine body of men" and then croaks his way painfully through the song, his voice on the ropes.

"We just recorded it as it was," recalls Eddie on the transition of these headbanging anthems from stage to the vinyl that made physical the performances. "We did do a little bit of fucking about in the studio, I seem to remember. I think there were a couple of vocals that needed just some tightening up. There might've been a couple of bits and bobs we fucked with. As you do. But the crowds were fucking great. We didn't need to add any crowds as far as I can remember."

"Capricorn" is next ("a slow one so you can get mellowed out," says Lem), and once again it is Phil who proves his prowess most with tasty fills and a display of strength that propels the track way beyond the original. "Bomber" follows at light speed and with punk rock fury, with Phil's double bass drumming prominent, leaving only "Motörhead," which is preceded by Lemmy's cryptic, "Just in case," a subject of controversy and query over the years. Just in case of what? Just in case the plug gets pulled on the gig? Just in case they keel over and die onstage? The mystery continues.

Exemplary of the band's do-no-wrong run of good luck at the time, "Motörhead," the album's oldest and trashiest track, as well as arguably the most haplessly written, would be issued as a single (backed with "Over the Top"), becoming the band's biggest U.K. hit ever, peaking at No. 6.

What's more, backstage in Leeds and Newcastle, the band was presented with silver records for *Overkill* and the *St. Valentines Day Massacre* EP as well as a gold record for *Ace of Spades*, making them fully sated big fish in a medium-sized pond, further confirmed when the album improbably vaulted to the No. 1 slot on the U.K. charts, by far the nastiest, most uncompromisingly heavy record to ever reach that loftiest of plateaus.

"It was our peak time," agrees Eddie. "The bummer, though, about the album, *No Sleep 'til Hammersmith*, we were in America when it came out and went straight to No. 1. And normally you'd be in the fucking pub and in the clubs, right? Everybody'd be buying you drinks. But of course we weren't there. Typical Motörhead. We were on the road in the U.S.A. with Ozzy in Beaumont, Texas, with Mountain, strangely, opening the show. Because they had to be somewhere else, Leslie, who is a very good guy, used my amps that night, and I can honestly say they never sounded so good. But we missed all the free drinks we would have been eligible for back in London, and it was all over by the time we returned to the U.K. It was a bad time to have a No. 1 album, but I can live with that."

Not only were they away for the accolades, but earlier on, they were away for the finalizing of the mixes. "Yeah, we were in America for that too, and as I remember it, they sent us a rough mix of some of the stuff, and we were having a rave-up. We were in Detroit, which would've been May. We were with our agent, Nick Caris, and we were at his office in Detroit, and we were partying that night at his place, and we played the tapes, and we thought it was terrible. It was the mix of the album we played him, and we hated it, just the mixes. So we sent a six-foot-long fax to Gerry Bron at Bronze Records, telling him what we wanted changed and all that. And at the end of it, we said, 'If you put it out on us, we're going to kill you.' He put it out anyway. It went straight to No. 1. They didn't do any changes. They put it out as it was, even after us sending him a six-foot fax telling him we're going to kill him. But of course it came out and went straight to No. 1. And as I say, we were in America at the time, so we missed all that."

But at least Eddie got to rectify the situation 20 years later, being in on the remix of the album for the hugely expanded version issued by Sanctuary/Metal-Is in 2001. "We had a situation with the record company, whereby I got involved with doing the mixing on it. What happened was, we didn't really want to change *No Sleep 'Til Hammersmith*, the original, because it was a classic record. But as it turned out, the record company would have expanded it anyway, as record companies do. They want to give away more later just to keep a little bit of something going. So I spoke to Lemmy and Phil about it and we agreed that because I'm here in the country, I should at least go in and keep an eye on it and do a bit of mixing on it. So that's how that came about. I didn't want people to think it was just being thrown out there for any old reason. We did as much as we could. We are all very pleased with it. The material we added on didn't have the overdubs. Because we replaced a couple of things on the original, because Lemmy's voice was a little bit shot because we had been touring a lot. So back then we had the opportunity to change a few things. But obviously in the second lot, we couldn't change anything; it's got more of a nice life feel somehow."

But nearly four decades on, people are still scratching their heads as to how Motörhead could have such a hit with such an egregiously noisy and distortion-drenched live album.

"It's to do with the whole Motörhead attitude, what we kind of stood for back in those days," answers Eddie, asked why *No Sleep'til Hammersmith* was so popular. After all, again, logic would dictate that Motörhead in the studio was already a pile of abrasive signals, one would think only accessible to the most metal-tolerable of potential consumers. And along comes a live record of those songs, played fast and loose, ferocious, naturally dirty songs played much dirtier. Who the heck was buying all these copies of *No Sleep 'til Hammersmith*?!

"I used to think the show had a lot to do with it," wonders Eddie, agreeing with the characterization. "Having the bomber and stuff like that, and generally so fucking loud you couldn't hear yourself think. But obviously you can't include that on the record. So I think it's just the thought that somehow we did capture that as well. When it came out, the kids and everybody who was a fan of Motörhead used to enjoy the live gig so much that a live album sort of takes them back there. So they get a little piece of the magic of the gig. Because our gigs were kinda special. Obviously the sound used to vary because of the volume and stuff, but it was always a good show. We were a great band and a great live band, and everything we did was for live. And I think with Motörhead, there was a charm with the live shows. People used to come to the shows, and it wasn't just the songs and the music. It was an event.

"I went to see fucking Queen," continues Eddie, drawing comparisons. "I saw Zeppelin, I saw Bowie, you know, back in the '70s, and you go to the show, and after halfway through you go, I've had enough this, really. I might as well go put the record on. Not Zeppelin so much, but Queen, definitely. And Bowie a little bit. But Motörhead wasn't like that. You went to Motörhead, you couldn't get that in plastic, you know what I mean? The whole event, the vibe you got at the gigs, the bomber, the sweat, the noise—it was an event. And I've spoken to people since, and they always talk about going to a Motörhead concert. When I'm talking to them, I'm thinking, they didn't just go for the music. They went to see Motörhead, but not Motörhead playing music— it was Motörhead: the event. And I think the live album was that. I think when people bought the live album and put it on, it took them back to the event. As opposed to, 'Oh, listen to that guitar solo. Isn't he fantastic?' It was fucking great in those days getting your ears blasted out, you know?"

Lemmy sang straight up so his throat was as open as possible.
| © Wolfgang Guerster

Lemmy had a way of bringing the fans into it as well. Even from the few lines he throws out on *No Sleep 'til Hammersmith*, there's a sense that he's (begrudgingly) glad you're there, and that he was going to treat you with a level of intelligence because you've made the effort to drag yourself down to the show. He's a frontman that detests the tropes of frontmen. This is not a "Hello Cleveland!" kind of pony show. It's more "We're Motörhead and we play rock 'n' roll" and brief inside jokes with the hundreds of people inside, including a shared laugh over just who, really, has bought the new album. In a sense, he's not going to suffer fools gladly, just like in his interviews, but he's pretty sure there are few fools in the crowd anyway, because after all, they have the good cynical sense to be at a Motörhead show.

"Lemmy was a very serious frontman," continues Eddie. "He took his job very seriously. Yeah, he was a funny man, but he loved every minute of it. He didn't have any contempt for the audience at all. He did it 100 percent. He was honest and he had a wry sense of humor. We were all honest; we weren't trying to lie. And I guess you've hit on it there. Being honest was our thing; we weren't trying to sound better than we were, but we were just doing the best job we possibly could. And Lemmy always had a nice turn of phrase; he always had a good vocabulary, Lemmy. So he could come up with good things. Whenever you hear his interviews, he's always got a little something to say."

"He was a very good guitar player," says Angel Witch bassist and Bronze Records label mate Kevin Riddles, assessing Eddie's place within Motörhead. "He used to rein it in a little bit sometimes. Because he could quite happily go off and widdle away, like most guitarists can for hours on end. But he knew what was required in Motörhead, and did it, I think, brilliantly. And yeah, he was the thinker, if you like. Lemmy is the tactician, if that's the right way to put it. Lemmy's the quarterback, Eddie was probably more like the wide receiver and that sort of stuff. He was brilliant at what he did, incredibly quick, occasionally had to rein it in for the good of the band. But that was classic Motörhead, to me, just classically brilliant."

As for the dynamic in a studio setting, Riddles continues, "I saw them once and it was the most chaotic thing I'd ever seen. Phil just played all the time. He never stopped hitting something. So there was always that noise of a drum kit going in the background. And then all of a sudden, Lemmy would shout, 'Right, here we go, one, two, three, four,' and off they go. And somehow it would all come together. But I know that at that time, the only time they ever did any overdubs was at the intro of the song, because they never came in all together. So by the time it came to like the verse, they were all where they were supposed to be. But leading up to the verse, they were never together. It was only when they got to the verse. And when they came to listen to it, they'd always go back into the studio and do the first bit again and splice it back together. That happened on three or four cases I know."

But on stage, the band was all black clothes and smoke, Eddie, the second coming of Blue Cheer's Dickie Peterson, buried in his long hair, Phil givin 'er, and Lemmy croaking up at his mic. "That was to help him to sing," explains Eddie on Lemmy's battle stance. "When it's that high, to sing up like that, it opens up his throat, and it makes a clear passage. The air goes straight up and out your mouth. If you have it down, you're almost cutting off your throat a bit. And Lemmy used to always be able to sort of shout up. He'd position it so he could shout up.

"I tell you what, I think we looked great," laughs Clarke. "Now that I look back on it. I didn't really pay very much attention to what we looked like, but on reflection now, we really did look fucking great. Bands out there now, they go out in their fucking pipe and slippers, or you had the spandex look not long afterwards with the hair and the makeup. But we didn't do any of that. We went on with our jeans and stuff, bullet belts, leather jackets. We wore those in the street. That's what we wore all day, really. And I just thought we looked kind of real. I think we looked quite serious, really."

But, again, it's not so much a biker look. "Well, not really. But like we had to say in an interview once, well, actually, I don't own a motorbike; I don't ride one. And so even though a lot of bikers had taken us to their hearts, we weren't actually bikers."

What they were was approachable. And fully anti–rock star. According to Rob Godwin, one might trace this ethic back to Lemmy's time in Hawkwind. In this light, Motörhead came honestly and naturally to their role as bridge band between long-haired rock and music by people with hair like Phil's. "At that point in time, by '75," says Rob, "when Motörhead first came on the scene, bands like Priest and AC/DC were just getting recognition, the punks come in and derail many different subgenres of rock music, including prog and psychedelia. And everything was being tossed out. But Hawkwind and Motörhead just plowed right through, because they had a connection with their fans that was more in sync with what the punks were saying. Which is, you know, we don't want these big rock guys looking down on us from 60-foot-high stages and from behind a moat. You want to go and have a beer with them at the bar.

"And that was something that Hawkwind had cultivated," continues Godwin. "I don't think they consciously cultivated it. It was just something that they'd been doing since the beginning, right from playing outside the gates of the Isle of Wight festival in 1970. While Hendrix was playing inside, they're playing outside the gates for free. That mindset, I think the punks sort of latched onto. It was like, these guys, they're the same as us. And I have to say that that mindset continued in the sense that you could always go and find Lemmy at the bar at the Rainbow. He wasn't going to go hide behind a castle wall. And it's the same with Hawkwind today. The last time I saw Hawkwind was a year and a half ago playing some theatre in Yorkshire, and before the show they were in the pub next door, with all the audience. I can't say what other bars they'd be in, but having said that, the Hammersmith Odeon was one of those places that Motörhead, obviously, played. It is a very well-known large venue in the West End of London, and it had pubs all around. Even now, they're still gathering places for punters before the shows. I went to see Kate Bush a year ago, and every pub within spitting distance of the Hammersmith Odeon was overflowing with the punters. Needless to say Kate Bush wasn't in the pub, but you can bet your ass Hawkwind and Motörhead would've been there.

"There's an authenticity about it, right? You could tell Motörhead was the real deal. I don't think they got into it for the money. They got into it because they wanted to be musicians. They wanted to play rock music. And like I say, in Lemmy's case, certainly, that whole mentality came from Hawkwind. They would play a paid show and then five minutes later they'd go and play somewhere for free. And I think that whole outlaw counterculture thing went all the way down the pipe to Lemmy as well."

Addressing the band's visual image, Rob clearly sees the connection of Taylor to the punks. "Yeah, I think so. His image, with the piercings and the spiky hair and sort of ripped clothes and everything else, he was always like Animal from the Muppets. And when he first came on the scene, yeah, I think he complemented Lemmy's image. Lemmy had started to cultivate a biker look. I have to say that the first time we really got a sense of that was that shot for the cover of the *NME* in the mid-'70s, a famous photo of him in shades sitting on a long-neck chopper, and there's a girl on the bike with him. That was like the first time that we saw him doing the sort of Hells Angel/*Easy Rider* thing. But he was just another one of the guys."

So like their fans and like bikers, the guys in the band lived fast, traveled light, and could always be available for a pint—Lemmy would indeed tell me at the end of every phone interview in advance of a show (and I'm sure everybody else he talked to as well), "Come say hi and we'll have a beer." Furthermore— between the three—there would be no marriages and only one child (Lemmy's son, Paul Inder). One can debate the number and

Phil bringing the thunder. | © Wolfgang Guerster

intensity of regrets, but I'm sure there are a few for each of the three members of the classic Motörhead lineup. There was not even much in the way of transportation or purchased accommodation, although, as Kevin Riddles relates, once the band had a bit of money in their pocket, Lemmy upgraded his digs, which nonetheless remained a rental until jettisoned.

"He used to live on a beautiful houseboat on the River Thames in London, in Chelsea," recalls Riddles. "And I walked in there one day, and the one thing I noticed by their absence, there wasn't a single piece of musical equipment. Not one—there wasn't a guitar, there wasn't a ukulele, there wasn't a juice harp, there wasn't a kazoo, nothing. And I just happened to say, 'So where do you practice?' And he goes, 'What the hell would I want to fucking practice for?' And that was it. He, by his own lights, by his own admission, developed his style. And the way he played during his Hawkwind days, if it was good enough in 1970, so it was good enough for the rest of his career, basically. And that's all he did. That's what he did. That's why it's unique."

Eddie adds his thoughts on no instruments in the place. "When you're in a band and you're rehearsing every other fucking day. I mean, I always had a guitar on the side, but I was too busy partying and shagging birds to fucking play the fucking thing. You know what I mean? Someone to pick you up and stick you in a fucking rehearsal room and put a guitar in your hand and say 'Go,' and you go off. Fucking great. It was a little bit like that. But Lemmy wasn't, like I say, about the jamming thing. Lemmy wasn't the greatest man for rehearsal. I used to like rehearsing; I used to enjoy it. And I know Phil did. But Lemmy didn't like it."

Back to the home on the river. "Fucking cold in there, mate," remembers Eddie. "Yeah, he had this fucking houseboat. I only went on there a couple of times to go and see him. And of course trying to get to it, you had to jump across all these other boats to get there, which, being a piss-head, could be quite difficult at times. But no, he stayed on there. That must've been about 1981, I guess. That might've been about the *Ace of Spades* tour; I've got to think it was. But it was very cold, very damp. Great in the summer, but in the winter, cold and damp. In fact, we worried about Lem on that. In fact, he tried to buy the fucking thing, if I remember rightly, but they wouldn't give him a mortgage on it. He fell out of love with it eventually, but there was something he kind of liked about it. I think it was the fact that he felt a little bit cut off from everybody there—he kind of liked that."

"Phil had his old green Camaro," says Eddie, on any other material possessions the guys had, now that they could afford them, albeit modestly. Confirms Phil, "I was out to buy a bike once, and my manager said, 'You'll be dead in a week,' so I bought a Camaro instead. I was dead in three weeks.

"What did I have? I had a fuckin' old piece of junk," continues Clarke. "I was never really bothered about cars. Lemmy doesn't drive. I never had a fancy car. Fancy cars never did it for us, especially me. You know, the last thing I want to be seen in is a fancy fucking car. It's not my cup of tea at all. We sort of tried to buy some houses, sort of after *Ace of Spades*, and after *No Sleep* in the early '80s. Phil managed to put a deposit on a flat, in I think '82, and I was going to buy something in '82. But then of course I wasn't in the band anymore. So that went up the Swannee.

"I mean, the thing with us, we didn't give a shit. We didn't think about things like that. I remember, I was living in this flat, and I was living in it for years. And the owner spoke to me and said, 'Do you want to buy it for X amount of money?' And it was cheap. I thought, what do I want to do that for? You're rocking and rolling, you just want to carry on what you're doing, going to rehearsals, writing songs, doing gigs and being on tour, you know? There was nothing else for Motörhead."

CHAPTER 8

Iron Fist: "It was hard work getting Lemmy out of the pubs."

With heavy metal all the rage in the U.K., Motörhead were well rewarded, for once, with being in the right place at the right time, issuing in 1981 a blistered raw live album to surprise mainstream success. Now wise sages of the NWOBHM, Lemmy, Phil and Fast Eddie were there to witness the rise of Iron Maiden and Saxon in tandem with their own pint-fueled notoriety. Where they would drop the ball is through not executing the transition to the United States like Maiden and Def Leppard had done, but instead experiencing somewhat the same fate as Saxon, who would continue their goodly run at least into 1984 before falling off the radar. As well, the all-important follow-up to *No Sleep* that they were about to make would be greeted with middling reviews and similar response from the fans. And, arguably, the whole thing was subliminally predestined due to the slapdash assemblage of the album jacket: *Iron Fist* featured a badly lit photo of just that, a true and physical item that might have looked impressive in real life, but couldn't hold a blowtorch to a Joe Petagno illustration when it came to sticking it on a record jacket. Plus the title felt recycled (and indeed it was—the band had once, for contractual reasons, billed itself as Iron Fist and the Hordes from Hell), and all the type on the album was uniformly rendered in tired fire-engine red. These things matter. Iron Fist looked like one of the many rushed and ill-conceived exploitation hits pockmarking the Motörhead catalog, and many a fan steeled himself, already making excuses and rationalizations, as he lowered the needle for the first time upon the inky blackness of his new purchase.

"We didn't ever have any that were too bad," says Lemmy, surveying the entire run of albums, "but the worst one was probably *Iron Fist*, because we were in the unenviable position of having to follow a live album that went straight in at No. 1. Which was kind of tricky, because you can't very well do another live album. They'd been waiting for that one for five years, so that's why it sold so quick so good. And every studio album you're going to come up with is going to sound tame next to that. And we didn't do a good studio album anyway. There were a couple of songs on there that weren't even finished properly, like 'Bang to Rights.' It could have been a lot better, and I was sorry that it wasn't. So I didn't like that album. Plus we let Eddie produce it, which was a mistake. Like I say, it was also following *No Sleep 'til Hammersmith*, which didn't help. The next studio album after a great live album is always going to sound a bit wet."

After 30-plus years of temporal distance, most fans have come to view assessments like Lemmy's as too harsh, and one figures the common narrative from Lemmy himself combines years of his own words on the subject with memories of the early reviews, mixed with the way journalists speak about the album today and with fan reaction over 30 years. In other words, the narrative has ossified, in no small part due to remarks from the band itself, and it takes a lot of will to sort through the legend of disappointment surrounding *Iron Fist* to enjoy the songs for what they are.

May 12, 1982, Toronto—second to last gig for Fast Eddie Clarke as a member of Motörhead. | © Martin Popoff

With the band feeling overworked, further cracks in the armor occurred when Phil decided he didn't want to work with producer Vic Maile anymore, this after two records, a studio album and a live album that vaulted the band to prominence as English hard-rock heroes, upsetters of the apple-cart, the real deal of British metal at a time when it was a bonafide bandwagon of a genre.

"Well, unfortunately, Phil, after the success of *Ace of Spades*, he got himself a brand new drum kit," explains Fast Eddie. "And this happened to Jerry Shirley in my band Fastway, as well, as it happens. Because a brand new drum kit, it's his pride and joy: 'I love it, I love it, I love it.' And unfortunately with Vic, it didn't work very well in the studio. Vic couldn't get it down good in the little studio where we had done *Ace of Spades*, as it was possibly a bit big for the room. I don't know what the row was about because I wasn't present, but they had a row about it and I know Phil was unhappy with the sound. And Vic, he was only a little fellow, but if he got the bit between his teeth, he could be quite belligerent. So they had this standoff situation, which I didn't think was that serious. But once Phil said, 'Man, I can't work with Vic anymore.' I said, 'Come on, sit down, it can't be that bad, what's the matter? What is this about never wanting to work with Vic again?' So that was that."

"He was generally cavalier," answers Eddie, asked if this was in character or if he was usually pretty easygoing about sounds, as one would surmise given Motörhead's excessively rough productions. "But there were certain things he got really uptight about. The sound had to be right; everything had to be right for him. I can remember one time, 'My high hat is not quite in the right place,' you know, right in the middle of a recording. So believe it or not, as Motörhead, we were very—it doesn't sound like it—but we were actually right on the money when it came to trying to get things right. People probably laugh at that, but I mean, Phil, I know he spent a lot of time on his drums and I spent an awful lot of time on my guitars, changing the strings, trying different sounds."

And so it would fall upon Fast Eddie himself, of all people, to produce *Iron Fist*, Eddie having proven his stripes by working with Motörhead-like NWOBHM upstarts Tank on their *Filth Hounds of Hades* debut.

"If you really want to know, that was very difficult," begins Eddie, on this odd turn of events. "I had obviously done the Tank album, and not thought much of it. The management wanted me to do it. I wanted to do the Girlschool album as well, because I'd done the demos. But Gerry Bron wouldn't let me, because he didn't want to interfere with Motörhead. Well, Doug Smith, the manager, he had his foot in the door with Tank, and I think he didn't give a fuck. He wanted his guys to sell, so if they could use me as a lead, they would. So at first we had got set up with Vic Maile and then Phil had his falling out with Vic Maile. I must add that Vic didn't like the kit much, and as I said, Phil and him had a fucking barmy, and Phil refused to work with Vic

Maile anymore. So we needed to find a producer. I said, well, I don't want to produce it. I can't produce and fucking play on it, you know? So that was how that went."

"So then we talked to Chris Tsangarides," continues Eddie, on the hot NWOBHM hand at the time, particularly through his work with Tygers of Pan Tang. "We had a chat with him. Nice guy, you know, sort of dope-smoking hippie type. And we had a drink with him, me and Phil; Lemmy wasn't there. Lemmy was very strange at this time. I don't know why, but Lemmy had got the hump about something. But looking back, I see that there was a problem. He had a problem with me, and I don't know what that was. He later claimed that it was some girl I was shagging that had something to do with him, but that wasn't true. I had a girlfriend, so I don't know what he was talking about. He'd got the hump with me, and I think the Tank thing might have upset him. Anyway, if I missed it, I missed it completely. But of course, Chris Tsangarides wanted ten thousand pounds. Well, ten thousand pounds to us was a fucking fortune. Because we've only got a couple of hundred pounds a week, you know? And so, yeah, when somebody says, 'Well, I want ten grand,' well, fuck off. Because it's all very well you made your kip if we're all on small money. But if one side needs to be paid seriously, we don't go for it, because it's too much money to us. And then we had another guy, John Antony, who we went to meet in the King's Road; all three

of us went for that, and he wanted twenty thousand pounds. He used to work at Trident, and he was engineer on the Queen stuff. We were desperately looking for somebody to produce us but of course he also wanted too much money.

"In the end, the record company was really pushing us to do this fucking *Iron Fist*. Because the record company was in trouble. And they needed us to put a record out, so they could make some money. The record company was going skint and they needed a Motörhead album. We weren't ready. And, so they're pushing us and pushing us. In the end, the management, said, 'Why don't we let Eddie do it?' And I didn't really want to. Phil says, 'Yeah, Eddie can do it. He did the first album on Tank; why don't we get Eddie to do it?' And so then it was just, well, I don't care. You see what I mean? So, of course, the record company is thinking, well, it will get the job done. And the management are thinking it was straight money, you see, because I never got any money for it. So of course it's like straight money. So see? There's this other stuff going on. So the whole thing was fucked, from the off. And like I said, Lemmy was not really on board generally."

So the producer's fee went from £10,000 to £20,000 to zero.

"Yeah, of course, and everybody laughed. So, in a nutshell, yes. Which is a fucking bummer. For that to come into play, at this stage in our career, was a mistake. But anyway, so we went on. And of course, we were struggling, right in the album. To be honest, we were struggling for material. It wasn't like, this was hard graft. And I didn't realize that the vibes were so bad. Phil was taking smack at the time. He also had a girlfriend who was doing a bit of smack. We didn't know that. But it explains a lot, what happened later. And so of course, I didn't really see much of Phil. Lemmy? I didn't see much of Lemmy either. We used to meet up down at the rehearsal room, but most of that was spent in the pub. It was hard work getting Lemmy out of the pubs, to do some work on the songs. And the riffs . . . I was pretty riffed out at that time. We needed a serious break. It had been a busy time. And we'd just come back from class and now we're struggling for riffs, which made the whole thing worse. All I remember about the songs is we struggled desperately in the rehearsal room to come up with the tunes."

Fated to pull double duty—it serves Eddie right for producing a classic kerranging feast of "baby Motörhead" music like *Filth Hounds of Hades*, in fact, in December of 1981 into January of the new year, immediately before work was to begin on *Iron Fist*.

"Oh, they were great," recalls Eddie, regarding Tank. "That was a great album; I actually really enjoyed doing that. But they had their own problems as well. Bands back then, there was a lot of drinking and partying going on, so there were these mood swings and stuff going on. But they'd supported us on the tour in Europe when we got back from America with Ozzy. They were really good. And hence, I got to know them and did the album. The guitarist, Peter—I had a lot of problems with Peter. I remember rolling around the fuckin' studio in a punch-up with him. We traded blows a couple of times. But I couldn't be seen to be beating up the fuckin' artist, could I?"

As for what Eddie brought to the Tank sessions, "Nothing really," laughs Tank bassist and vocalist Algy Ward. "He just brought a lot of drink and a load of amphetamines, that's all. And said it wasn't loud enough. But no, Eddie he had to finish *Filth Hounds* quick to go and do *Iron Fist*. And then he pissed off to what would become *Fastway*. A couple of the songs on the *Fastway* album would've ended up on the *Iron Fist* album, or, well, whatever the next Motörhead album would've been. But he'd just had enough of that sort of nonsense."

Similar dismissive missive from Tank drummer Mark Brabbs: "With all due respect, not much, really. Because on the first album we'd spent a year writing it as such, just in the studio writing songs. Then we spent a good nine months touring it before we actually got in to record. We went to DJM Studios to put down demos, with the DJM engineer. And then Eddie came along and produced the single, with a guy called Speedy Keen, which was quite good. But as it happened, nearly everything was done. Not being disrespectful to Eddie, because he's done a good job, but there wasn't really much left for him to do apart from get a sound up, possibly, which the engineer would've done anyway."

"We were kind of on ice anyway," furthers Eddie, who, if Lemmy was to be believed, was quitting the band every other day by this point. "And you get a lot of time off when you're in a band, so I said, okay, I'll have a look at it for them. And like I say, the management, they also managed Tank, and they wanted to use my name to sell the record. So it was a bit more like that than anything else. But I had done, previously, a single with them, for DJM Records. This would've been a year or so before. It was also when I did the Girlschool demos. See, I used to love being producer, because I used to love recording. I mean, when I was a kid, 10 years old, I had sold me train set and got a little tape recorder, so I'd always been into that. I just wish computers and that had been around earlier, so I could have had a 24-track in me living room, you know?"

The *Iron Fist* sessions had started at Jackson's in Rickmansworth, but once the dust-up between Phil and Vic happened, the guys had to uproot and go elsewhere.

"We went to Morgan Studios," continues Eddie, "and I used Will Reid-Dick, my old friend engineer, who's a good man. We went through every day religiously to try to put this record together. Did the backing tracks. They went down relatively not too bad. They weren't perfect, but no one was interested. Phil wasn't interested, fucked off and we never saw him again. Lemmy had done his bass at that time, and then it was down to trying to get to the vocals. 'Well, look man, I want to go to the pub.' 'I've got your vocals to do.' 'I'll have to do it some other time.' It was all that. In fact, when I tried to get him to do a replacement bass—he did a bum-out on one of the tracks—I couldn't get him to do it. We had to fly in and out—in the old days, you had to fly it in on the quarter-inch, so you had to record a note back onto

Front cover of the Iron Fist *tour program.* | © Bill Baran Archive

a quarter-inch, and then fly it back onto the 24. Because I just couldn't get him to play. He was just not interested. They both were not interested, and I never understood why. I never got it."

"I don't know if *Iron Fist* was rushed or not," reflects Phil on the situation. "Certainly as each album came and went, it got quicker, as in the time it took to record an album. We were never ones to stay in the studio for a lot of time. For one, we couldn't afford it, and for two, we weren't that kind of band. Most of the stuff we played live in the studio, and then there would just be, obviously, guitar overdubs and bass overdubs and vocals. But all the albums were always live—I never did any overdubs—and the rhythm guitars are always live. I seem to remember there was a bit of animosity or shit going on, because it was produced by Eddie and Will Reid-Dick. But it was very low-key and it was mainly between Eddie and Lemmy."

Iron Fist, recorded in fits and starts between January 26 and March 1 of 1981, would be issued on April 17, hot on the heels of the opening title track emerging as a single (backed with non-LPer "Remember Me, I'm Gone") two weeks earlier. All of the nagging issues with the wider album can be heard within this dog's breakfast of a title track itself. "Iron Fist" opens, ill-advisedly, with the exact same Lemmy bass strum as "Ace of Spades," after which it proceeds to become a weaker version of that top-shelf Motörhead classic. Eddie and Will's production is essentially correct, not gravely lacking in any department, but it's not particularly powerful. And then when Phil sounds sloppy on top of it, and maybe too loud, compounding the wobbler of a performance, it's not a grand opening statement, even if the song's anthemic chorus helps render it the album's most enduring track.

"Heart of Stone" is similarly fast, rickety and under-written. Compression would be a debate primarily of CD-era production, but whatever is going on here results in a similar level of ear fatigue to the most egregiously heavy records of the 2000s that are victims of too much compression. Thankfully, the guys then switch gears with "I'm the Doctor," offering a simple, old-time rock 'n' rollsy number punked-up beyond recognition, but easy on the ears nonetheless due to its rootsy charm and Lemmy's comfort with the historical rock idiom.

But then the album begins to exude a degree of hue and dimension. "Go to Hell" and "Loser" both hang on melancholy heavy metal riffs and all of a sudden *Iron Fist* is beginning to look desperate in a heroic way, white-knuckled, producing hidden gems of quality art through the fog of exhaustion. Closing side one of the original vinyl, however, is another nondescript quick one, "Sex & Outrage," reflecting a similar degradation in the quality of Judas Priest's fast songs as they went from the high integrity of *Sin After Sin* and *Stained Class* to the sawed-off Kiss songs all over *British Steel*. Motörhead didn't have quite as far to fall as Priest in terms of riffic complexity, but the valid complaint was that these fast songs offered nothing more in terms of creativity over the band's previous proto-thrash numbers, and maybe even less when it came to the disintegrating chemistry between the pillars of the rhythm section, namely Kilmister and Taylor.

Over to side two and *Iron Fist* punches above weight with another quiet classic, "America," which is a newer, groovier kind of metal for the guys, on top of which Lemmy barks compact and colorful words of both praise and damnation of what would soon be his adopted homeland.

Of course he also comments on American women. "I like them because they're crazy," quips Lem. "If you get a real good American girl, then she is fucking nuts. She is open to any idea and any avenue of thought. American girls—and American men—are eager to learn stuff and they are not afraid to say so. The other side of it is that Americans are always full of extremes. They have an attitude of, 'I know it all so don't try to tell me nothing.' If you get a good American person on your side then that is a great friend to have."

"Shut it Down" is another very cool potential Motörhead anthem that never rose to widespread recognition, cruising briskly, topped with a malevolent riff from Eddie who picks his places over a signature skittery Phil Taylor shuffle.

"'Speed Freak' I really like," laughs Eddie, on yet another very fast one, but a fraught mess not without punk charm housed within its yobbish verse melody. "I love that fucking track. 'America' wasn't

Toronto was never the same. | © Martin Popoff

bad either, but it all sounds a little unfinished. It didn't have the input of the three of us. It was left to me to put all the input into it, and as I say, I considered in the beginning that I couldn't play and produce at the same time. I never thought that was possible. And I thought we were doing it together. But they weren't interested. I'm upset, still, to this day. Breaks my fucking heart."

"(Don't Let 'Em) Grind Ya Down" is arguably *Iron Fist*'s greatest triumph. Opening with a strident drum flourish from Phil, it then settles into a mid-paced groove over which Lemmy spits out the nasty version of Motörhead's credo, the cynic's view of why they do what they do, us versus them in a world of miserable thems.

Strength to strength, as we draw to a close, "(Don't Need) Religion" is Lemmy's snorted grand statement of his steadfast atheism, augmented best if and when an interviewer can get him on the topic.

"I have always hated organized religion," spits Lemmy. "If I believed in God, I would not need an interpreter. God is the first to do everything, right? You should be able to talk directly to him. You don't need some special building with some guy who has a degree in God. Every army in the world has had their tanks and guns blessed by their respective priests. It is kind of weird since the Bible says, 'Thou shalt not kill.' Blessing a weapon is kind of odd to me. So many people claim that God is on their side that I wonder if God sometimes wonders who is on his side. So I am kind of anti-God. If there is a God, then he is a miserable bastard. Sometimes I think he might be the devil dressed up as God. I say fuck God and fuck the Devil; I'm responsible for what I do. I don't have to hide behind anything. If I am anything, then I am an anarchist. You can't trust people to get it to work right."

There's a sophistication in the musical presentation of "(Don't Need) Religion" that, again, coupled with other songs on the album that are less than breakneck speed, makes for a sincere and true advancement in the band's catalog, even if the magic of chemistry and fire and emotion is located in greater abundance on, say, *Overkill* and *Ace of Spades*. Still, all told, it was good to

Eddie in a mean pair of boots. | © Martin Popoff

see Motörhead working with such sophisticated chord changes, combined with a memorable central riff, no less.

Last track on the record is "Bang to Rights," which depicts neither Lemmy at his best lyrically nor Eddie playing anything too interesting, Clarke turning in one of those circular riffs vaguely anchored in the blues but then made metal amidst the mayhem that is Motörhead. It is of note that non-LP track "Remember Me, I'm Gone" is little more than a variation on the tired "Bang to Rights" construct, same mindless beat from Phil, strumming, chord changes, the end.

Wrote *Kerrang!*'s Steve Gett favorably, surely maintaining the peace and the magazine's cozy relationship with the band, "Crank up the stereo, open the windows, scare the hell out of next-door's tomcat, have their mutt yelping for its kennel and set the neighbors themselves fleeing in a state of total disarray. Your folks might threaten to kick you out . . . But what a way to go? The bottom line of my ramblings is that Motörhead have remained loyal and true to their cause, never getting into fashions or ephemeral trends. Basically, they've stood their ground without compromise, and I can think of only one word befitting such action—HONESTY!"

And yet, conversely, "Lemmy hates the record," says Eddie. "I mean, Lemmy hates it. I never thought an awful lot of it, because of, obviously, the history in it and the fact that we weren't as enthused by the material. And like I said, I didn't realize what was going on. I blame the management to some degree. The record company were desperate for product, so they looked forward as well by forcing us to go ahead so quickly. You know what the fucking joke was? We did the fucking album, and we're coming down to the studio with the fucking album sleeve. Then there's a fucking tour booked, we go out on the fucking road, do the first gig, and the fucking album's not in the shops! Can you fucking believe that?!"

"So we're on the road and it's like terrible because nobody knows the fucking tunes. So we said, look, we have to do evasive action. We're going to have to do the old set. So, oh, we do the old set, fantastic. So we did the old set, and Phil said, 'If you don't do the new set, I'm leaving the band.' And I wish I'd said, fuck off then. Oh, I do, because then I wouldn't have had to leave the band. Because he did what I did. But of course, what did Lemmy and I do? We said, 'All right, then, all right, Phil; at sound check tomorrow, we'll go through half a dozen of the songs, and we'll put them in the set.' So we did that and we put them in the set. Well, of course, it was the worst tour we'd ever done. Because the kids were standing there wondering what the fuck we were playing. Because they couldn't get their hands on the record. So it was a nightmare! It wasn't until we hit the last six, seven numbers, that the fucking crowd came alive. Well, by then, we'd all died a death on stage. So that didn't help either. Plus Doug came to Lemmy and wanted us to take Tank out on the *Iron Fist* tour. But something had happened to them and they were fucking awful. And in fact we were awful. The record's not in the shops and so right there, the tour was actually a bit of a fucking disaster. I could almost say it's the worst tour we ever did because of those two things. So things were bad and went from bad to worse. It seemed like all the fucking stars had aligned to destroy the band. And true enough, that's what happened."

CHAPTER 9

Eddie's Last Meal: "A bottle of vodka on the table, a glass, and a little pile of white powder."

Essentially, the demise of the classic Motörhead lineup came down to arguments for integrity on one side—Eddie's—and arguments for maintaining a sense of humor on the other side—Lemmy's. Both are positive qualities and both are reasons rock fans love the original Motörhead so much. Those disposed exclusively to the serious side or the jocular side exist, but most Motörhead fans appreciate both: that the band could rock deadly hard, and that Lemmy was a serious wordsmith with a complex, though mostly cynical and near nihilistic, point of view, balanced against the idea that the guys can take a joke.

The summary of Eddie's gripes included the previously discussed hassles over the construction of *Iron Fist*, the cock-ups in getting the record into the shops and arguments over playing the new songs. But if we had to pick one isolated event big enough to bust up the band, it would have to be Lemmy's intention of recording a single with Wendy O. Williams of shock rockers the

Plasmatics, specifically a cover of Tammy Wynette's country classic "Stand by Your Man."

"It all started at the beginning of the *Iron Fist* tour [May 1982]," begins Eddie. "We were going to start in Toronto, funny enough. The *Live in Toronto* was done there [Castle issued the show as a VHS in 1982, with the audio used on the reissue of the studio album], at Maple Leaf Gardens. That was done that night, and yeah, they made a little movie out of it. But before that we went to New York, met up with Wendy and them and did some rehearsals, doing 'Stand by Your Man.' Lemmy always liked women performers. And I was trying to get them to do it a little more rocky, you know what I mean? I'm saying, 'For fuck sake, could you take some of the chords out?!' I'm saying, 'Why don't you turn it up a bit?' But they wanted to do all this poncing about with it, these sappy chords.

"That's really when I started to notice Lemmy was fucking having it out with me. He's like, 'Mate, why don't you just fucking shut up, man? We're doing it this way.' It was all that, you know? Lemmy got mad and started arguing. I got mad and was yelling back but what I didn't realize at the time is that he had already had enough of me. And I was thinking, oh, what the fuck have I done? So of course when we got up there to Toronto, and I'm producing it, and they've laid the fucking tracks down, and of course Wendy goes out to sing and she can't fucking sing in the key they've done it in, so then we have to transpose it and do it again. Of course, when she does finally start singing, it wouldn't've made any difference what fucking key it was in, because she couldn't fucking sing. I didn't realize that, and I don't think anybody did, but of course, Lemmy wants to . . . you know, he's got a soft spot for her. And one thing leads to another, and Phil . . . Phil's already been talking to Brian Robertson. I didn't know about that. So he wants Brian Robertson in the band. So suddenly an opportunity appeared for them to get me out of the band."

We've heard all about Phil's and Eddie's punch-ups. Lemmy

always maintained that it was a brotherly type love/hate relationship, and that the violence would always end as quickly as it erupted. But obviously over time, resentments set in. It didn't help that Lemmy was accusing Eddie of drinking too much to function, with Eddie counter-accusing, pointing out that Lemmy could often barely make it through gigs having been speeding all day and night, passing out the minute he got off stage. It also didn't help that the guys still weren't making much money, primarily from their lack of progress in America, and that creative energies and excitement and motivation had all been depressed for the last record. So there was this undercurrent with Phil's reservations about Eddie, but let's also not forget that Eddie had been threatening to quit on a regular basis.

At least that's always been Lemmy's assertion. Doug Smith? Not so much. "Oh dear, I suppose, you know, a few times. I suppose a few times. But it's difficult for me to decide whether or not it was him playing power games. And when I say power games, you know, throwing his weight around, or in actual fact, that he had had enough. You just have to sort of take it as it comes. And with them, it comes with the fact that they were like a little three-piece marriage. They would have arguments all the time that would cause them to sort of sometimes not speak to each other. But it was part of it.

"But sure, they always had arguments, terrible arguments. It's all part and parcel of, I suppose, being and working with people. Rock 'n' roll bands are like marriages. Everybody's got an opinion and everybody feels they've got a right and all the rest of it. It's very hard to make a lot of people work in the same direction. But it doesn't matter, because at the end of the day, that angst and anger and everything that they had came out in very hard-played music.

"In reality, Eddie was the one who probably was more responsible than Lemmy and Phil," continues Doug. "I think that's the easiest way of saying it. Eddie was responsible for a lot of the melodies, and probably pushing along rehearsals and pushing along recording. He would have to work hard to get Lemmy working, because he'd usually been out all night. He was like that in Hawkwind as well—exactly the same. Just as long as everything was organized, he'd try to be there. As far as I was concerned, I worked with him for so many years, I thought he was a friend. But it didn't turn out that way. But I hold no ill will."

Most definitely the cracks were beginning to show. When I asked Eddie what Phil might not have liked about his guitar playing, Clarke says, "Oh, he always used to moan about it, and he didn't think the sound was right and I twiddled too much. He was a funny bugger, Phil. You know, he was out of his head most of the fucking time, so I never quite got it. I was actually the only one who could fucking do anything. That's why I ended up doing all the fucking administration shit. Getting them to rehearsals on time and all that. And I think they resented it. But they got me out in the end, so they got their wish."

And as alluded to much earlier, Eddie's running of things has its pathology right back to the very first time the guys even played together. Phil as loose cannon, Lemmy as aggressively lazy with certain aspects of his career as a part of his complicated live fast and loose philosophy . . . it was there in the beginning and it was getting worse at the end.

"Yeah, well, without me, the band would've never got back together," laughs Eddie, referring to the very beginning, when it was threatening to fall apart before ignition. "When I first got my audition, I had to pay for the audition, I had to go pick them up in my car, pick up their equipment, take it to the rehearsal room, pay for the rehearsal room, have the audition and take them all home again. You know, if it wasn't for me, Motörhead would never've got started again. I mean, don't get me wrong, I'm not blowing me own trumpet. But I was always the one who did the administration. I had the get up and go. All they had was the get up and go from the speed and take me to the off-license and get me a can of beer. That's all they could manage."

Lemmy wearing a T-shirt of the band that would break up the classic Motörhead lineup. | © Piergiorgio Brunelli

The Rise of Motörhead ♠ 201

Clarifying his role in the business affairs, Eddie says, "Not so much what the manager should be doing, but if there was a question about contracts or whatever, it was, 'Oh, go ask Eddie. He's in charge of that.' So in that sense I was kind of like the one who could do that. If something had to be discussed, they would say, 'Well, you better speak to Eddie.' But no, the managers did their job. I had obviously kept things rolling as I would. You have to keep rehearsals going and make sure you put the work in. I was a bit of a stickler for doing rehearsals and making sure that was spot on. Whereas Lemmy preferred to go down to the pub. And Phil was a bit like that too. There were some disputes where we were trying to get Lemmy into the rehearsal room to write new tunes and all that. He could be a tad disinterested in that side of it. And over the years it became pretty frustrating for Phil and myself.

"I was always the one who cracked the whip. I was the one who did the production and I was the one who was involved in any business deals. They were always saying, 'Eddie, what do you think?' It was always me that had to go in the room and do the talking. I think Lemmy just got fed up with it. It wasn't my fucking idea to do it but they were always asking me and I was always the one who would say, 'Fuck, I'll just go in and talk to them.' I knew a bit about putting bits and bobs together, on the other side of the business, as it were. I was working; I used to do odd jobs for a living. I'd do all sorts of things. Because I was trying to finance a solo album at the time. So of course I was doing laboring work, so I could pay for the studio. You know, I was full-on dedicated to my art. I loved it—and I would do anything."

Right there we see a level of integrity out of Eddie that fans surely found palpable and inspirational. And despite Phil's punk rock slash through life, we know that he also took drums and his sound and the making of the records seriously. Lemmy, too, was loaded up with integrity, but it was also in his nature to downplay caring too much about anything, and it's almost as if against his will, he had to act that way with his band mates, be that Clarke and Taylor or Campbell and Dee. No question though, it was Eddie who took industry barbs about Motörhead being a joke most to heart.

As Angel Witch's Kevin Riddles alluded to earlier, Eddie was reining in his playing to support the band's strength, its raison d'être. "Obviously, it was very restricting," agrees Clarke. "It was very restricting. I didn't quite realize how restricting until I got to my first rehearsals with the new band Fastway. I was playing with Pete Way and Topper Headon and we had a fucking ball. Suddenly I realized there's this whole new world out there, you know? It was nice. But there's something else that made Motörhead great though. You know, if you've all got to fit into a sort of box and find your niche together, that makes you unique. But there's a lot of pressure as well, because you're always having to fucking work on what you're doing to make it work—which created tensions in itself. And of course those tensions eventually led to the split in the camaraderie."

As for having to take the reins, especially during the *Iron Fist* sessions, Eddie says, "We put in a lot of time, but Lemmy's Lemmy. He's always been Lemmy. His thing is, hey man, I play in a band and I play bass or whatever. I play and that's it. And I would have to ferry him everywhere. You know, he expects to have a chauffeur taking him wherever he's going. I get up on stage and do my thing and that's it. He was the powers that be—Lemmy was Lord, you know?

"Lemmy didn't drive," chuckles Eddie, back 'round to that interesting wrinkle in Lemmy's reality. "He got taken wherever he wanted, because he didn't drive. I don't think he ever wanted to drive so he could always be chauffeured around. But at least that way he could stay high on Valium and having a few drinks and not have to fucking worry, you know? Oh yeah, he had it all worked out. As things go, Lemmy had it pretty much all worked out. Ol' Lem, as we used to call him sometimes. But you know, barring that, we were still a three-piece; it was still three of us together. It would not have worked without Phil being who he was, me being who I was and Lemmy being who he was. That's the only reason it worked. And with Phil being quite ill up to the end, obviously I'd been thinking a lot about Philip, when I first met him and everything, and I love the little fella, and we made some great music together. But there's no way Motörhead was anything other than three people locked in—that was the only reason it was there. And once I wasn't there and Phil wasn't there, it couldn't possibly survive as it was."

Back to the backing tracks that broke the camel's back: "So, right, we did the rehearsals in New York for the Wendy O. Williams thing," continues Clarke, "and then we drove up to Toronto, and then we had three days in the studio in Toronto. Lovely studio, quite new, and it had a lovely Neve desk in it. The studio was in a new district, and I remember thinking Toronto is quite nice, to go out and have a coffee on the street and all that. But of course, once that happened, I said, 'Look man, this is garbage; we can't possibly put this out.' And they said, 'Look, man, we'll put on the cover that it's got nothing to do with you. It'll say, "This has nothing to do with Eddie Clarke."' I said, 'Man, you're missing the point, Motörhead is my band as well. It's our credibility that is on the line here.' I thought Motörhead was in danger of becoming a laughingstock. But they were already thinking like it wasn't my band anymore. The bastards. So anyway, we did the Toronto gig and then we jumped on the bus and then we drove down to New York for the New York gig."

Which is pretty much the way Phil Taylor says it went down at the time, speaking with Jon Sutherland from *Record Review*: "It was a bit stupid because even Will Reid-Dick, who came to Canada to produce the single, knew it wasn't supposed to be something like Paul McCartney or a big production. Everything was going fine, we had all the backing tracks down, no fights, no arguments. Then Wendy arrived and started singing. Will Reid-Dick and Eddie took a break and said they wanted to get something to eat, and they never came back. They hid in the TV studio, which was away from where we were. After couple of hours, Lemmy and Rod Swenson, Wendy's manager, started thinking, where are they? Finally I walked around and found Eddie. I asked him, 'Don't you think you should be over there?' And he said, 'Fuck that. I don't want my name on that garbage.' I had a feeling he was bubbling. So I left and I could hear him saying, 'I'm gonna leave the band if this shit comes out. It sounds like Mickey Mouse on nitrous oxide,' which is quite true, actually."

So Phil assumed the role of peacemaker, a position he claims he had in the band. "Yes, on stage, I've always been in the middle, and in life, I've been in the middle. The sort of peacemaker of the band. The stable part of the band. Eddie hadn't spoken to Lemmy for three days and I kept saying to Eddie, 'Don't leave the band.' The guy had quit the band once a week for seven years. And I thought this was a stupid reason to leave the band. We offered to put out a press release that would say that Eddie wasn't on the record and didn't like it. I offered to put on the back of the record, 'This record contains no Eddie Clarke; he had nothing to do with it and he thinks it's crap.' Wendy's manager or any of us wouldn't have cared at all. So it was no big deal. That still wasn't good enough for him. Nobody runs the band. We all run the band. Our manager takes care of the business affairs, but luckily we're a three-piece and we vote. The one who's odd man out has to bite the bullet."

To clarify then, the single wasn't completed in Toronto. "No, we recorded the backing tracks, two lots of backing tracks, in Toronto,' explains Eddie. "Wendy went out to sing, I went to the off-licence and bought a bottle of Jack and went to the hotel and got drunk. Because I just couldn't stand it; I just couldn't picture it. It got to the point with that song that I couldn't live with it. I told Lemmy, 'If you're going to do this, then I'm going to leave the band as this is rubbish.' I said to them, 'What we should do . . . we've got Will Reid-Dick here, why don't we put a blues thing

Not exactly right—Eddie played the Palladium in New York two nights later.

together? We can do a Motörhead play the blues. You know, do "Hoochie Coochie" and a 12-bar, maybe something else, a bit of harmonica. We can lay that down now and Will could take it back to London and mix it and put it out while we were on tour in America. How about that?' 'No man, we want to go with this Wendy O. Williams thing.' And that was it for me, really. It was a terrible piece of work."

As for why Will Reid-Dick was on the trip, Eddie explains that, "He was the engineer/producer on *Iron Fist*, and he also came over because when they did the Wendy O. Williams thing, they didn't want me to play on it—they wanted me to produce it. I don't know why. They were obviously already fucked off with my playing back then. I don't think they liked my playing. I think that's kind of why they got me out of the band. I think they went off my playing. And so they didn't want me to play on it, and they said, 'Well, why don't you produce it?' And I said, 'Look, if I'm going to produce it, I'm going to have to get Will to come over and do the engineering.'"

Phil kept trying to keep tempers tamped, telling Sutherland

that Lemmy was "totally amazed" at Eddie's anger about the session. "I didn't say much to Lemmy because I was still trying to make peace with Eddie and try to get him to stop his ridiculous attitude. He asked me about it, and I said, 'Eddie's mellowing out a bit,' which he really wasn't. See? You have to tell little white lies occasionally, even to your friends. But Eddie wanted the record stopped. He was doing this Vic Maile trip and he started sounding like him. His attitude became, 'I'm the producer. I say what goes on, and how you play it.'"

"So I'm in the bus on the way to New York," continues Eddie, "and of course they're playing Wendy O. Williams all over the place. They carried on doing the recording without me and they were playing it in the bus on the way to New York. I was losing it. They know I'm really upset. They've got Plasmatics T-shirts on; they're taunting me all the way down. The manager's with us, and I'm saying to the manager, 'Man, this isn't gonna work if they carry on like this, because apart from me knocking 'em both out, I'm going to have to fuck off.' Because I was going to knock 'em out and fuck off anyway, because it was pissing me off so much. I really got the fucking hump that they weren't getting it. I told them, 'Man, you've got to stop playing this song or I'm going to fucking lose it.' I told the manager that he needed to do something or war was going to break out. And the management wasn't helping. Doug Smith was being a complete ass. You could see that the band is splitting up in front of him, and what did he do? Nothing! You know, he let these two cunts fucking get away with it, and it really pissed me off.

"And so when we got to the hotel in New York, it had reached a fever pitch. So the manager called a meeting of the people that were around us in Toronto, and Phil and Lemmy, and this road crew, you know, the head of the road crew and that, and a couple of business guys that were there looking after us in Toronto. And they're sitting there, and they're saying, 'What's the problem?' And I said, 'Well, look, this is a piece of shit.' I said, 'Ask him;

he said it was shit.' I had talked to management and told them that the track was rubbish and they all said they agreed with me. And I turned to this guy, and said, 'Well, you said it was shit.' He wouldn't speak. Nobody would speak in my defense on how bad this fucking music was that they wanted to do. They were all standing there being silent. All of sudden I was all on my own with six or seven people who were all saying I was a twat because I didn't like this record. In your heart of hearts, you know it's rubbish but they won't say it in front of the band."

"So in the end, I said, 'You're all a bunch of cunts' and I fucking stormed out. One of the fucking big road crew guys, the gorilla, started to chase me down the fucking corridor. I had to fucking floor him. I had to drop him in the corridor so I could get to the lift and get away. It was all a bit over the fucking top. And the other fucking road crew jumped on him, fortunately, or he would've killed me. And I just ran off. So I ran off to the road crew's hotel around the corner. Well, I got a cab. All I had was a bit of Canadian money. I said to the guy at the desk at the Holiday Inn in New York, 'Give me 20 bucks, quick.' I wanted to jump out in the street and get in the first cab.

"It all got funny that night," continues Eddie. "We were supposed to play the following day. I sat up all fucking night waiting to hear some news. There was no news. They had two roadies minding me at this time so I couldn't leave the room. When I look back on it now, it is all quite funny. They kept me prisoner all fucking night, didn't they? They wouldn't let me out and all this and so in the end it was past the point of no return. Anyway, I get a call at quarter of ten the next morning and am told that Lemmy said he would do the show under one condition. That condition was that I had to go to the show and do my sound check first and then I would have to leave the building and then the rest of the band would go in and do their sound check. I am in fucking New York, man. I've flown all the way over here from England, so I want to do the show. I do what they want, and then I am ready to go to the dressing room. I had to go and do my sound check, and I had to be escorted out, back to the hotel so that they could then go in and do theirs."

"So when I get to the fucking show that night—this is really quite funny—I'm being led in, I'm almost handcuffed to a guy, a minder. They have this huge dressing room but I don't get to go in there. He takes me in my dressing room, and it's a little boiler room about six foot by six foot with one chair. There's a bottle of vodka on the table, a glass and a little pile of white powder, right? And that's it. And I'm sitting in there on me fucking Jack Jones and I'm thinking what's the matter with these cunts, you know? I did the show but it was a funny show as we were obviously fucking hating each other.

"So after the show, which was pretty fiery, I went into the dressing room with the agent, Nick Caris from DMA. He's saying, 'Why don't we go talk to Phil and Lemmy?' I agreed as I was high off the show and I wanted to do more shows. I didn't want it to end there. I go into the dressing room and there are about two hundred people there and they are all playing the Plasmatics, and this huge dressing room, the size of a football field, is all full of smoke. This guy goes over and gets Phil and Lemmy as I wait just inside the door. They come over to see me. Lemmy looks at me and says, 'Go on and speak.' I said, 'Guys, I know a lot of shit has gone down here but I'd like to carry on and do the rest of the tour.' I said, 'Look, guys, this is ridiculous. We've got to carry on. We can't let this get in the way.' They said, 'No man, fuck off.' And that was it. So I was out the fucking door."

"I liked Motörhead," begins Nick Caris, offering his version of events. "Motörhead had melodies. They were aggressive music, but there were melodies; they were kinda like Metallica version one. Anyway, yes, I brought Motörhead over for their first headline tour, which we sold out all the three-thousand- and four-thousand-seaters. Some promoters didn't want them in hotels; they were famous for trashing Holiday Inns in Germany or something. So

I was on my way to New York. We had sold out two shows, first time in New York for Motörhead. This was with Eddie, the real Motörhead. I land at Newark airport and I call my office and they say you gotta call Doug Smith, the manager of Motörhead, who is in England, there's a problem. So I call him and he says, 'You gotta get to the venue. Eddie just quit the band.' Oh jeez. I didn't have the venue's backstage number, so I called up Ron Belzer's office, who was the promoter. I said, 'Ron, Ron, you got 'em sold out for two shows, tonight and tomorrow; I need to talk to them.' 'Oh, okay.'

"So I went to the venue; this was still early, about 4 o'clock, and I talked to Eddie. I said, 'It'll be okay; I'll go and talk to Lemmy.' And I thought I had everything worked out. I walked Eddie back in with his head down, and Lemmy said, 'Nope, you're out of the band.' I remember Phil was sitting back in the corner, just quiet. And that was it. That was a great band. But of course Lemmy and Phil were really powerful. Because remember, that was a rhythm section. And they were powerful, and it almost didn't matter who was playing guitar, although Eddie was obviously excellent and he was part of the original thing. But I met Lemmy when he was in Hawkwind, and Motörhead was like a straighter band compared to Hawkwind. But I love Lemmy. You wouldn't think it, but he's so intelligent it's ridiculous. But by this point, they were always at each other, and I know Eddie didn't like Lemmy doing 'Stand By Your Man.'"

As for Phil's recollection after 30-odd years of what went down, he told me, "I still don't really know what happened with Eddie, because he was always leaving the band and we never took him seriously. And then when we went to Toronto to do that thing with Wendy O. Williams, I mean, he'd already heard— we already went to Bronze Records and listened to Plasmatic songs, and Eddie heard her voice and what it sounded like—he knew what was expected. And he was going to produce and play on it. And then for some reason, when we got into the studio, when Wendy started singing, he just kind of freaked out and

Lemmy with the incomparable Wendy O. Williams, who died by her own hand,
April 6, 1998. | © Ray Palmer Archive/IconicPix

changed his tune. It's almost as if he went into the studio not as a member of the band and had never heard of Wendy O. Williams. He just freaked out, 'What the fuck is this? This is garbage! I'm not having anything to do with this. This is making Motörhead look like idiots. She sounds like Mickey Mouse!' And the thing is, I said to him, 'Eddie, what are you talking about? You knew what we were doing before we came over. We're not doing it with the intention that the world is going to think it's the next best thing since Jimi Hendrix. We're doing it for a laugh, you know? I mean, not to ridicule ourselves, but it's a fun single. That's what we're doing. We're doing it for fun, and then maybe we'll make a bit of money, great. That's what it's about. It's not something that's going to be split up and analyzed by people, like we're trying to be the world's greatest band or producers. We're just doing it for fun, you know? That's all it is. Take it for what it is. And you knew that before we came out here.'

"And he didn't want anything to do with it," concludes Phil, "and so he left the band. And me and Lemmy said, well, fuck it if he comes back and says 'I didn't really mean it; I want to come back' like he did before—fuck 'im! We've had enough of this. But he never did, actually. He never said he wanted to come back. So we just left it at that and that's where we got Robbo in."

Eddie, to this day, doesn't know how far in advance Phil and Lemmy were musing over getting Brian Robertson in the band, but according to Phil, speaking with Jon Sutherland in late 1982, "He was the first person I thought of when Eddie left. It immediately came to mind. He was doing something, but he wasn't tied down to a band or anything. He was making a solo album at the time, combining all sorts of sounds, instruments, and styles. He has rhythm tracks for synthesizers, real drums, real instruments, electronic drums, electronic instruments already done. We knew, though, that he wasn't doing anything permanent. Lemmy rang him up and said, 'Oh, Robbo, how'd you fancy touring with Motörhead?' Without delay, he said, 'Sure, why not?' As soon as he got his visa together, we met him at the airport. We had known him for a few years, but we never played with him. Robbo, Lemmy and I, among others, were social drinking buddies, so we knew him quite well. We'd see each other at the same pubs and face down in the same gutters. We knew he had a bad reputation. We thought, if there was anyone crazy enough to do it, it would be Robbo. Our main objective was to survive, not die. Robbo had just had a little spell in hospital just before he came over here. He was doing a bottle of Remy Martin a day and his liver was really screwed up. He hadn't been out on the road in four years, and here he is joining Motörhead, which is really jumping into the deep end."

"That's one reason why I'm so pissed off at Eddie," continued Phil, reminded that there was a Japanese tour planned and a U.S. tour to finish. "It's one thing to leave a band when you're not doing anything, but to leave right in the middle of an American tour is the most inopportune time. He said finally that he was thinking about leaving back when we were in London. And I said, 'Thanks very much, you bloody shit. That's really nice to tell us this.' It used to be, when we had a disagreement, it was just a smack in the mouth, a couple of apologies and everything was normal. I would've preferred to have parted amicably without any violent thoughts towards each other. We're really pissed off. How else would you feel about a guy who dumps on you like that? If we had bottled the tour, we may never have been able to come back. Instead, we're going ahead with it, playing a half-hour set, sometimes less than the support band. So far the audiences have been really great. When we get back to England, we'll have three days off and we'll get in as much rehearsing as possible."

Lemmy, part of the same conversation, was hopeful about the path forward. "When we started playing with Robbo, we started realizing how much we repeated and how much we really didn't know what we were doing. It sounds quite different. With Robbo, it will still be Motörhead. Robbo had a difficult time getting used to the sound because it was like playing without a bass player and having two rhythm guitarists. In fact, he's used to a four-piece with another guitar and a bass player; so far, he seems to like it." He then repeated the oft-quoted tall tale about just how loud Motörhead was, describing the band's PA as the "biggest I've ever seen: 117,000 watts. A guy called up during one of our outdoor gigs from six miles away and said he couldn't hear his TV, and we were just sound checking. I'm sure it was better than what was on the telly anyways."

With the story having grown from four miles to six miles, journalist Sutherland nonetheless underscores Motörhead's effect on people, writing that, "Trying to explain Motörhead to people is like describing the numbness of a sledgehammer to the forehead with glee. It takes a certain amount of wildness to accept the band. Audiences that see Motörhead are forced at a multi-decibel point to make a decision on the band. Usually they are totally absorbed or outright stunned. Motörhead is definitely powerful. Motörhead is pretty much an unknown commodity here in the United States. Those who have seen the band have had a chance to see why the band has dominated the English heavy metal scene. Motörhead is the largest draw and merchandiser on the English metal scene and does fantastic business at live shows, and with buttons, T-shirts, patches and rock 'n' roll paraphernalia. They are headliners topping the bill at huge outdoor festivals where the sheer speed, volume and intensity of their performance makes it hard for other bands to consider following them on stage."

But back to the rending, the events leading to Clarke's departure from the band were accelerating once they got to New York. This was all going down at the Palladium, May 14, 1982, which would mark Eddie's last show with the band. Clarke wouldn't be around to see the single finished and issued.

"No, I had done the backing tracks. We laid down the backing tracks in Toronto, and then I think Lemmy finished it off later. He'd finished it off later and produced it later. But yeah, Brian

Robertson was already on the fucking plane, I think. Or he was already over there. Phil was working some number. Yeah, some number was going, and I had no idea, mate, to be honest. I had no idea. I was pretty fucking heartbroken by it. I had to get back . . . I had to get out of there. I thought this is ridiculous. I don't understand it. I thought we would die together as a band. I did my usual, 'Listen, I'm leaving,' but I wasn't leaving. They said fuck off

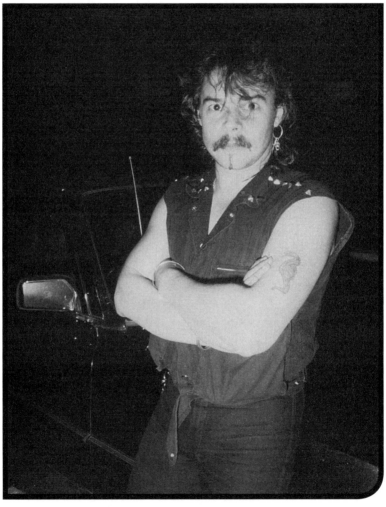

Do not accept a ride from this man. | © Piergiorgio Brunelli

then. They threw me out, really. And it all started over that bird. I think Phil was just sticking to Lemmy's coattails, because he saw Lemmy as the leader, and I was left out in the fucking cold. I never foresaw not being in Motörhead. I just never saw it. I thought—some of the things Phil got up to—if anybody needed firing out of the band, it was Phil. But it didn't even cross our minds—we wouldn't do that. But it's all history now."

"He left the band over that," is the point-blank way Lemmy characterizes it, thinking back specifically to wearing the Wendy O. Williams shirts on the bus ride. "Yeah, I remember that. It was really funny. He was mad, but it was really funny. If you haven't got a sense of humor about you, then you might as well check out."

CHAPTER 10

The Aftermath: "God bless him, little fella."

"I am not one to hold grudges," reflects Eddie, soon to have a considerable hit on his hands in America with his new band Fastway. "I had to pick myself up and was fortunate to run into Pete Way. We had such a blast putting Fastway together, when I was asked by my new accountant what to do about the Motörhead money, etc., I said, 'I am doing okay. I do not want to give them any trouble; we had some good years.' But first I had to fly back to England and I had nothing. All of my equipment, my guitars and everything, was still on the road with Motörhead. I remember kicking along the streets with a half a bottle of vodka in my pocket and hardly any money and thinking, 'Fuck, I'm not in the band anymore.' It was devastating.

"Fortunately, I was young," continues Eddie, stressing it didn't take him long to sort out a next move. "I also had a bit of a drink problem so that kind of helped, as well. You can drink yourself every night until you forget things. It was not long after that when someone called me and said, 'Pete Way has left UFO and would you like to get together to have a meeting?' I had to do something so I agreed. Pete was in a similar situation as me, as he had been kind of forced out of his band because of his behavior. I was forced out of my band due to my behavior. We both also liked to have a drink. So I met with Pete and we had a drink and then I went to see this guy I knew and asked him if we could use his rehearsal room on credit because we didn't have any money. He agreed to let me pay him later. Topper Headon from the Clash was just down the road and we got chatting and he said, 'Ah, this is fucking great, I'll play drums.' The next thing I know we get to rehearsal the next day and Topper is on drums, Pete is on bass and I'm on guitar and it just sounds great. It was the first time I had played with a proper bass player in seven years."

Explaining his optimism for this new band versus the hard graft that Motörhead had become, Eddie notes that, "Pete is a wonderful bass player. I was playing some solos and my guitar had never sounded so sweet. The underlying sound of Motörhead made it so I had no bass to lean on to play a solo. I was always struggling with my sound. I didn't realize until I played with Pete that the problem was that I didn't have a proper bass guitar for my sound to be soaked into. From there on it was fantastic. Topper was great but he had some issues and problems and he had to leave. We were really three outcasts. He told me that he was not in the right place and that he had to leave. One of Pete's fans told us that Jerry Shirley was painting and decorating in this town just outside of London. We met up with him in a pub in London and he comes in all covered in paint. Jerry was one of the greatest rock drummers of our time and he is standing there covered in paint. He liked to drink too, which was handy. We sorted it out and he agreed to join the band. We started rehearsing with Jerry and it sounded great."

"There were some drugs around but drink was the main drug," continues Eddie, on whether booze got to be a hindrance at any point with either of his bands of brothers. "I suppose sometimes it caused a few problems but other times it was helpful. I am sure some of my drunken antics pissed people off. I think it comes with the territory, but it didn't really have a negative effect. A lot of the fun was down to the heavy party lifestyle. But of course, I may have a twisted take on these things. I had some of the best times of my life with Motörhead, although it was a struggle with that band. We finally made it through sheer will and determination. Motörhead was very intense and suddenly I walked out of that intensity into this breath of fresh air that was Fastway. I started playing like I always knew I could. Of course, the problem with Fastway was that Pete left and then Jerry left and then I was drinking too much and I got out of control. There are a lot of bad memories surrounding Fastway."

It's well known that Fastway's fortunes declined quickly, along with Eddie's profile in rock, which persists at no more than a low hum to this day. But first there was the self-titled Fastway album from 1983, which spawned the hits "Easy Livin'" and "Say What You Will" and almost went gold in the States, followed by a second solid CBS-issued record in *All Fired Up*. And back in the Motörhead camp, even if Eddie was never to rejoin forces with Lemmy and Phil, relations soon became cordial again.

"Yes, well, Lemmy buried the hatchet at the Reading Festival in 1982 when Pete and I did a guest spot with Twisted Sister. We got on stage and suddenly Lemmy appeared! So, it was all good from then on. Phil was a different story, as he was the main instigator in my being excluded from the band. Notice I do not call it leaving, as it was not my choice. Everyone else says I left—not me! It is funny how I am still a little raw about the whole thing of not being in Motörhead anymore. Some things you just don't get over. I had imagined dying onstage with Motörhead."

Twisted Sister vocalist Dee Snider remembers this quasi-reunion between Lemmy and Eddie quite well, which he relates. But first to mind is a tale that demonstrates the graciousness of

SUN JUNE 10 (11AM)

HEAVY SOUND FESTIVAL 2

POPERINGE-BELGIUM

MOTORHEAD
TW. SISTER
METALLICA
MANOWAR
MERCYFUL FATE
LITA FORD
FAITHFUL   BREATH
H BOMB

TICKETS ENGLAND MEAD GOULD PROM
(0273-204101)
★ RETURN COACH FROM LONDON + FERRY + TICKET:
PRICE 43 POUNDS
★ RETURN COACH FROM LONDON + FERRY + TICKET
+ 1ST CLASS HOTEL: 59 POUNDS

Last hurrah before the changing of the guard, Heavy Sound Festival 2, June 10, 1984.

Lemmy, one in which Lemmy supported the gaudy and glam Twisted Sister against a hostile English crowd. Indeed, for all of Lemmy's gruff pronouncements that his focus is Motörhead and Motörhead only, he's always been one to provide moral support to anyone crazy enough to get into this most demoralizing of businesses (more the women, of course, but the guys too).

"Lemmy became our guardian angel," begins Dee, one of many metal stars to sing the praises of many days playing with Motörhead over the decades. "He saw Twisted Sister, and his first kindness to the band was just as a personal favor to Pete Way. Pete Way was producing our *Under the Blade* record, which we were recording in England. And Pete said, 'Hey, watch out for these guys; Dee's a good guy.' And Lemmy, being this great guy, 'All right, I'll take care of them.'"

"So we did Wrexham Football Ground, April of '82, which became a game-changer for us, but we were terrified as a band. It was our first big show in England, and it was in the daylight opening for Motörhead. Suddenly where we desperately needed to have this sort of veil of secrecy, we were walking out on stage with makeup on. I mean, we were very terrified for that show. It was a stadium show, we ended up second on the bill to Motörhead's crowd, and the guys were better looking than the girls. With Motörhead's crowd, you'd sooner go with a guy than one of the girls. When we saw that audience, we hadn't had one record out in the country, and there was a hatred. Hair metal wasn't around—there wasn't any hair metal in 1982. There was no glam. Glitter was dead, and Anvil was canned. They called them Canvil, because they canned and bottled them on stage because Lips wore those fishnet arm things. And so he was gay. Girl had been bottled off the stage—Phil Collen and Phil Lewis's band were wearing makeup. We were coming out with faces of makeup at a time when there was a hatred for the remnants of the glitter rock.

"And Lemmy literally walked out on stage and stopped the audience from bottling us. They hadn't started. They were getting ready; their arms were cocked with the bottles. And he introduced us, saying something like, 'I have some friends of mine here from the States! You will listen!' Which gave us just the briefest of pardons, and the audience welcomes us. And they listened to us for a minute, and they said, 'What the fuck? These guys aren't gay. These guys are fucking linebackers with lipstick.' You could see them; they were like, 'Lemmy and *those* fags?!' But it just gave us enough time to play, and fire was shooting out of my ass for that show. It was one of my most memorable victories. I remember walking off stage and ten minutes later—this was a football stadium—someone said, 'Listen.' And they were still chanting 'Twisted boom boom Sister boom boom Twisted boom boom Sister!' And I was like holy shit!

"And then Lemmy came down and said, 'I introduced you; now you introduce me.' And I was like holy shit! And I stepped out on stage and introduced Motörhead and the place went fucking nuts. That was a huge breakthrough for us. I mean Lemmy, I love that guy forever. If he hadn't done that, it might have been a whole different story and we would have been bottled off the stage, and it would have read 'Twisted Sister went home with their tails between their legs.' And England turned out to be the place that broke us first. But what star goes out three bands early, walks out on stage and effectively destroys his 'entrance' by bringing on an unknown band and saying something like that? I certainly don't."

As for Twisted Sister's part in thawing relations between Lemmy and Eddie: "So Lemmy had fallen in love with our band. He started showing up at the Marquee and introducing us and even playing with us, of all things. But we were at the Reading Festival, coming out, and we were being bottled on the stage at Reading, bottled! Again! And he comes out, he joins us and says, 'Come on, I've got a couple buddies.' So Pete Way and Fast Eddie are on stage with us, and he reconciles with Fast Eddie. They are having a heated, hated breakup, 1982, and Lemmy, for the first time, walks out on stage with Twisted Sister and Fast Eddie and Pete Way, and I have those pictures."

"Yep, that was Reading, the summer of that year," reiterates Eddie. "We had been working on the Twisted Sister album. Peter produced the album and I played on one track. And then of course Lemmy jumps up and has a go as well. It was quite funny. So it did break the ice a little bit. It was kind of nice actually as it forced us to talk to each other. I certainly didn't have an axe to grind. It took Phil a bit longer as he was a bit bitter and twisted. It was a sad end really, as I never thought it was going to end. I didn't have a problem with him—they had a terrible problem with me. But I'll still never work that one out.

"Lemmy was all heart, really," continues Eddie, on the subject of his ex–band mate supporting Twisted Sister. "I mean, he would always have a kind word to say to anybody. And he would talk to anybody. And we all were like that, but Lemmy had pearls of wisdom. He had been around a long time. It's another reason I think we did well is because we had Lemmy. When we were getting bad reviews and that in the very beginning, Lemmy would always say, 'Hey, listen, man, you're going to get a lot of those.' And he just, at certain points in my career, I can remember Lemmy saying things and it really helped. Because he had been there before and

I hadn't. So there was a bit of the old wise man about him. And especially Dee and the boys, I mean, a lot of people used to look up to Lemmy because he was such an icon."

"It's true," agrees Dee. "I mean, again, each of the shows, Wrexham, Reading, we were in danger of just being obliterated and sent packing. And Lemmy Kilmister uses his influence—he was huge and Motörhead were huge. And when Lemmy says, 'Hey, check them out,' you fucking checked them out. He's fucking Lemmy. He has spoken. He's that guy. Another example, *The Tube* television show: we were floundering at the beginning of that show. And, you know, it wasn't just Lemmy, but he comes out with Robbo and joined us for 'It's Only Rock 'n' Roll.' And that's the show I took my makeup off on stage, and that took it over the edge. That was legendary. The next day we had multiple record company offers and we got our deal with Atlantic. He has been our fairy godfather."

I asked Dee to sum up what Motörhead meant to the rock world at that magical time, and it's a question that gave him pause.

"Motörhead . . . man, I'm going to give some thought to how I'm going to verbalize this. Like AC/DC, they deconstructed heavy metal and infused it with a new vitality and transformed it into a new element. Lemmy will tell you that they were more a punk-driven thing. They weren't metal-driven. They weren't a metal band. AC/DC, they never viewed themselves a metal band. They were accepted by the metal community, but it wasn't necessarily their goal. None of the brilliant ideas, the brilliant musical changes of our time, happened on purpose. Alice Cooper was trying to be a Doors-y psychedelic band, and they sucked at it! And he invented shock rock. And Bowie wanted to be the Beatles and all of a sudden he's the king of glitter. Nirvana wasn't trying to be the first grunge band. They were just trying to play rock that appealed to them and they were infusing it with this garage element. So, great new ideas happen that way. And I think that's what Motörhead brought. They brought back a simplifying of hard rock music, stripping it down to its rawer elements, its most primitive elements. Which just set bands like Metallica down a whole new path of rock 'n' roll."

Another couple of New York heavy metal legends who wholeheartedly sing the praises of Motörhead are Charlie Benante and Frank Bello of Anthrax fame.

"Motörhead influenced us in a very specific way," reflects Benante. "Motörhead didn't look like your polished rock stars. They were just these . . . do these guys sleep, did these guys bathe? They just looked like this crew, this gang, and they had an awesomeness to them. And the cool thing about Motörhead back in the day is that a lot of punk and hardcore fans appreciated Motörhead as well. It was one of the first real crossover bands. But as a drummer, the way Phil Taylor attacked his drums, in songs like 'Overkill.' He was like a punk rock drummer playing metal and I always looked up to that."

"Everybody was inspired from Motörhead," adds Frank Bello. "And to me they're just good time rock. Lemmy always says, 'We play rock 'n' roll' and I love that. I've toured with Motörhead a million times, we've done Motörhead shows forever and I just found that there is just this great rock 'n' roll thing that they have going, yet in a metal way. Rest his soul, I met Phil a few years ago, a really nice guy. I'm friends with the band now, but the original band is the band I got into in the beginning. And what I get from them is just a lot of heaviness. Fast Eddie with those great guitar parts, complementary with Phil's kick drums and Lemmy's bass and vocals—that was Motörhead, man. This great three-piece band playing the heaviest shit ever.

"I'll give you a quick story," continues Bello. "This is one of my favorite moments in my bass life, okay? All right, so me, being Mr. Fan Boy, over the side of the stage for this sound check every day, because I'm a bass guy. I just love Lemmy's tone. I love the way he plays, everything about it. So I was a fan boy on one of the tours. I just started watching every sound check at the monitor board.

So Lemmy sees me. He's checking out his bass, he's playing the song, and he looks over at me and he goes, 'Hey, come here!' He calls me over, and I say, 'Hey, Lemmy, how you doing?' He goes, 'Try this on.' And he puts his bass on me, dude. He puts his main bass on me, and he goes, 'Go play.' He hands me his pick, and I swear to God, remember the movie *Back to the Future*, the opening sequence, where Michael J. Fox plays that opening chord and gets blown away by the speaker? That's what it was for me. It was so fucking amazingly loud—in every cool way in the world. It was one of the highlights of my bass career. I didn't mind how loud it was and how much it hurt my ears. The fact that Lemmy gave me this opportunity, I will never forget that; it was a very special time for me. Because he actually acknowledged me and brought me over. And then the cherry on top, he goes, 'Here, this is the one I play with. This is the one I throw out.' So he gives me a pick, the one that he actually plays with—there are two different picks. There's one he has a better feel for. 'This is the one I play with. Keep this one.' I'll always be fan boy, dude—always."

Meanwhile, as Eddie found his legs with Fastway, Phil Taylor remained with Lemmy for the band's next album, *Another Perfect Day* (featuring new guitarist Brian Robertson, ex–Thin Lizzy) and *No Remorse* (a mix of compilation and new songs). He would be out of the band for 1986's *Orgasmatron* but back for 1987's *Rock 'n' Roll* and 1991's *1916* before leaving for good as the band began the recording sessions for what was to become 1992's dog's bollocks of an album, *March or Die*.

Lemmy's first stab at replacing Fast Eddie Clarke did not go so well. As much as people appreciate the *Another Perfect Day* album now, much scorn was rained down upon Brian Robertson, with some of that being testimony to how much Eddie was beloved by fans as part of the band.

As Phil explains it, Lemmy was having a hard time adapting to the new six-stringer as well. "For me it was great, but for Lemmy . . . you see, Lemmy had the stupid attitude, just from Rob being a Scottish guy, like [in a Scottish accent], 'If Lemmy tells me not to do it, I'm going to fucking do it.' It was just ridiculous. Because Lemmy had nothing against Brian's playing. His playing speaks for itself; it was just the way he looked. When he joined the band, it was the tail end of the summer, and Robbo joined us in America and it was very hot and subsequently he wore shorts just like anybody else did. But unfortunately he didn't change from his shorts when we went on stage. But he didn't give a fuck. He's not the kind of guy. And admittedly, I said to him, 'Rob, you should at least put a pair of pants on.' 'Aar, aar, all right.' And Lemmy would go, 'Fuckin' hell, Rob, you look like a fucking wanker!' Instead of being reasonable about it. Well, of course, that got Robbo very pissed off, and it just got worse. And he started wearing headbands and all this kind of thing—that just set Lemmy off, really."

"And Rob was the sort of person, unfortunately—and in a way, I agreed with him—it's like, why should they give a fuck? Go listen to the music instead of looking at my fucking shorts. Which is fair enough, but on the other hand, I would say, 'Damn, well, Rob, it wouldn't hurt just to put a pair of pants on if that's what it takes to get the fans over.' Because after all, unfortunately, if you want to call them shallow or whatever, they are seeing the shorts, not the man, not the music. And unfortunately it's not very good.

"Because that lineup was good," continues Phil. "I thought *Another Perfect Day* was the best album Motörhead ever made. And so does Lemmy, as it happens. He just couldn't stand the image that Robbo projected. It's always down to—which was really stupid, because I used to have chats with Lemmy—'Lem, when you speak to him about it, speak to him like a normal human being. Don't jump down his neck. Because you know he's just going to get worse.' 'Oh fucking, grrr . . .' So anyway, he said Robbo had to go. It's the shorts or you, so it was him."

"Apart from that, we got on really well, and musically it was really good, because Thin Lizzy has always been one of my favorite bands, and playing with Robbo was great. That whole album was virtually written by Robbo and me, I mean, not me from a musical point of view, but Lemmy was hardly ever at rehearsals. He came in and mostly did his bass parts in the studio. The arrangements were already done, and I think you can hear that just by listening to the album. There's not a great deal of Lemmy influence in there. And of course, Lemmy I think is one of the best lyricists of our time, for that genre. He could always write good lyrics. So yeah, that was an unfortunate time. But Motörhead with Brian Robertson . . . I regret that it couldn't have gone on longer, because it would have developed into a hell of a good band."

"I really enjoyed it, from what I can remember," laughs Robbo, with regard to his one record cycle with Motörhead. "Because that was crazy. I mean, we were traveling in a bus. I'd never even done that before. Straight off the stage, into a bus, off to the next gig, blah blah blah. So it was a severe amount of Jack Daniels consumed, and other things. I enjoy the album thoroughly, but I did say to the boys when I joined the band, when they asked me, because I only went out to do the tour, just to help them out, because we were mates, right? And then they asked me to join, and I said if I do, and if we're going to do an album, it's not going to be like the old Motörhead, because it just won't be. And they were like, 'No, that's cool.'

"I mean, I know that Lemmy is quoted as saying that Robbo thought it was his solo album, right?" continues Robertson. "Now, that just makes me laugh, because the fact is, you know, Phil came in and got his drums down. I mean, I wrote half the music actually on my own, in the rehearsal studio. I wrote the bits that I did on my own in the rehearsal studio by recording myself on drums and then using the guitar to write the riffs. Because Lemmy was in the pub doing his one-arm bandit thing, and Philthy was already gone. He just went home. Phil really wasn't interested once he got his drums down. He would come up for the mixes for a little while or whatever, but Lemmy was busy off writing his amazingly funny lyrics that he comes out with. I thought the lyrics were absolutely incredible. There's one track there that I really had a hard time doing the solo on, because, every time I heard the vocal, I burst out laughing. And Tony Platt, the producer, kept saying, 'Robbo, come on.' And I said, 'Look, you're going to have to take the vocal off. Take the vocal out and I'll launch into the solo.' It was 'Back at the Funny Farm,' and 'I really like this jacket, but the sleeves are much too long.' What a thought. He really had an amazing mind. He is a really good lyricist—weird, but it's tongue-in-cheek."

"It's a long story, but I'll give you the short version," begins Phil, when asked about his own eventual departure from the ranks, concluding the death of the classic Motörhead lineup. "Lemmy was under the impression that I was fucking his girl-friend, which I wasn't. And for a start, she wasn't even his girl-friend, and it was as simple as that. And Lemmy and I had been at loggerheads for a long time. I had rejoined the band two or three years earlier, when I was away for about a year, and my mom had passed away the summer of . . . I left in the May of '92, and my mom passed away in the late summer of '91—and that hit me very hard. And I mean, it was still affecting me a lot, so I wasn't exactly the person I had been. I guess looking back now, you could probably say I was depressed or something. But my heart wasn't in anything. And I guess Lemmy could see that. I was just very quiet and not me.

"But the thing is also, when I rejoined the band [Note: Phil left in '84, returned in '87 and was gone for good in '92], Lemmy had a different attitude toward me. It was like, once I left the band, I was the last original member to leave, and then so he really became God. He was the boss, it was his band, and whatever he said went. Well, when I came back in the band, as far as I was concerned, it was still the way it used to be. If I saw something, I would give my honest opinion no matter what it was or who was asking the question. Considering those two or three years I was back with the band, Lemmy didn't like that anymore. Because I would chal-lenge him on something that I didn't think was right.

"For a start, there were things like when we got the record deal in America, Lemmy moved over to America before I did, and me and Phil Campbell and Würzel [born Michael Burston, the first guitarist hired after Brian Robertson's ousting] were still back in England. And I found out that it became obvious—not so much by actually saying so, but more by omission—that Lemmy was lying. Because the record company would get in touch with Lemmy in L.A., and they just believed that he was like an Ozzy sort of figure. They would tell Lemmy everything. They would ask him everything. They wouldn't bother with the rest of the band because they thought they should meet with the leader. He always did everything, and if there was anything he wanted the rest of the band to know, he would pass it on.

"Well, that was the case in a democracy," reflects Phil, "but it was lying by omission, and that's how it ended up. I got pissed off with it, but Phil Campbell and Würzel turned out to be two brown-nosers who just went along. So I went to Lemmy and said, 'What the fuck is going on?' One of the things that really brought it to a head was over the 1916 album sleeve. I mean, we'd finished doing the album, and me and Phil Campbell and Würzel had just flown over to America, and well, Lemmy'd already been living there. Obviously, we were getting ready to start the new tour, and the first thing we had to do was get off the plane and go straight to the record company for a meeting about the album launch and this, that and the other. We got there, and I was completely blown away. What the fuck was going on here?! We got to this conference room, and there was a big easel up there with one cover after another. Lemmy, he might as well have had a pointed stick, 'Right, boys,' and that's how it was. He kept pulling out all these 'I like this one,' and they came up with this sleeve—rubbish. And apparently, while Lemmy had been in L.A., they went through about four different artists for this album sleeve for 1916. And Lemmy rejected them all. And he rejected them all at a cost of approximately fifteen thousand pounds a time.

"So he was making decisions like that, but he never even told anyone. And so he was throwing our money away. And so I blew up at him and said, 'What the fuck do you think you're doing? If you want to be the fucking big cheese, and you want to hire and fire and just pay us a retainer, fine. That's fine, we'll do that, and pay us a good retainer. But if this band is still a democracy, you've got no right. How can you make decisions like this that are costing all of us money? And then, number two, you can make all the decisions you want without any problem from any of us, like rejecting artwork, as long as it comes out of your pocket.' But that's not what was happening.

"And then on top of all that, we find out that he charges us . . . he ended up, as he says, actually designing the final sleeve that came along, and he charged the band eighteen thousand pounds for doing it! Exactly. I think he spent about sixty thousand pounds of our money, and Phil Campbell and Würzel, after that, made a big stink about it—only afterwards. And we decided, I said to them, 'Listen, you've got to fucking speak up. Because Lemmy just thinks it's me being an asshole.' And they never fucking did; every time it came down to it, Campbell and Würzel just sat there and went, 'Oh.' And Lemmy goes, 'What do you think, guys?' And they said, 'Well, I don't know, Lem. We're with you.' And I just turned around and said, 'You fucking wankers! That's not what you fucking said.' And then of course Lemmy would look at me and smile with that shit-eating grin, 'Oh yeah? I thought you said it wasn't just you then?' And so that really put it in a bad light, and then I think Lemmy was just looking for any excuse to get rid of me, because he didn't like being challenged. But at the same time he wasn't prepared to say, 'Right, okay, I am the boss, and I'm going to put you all on retainer and I'm going to take all the royalties.' Because that would have been fine by me. But don't fucking claim it's a democracy and everybody sharing everything fair and square, when you're doing shit like that.

"And then the final straw actually came in Japan. We went to

Japan on tour, and the very first gig—very first gig—Lemmy refused to go on stage, in Japan, right? And there's all these fans. And he refused to go on stage because the merchandising was all wrong. Which was totally ridiculous. And during that particular argument, it was just me and him in the dressing room, and we had a big fucking fight. And the last thing I said to him, I remember saying, 'Fucking 'ell. Whatever happened to you? Is this band a democracy or not? Is this a democracy anymore?' And he looked at me and said, 'Yeah, it's a democracy. It's a democracy when I say so.' And I looked at him and said, 'Well, at least, Lemmy, you're showing your true colors. Fuck it.' And then after that tour, we got back in the studio and it all came to a head and he accused me of fucking his girlfriend, which was totally ridiculous—absolute bollocks."

To add insult to injury, not much head-held-high Motörmusic got made during Phil's second stay in the band either.

"I didn't like *Rock 'n' Roll* much," tells Taylor. "It was a bit uninspired and dead, I thought. And the title was a bit iffy. I didn't like *1916* that much either. The one song on it was really good, but that album was written by me, mainly, and Phil Campbell and Würzel, in a dingy, damp little studio in Suffolk, in south London, while Lemmy was in Los Angeles. All the songs were put together by us three. The ideas for the riffs obviously came from Campbell and Würzel, but when we got over to L.A., we had about a week's worth of rehearsal and Lemmy just put his bass parts on. But he would never admit to that, of course, and of course he wrote the lyrics.

"Oh, and that's when he dropped the bombshell of—that was another situation—from that album forward, he decided that he was getting 50 percent of the royalties. Which fair enough, that's the law. The person who writes the lyrics, they are entitled to 50 percent of the royalties, because that's the way it worked. But he never did that before, and all of a sudden he's doing it. So, I mean, I was glad when he fired me. I said, 'You can't fucking fire me, I'm fucking leaving! I'm glad. Thank you very much. You're such a prick. And guess what—you are firing the only fucking friend you've got in the world. Because these cunts are just fucking sycophants, and the only thing they want to know is how far they can stick their noses down your trousers, and that's it.' I get a bit emotional about that because I loved Lemmy as a brother. And it's true, he doesn't have any friends and he got rid of the only real friends he had, which were the ones who would tell him to his face what they thought. But now he just hires sycophants and people who tell him how great he is."

"Ah yes, Phil Taylor, that's a different story," counters Lemmy, asked about Phil's departure from Motörhead. "We were family for years and years, me and Phil. Then one day he did something that I considered unforgiveable, so I haven't forgiven him. So no, I don't keep in touch with him at all, even though he's in L.A. somewhere."

"Once Phil got kicked out of Motörhead by Lemmy in the early '90s, he never did anything else after that," sighs Eddie. "He fucked about a little bit with an electronic kit, but he never played again. And it's a waste, because he was a fucking brilliant drummer."

＂＂

Motörhead would of course soldier on, making some of the best music of their career with Phil Campbell and Mikkey Dee. "I know this is the best version of the band, because I'm playing in it and I know," says a somewhat exasperated Lemmy, having to perennially defend the current band against the legend of the original. "This is certainly the best band I've ever had, but people are just stuck with it, you know? People won't come out of 1981. The old stuff is pretty ropey when you listen to it up against this band, without the benefit of nostalgia painting it gold, you know?"

There's much to be said for that supposition. Whether it's dark horse *Bastard* or *Motorizer* or *Aftershock* or the band's last album ever, *Bad Magic*, there are piles of great songs everywhere, recorded with grit and heft and determination, year after year, the modern Motörhead distilling rock 'n' roll to its hard essence (and yes, please do call it heavy metal). And yet there's still a boozy romance with the original band that cranked those six records—bang, bang, bang—from 1977 through 1982, *Ace of Spades* the evergreen pop culture icon amongst the stash.

Staring down mortality, Lemmy told me with a typical smirk and snort, "I figured I've already gotten away with it, you know? I've made it. And a lot of my contemporaries really didn't. I keep doing it because I love rock 'n' roll, I really do. Almost ever since I could remember, I've been doing it. I mean, it's been good to me, and I've been pretty good to it too. I don't think I have any reason to stop doing it."

And of course, doing it means living on the road. When I asked Lemmy how he stays mentally fit during all those miles, he counters, "I'm mentally unfit. That's the secret. There's no way of going on the road and being normal. I mean, what the fuck are you on the road for if you're going to be normal? You've got to be fucking nuts to go there in the first place. I mean, to stay there, you've really gotta be tragic. Going home scares me. The road is where I live, you know. I live on the bus—that's it." Lem clearly doesn't like those four walls: "Well, why do that when you can have 150 fucking walls on tour?"

"But the business has always been a pain in the ass," adds Lem, always able to find the cloud inside the silver lining. "The music business is cutting its own throat, and it doesn't even know it. Because all they promote is singles by faceless bands who are going to disappear immediately. And you wonder why they have no fan base. They're just destroying the fan base by making it disposable. And MTV is helping them as well. I mean, MTV, I've never seen such an abortion in my life. Game shows on Music Television—that's what we need! Like there weren't enough game shows on TV. It is wonderful, isn't it? You have to keep a sense of humor about this shit. Mankind, as a race, is hilarious. We just keep killing each other. The only thing we improve is that we can kill each other from farther away. We don't need to see the hand-iwork that we did. I think if we still had to see the dead man with our sword stuck in him then there would be a lot less fighting. How they do it now is cowardly. You are killing a guy from several miles away and you don't even know what he looks like.

"I just do what I do and that is to be the bass player and vocalist for Motörhead—that's my title," continues Lemmy, true to the rock world's assessment of his noble role as well as his harried band mates' and managers' assessment of his lack of cooperation and ambition. "What we do is we kick ass. As far as the popularity goes, I never saw the point of letting them win. If you let them win then the whole thing was for nothing. You've got to prove it. You've got to say, 'Yeah, I was here and I shit on your hydrant'—you've got to leave your mark. Seriously, I've always felt that we were a pretty good band and I always have thought that we deserved more attention in America. We've been putting albums out here since 1982. If it takes making a movie about one of us [*Lemmy*, 2010] to get us more recognition, then I say, 'Let's do it.' Most of our dreams have come true. There are only a couple left that have not come true, like having that hit in America. But I never did see the point in it. I am not going to throw my heart away for money. You may be able to do that, but you will lose all of your original fans because they will know you're selling out. Plus, we've never played in Africa or China or Thailand or places like that. I'd like to do that before we go. Sure, I'd like to have a giant hit in America before we go, but I don't see that happening. Because we've never even been in the Top 100 here, you know? Other than that, I'm pretty satisfied with my life."

Doug Smith figures that Lemmy hasn't yet received the respect due to him for his lyrics, his world view and the amount of integ-rity that he represented to his fans.

"His lyrics were always great," chuckles Smith. "I actually have some of Lemmy's handwritten lyrics and a few short stories that he wrote. Oh yes, he tried to write short stories; he would do it when he had nothing better to do and he had a good line of speed. And he would work hard at it. No, he was a great lyricist. As far as artists and musicians go, when people actually read his lyrics, they get a real shock. They are really political. He had his own way of saying what he felt, and I think he should be even more immortalized than he is, that's for sure.

"He didn't like sycophants," continues Doug. "He didn't like people who pandered to him—and people always did. Which was terrible. Because, you know, he was as ordinary as everybody else. He felt that he had to be, otherwise he wouldn't connect with the punters in the audience. He connected with these people. And they loved him for it.

"I remember a gig in Newcastle, watching them play, and they were really so hot at this particular point; they were just boiling. And I was standing at the side, in front of the stage in the audience, and looking up from that point of view. And the front row had this kid who had medical glasses on. Now you may not know what these are, but if you come from Northern England, you'll see kids with these old things; sometimes they had pink rims to them. This kid is sitting there watching the band, going crazy. And suddenly, they go into this great guitar riff, and he just leaps up and jumps up onto the arms of the seat. And he can't be more than 14 years old—he shouldn't even have been at the gig. It was a magnificent sight.

"And that's how he connected. They were idols. And at the same time, you look back on the lyrics and realize what he was trying to say, basically that we are all the same people in the world, one global village. I was with them for many, many years, and I've got to say, that original material . . . all this recent Motörhead, isn't, to me, what the real Motörhead is. The real Motörhead was Lemmy, Phil and Eddie. That's it—always will be. And Lemmy knew it. I don't think he would agree with me on that, I think he'd get really fucking annoyed with me, but it's the truth."

"We were called 'The Best Worst Band in the World,'" continues Lem, on the subject of getting little respect, which rankles him almost as much as it does Eddie, even if his nature is to, well, stare it down. "I remember seeing that for the first time and I really thought that was unjust. You've got to read the reviews just to see what people are saying but just don't believe them—the good or the bad. You've just got to figure out what is relevant. Most of what they say is irrelevant. The best rock 'n' roll has always pissed off parents. The best stuff makes them go, 'Turn that rubbish down.' If they are saying that, then you're on the right track." But respect from direct peers, like Ozzy and Metallica and Slash, who have all heaped respect over the years, is important. "Yes, of course it is. It means that you're doing it right. For me, music and friendship come together."

Lemmy also leaves behind an improved relationship with his long-estranged son, Paul Inder, something he never had with his own father. "I thought it was great; I thought he should know," reflects Lemmy, when Jeb Wright points out the scene in *Lemmy* where he says he loves his son. "I'm not very good at saying things like that to people. I just thought I should say it. British people keep it pretty close to the chest, you know what I mean? That is kind of why I like Americans; they are keen. They are eager to get out there and they want to get the most out of things. They want to find out how things work. It is certainly different than the British, as they are so fucking stuck on their manners. Manners do not make for progress."

And Lemmy wasn't about to look back. Even when everybody was hearty and hale, the high quality of the longstanding current lineup—tour in, tour out—was enough to ensure that no one was calling for a reunion of the original classic lineup. Might have been nice to see, but there was never much cry for it.

"The thing is that I've had this band together with these two guys now for a lot longer than the original band," answers Lem. "They have been through a lot harder times than the first band. I don't see why I should put this band on hold for a bit of nostalgia. I don't see why I should put these guys out of work while I go and tour with the old guys. I don't think it's fair of us to do that. I don't know if Eddie and Phil can still do it at this point."

"Well, it's me; I never gave up," says Lemmy, when asked how the band had endured to last fully—and exactly—40 years, along with 22 studio albums and, depending how you count, another dozen or so live albums. "So I have to have a band with me, so that's it, I guess. I mean, a lot of bands break up because they can't decide who's the leader, you know? There's always infighting going on, and a lot of bands are jealous of the fucking singer. I'm sure Bill Wyman and Charlie Watts and Keith Richards bitched about Mick Jagger getting all the interviews. It's always the same. You have to get on with that too. Tolerance again, you see? Everything is tolerance."

To persevere for 40 years is one thing, but to do so while generating the kind of amps-buzzing racket Motörhead was known for is impressive. Really, it's a hard music to love, music made for lovers of hard music, and hence it's easy to understand the lack of wider acceptance in America.

"It's passionate music, isn't it?" continues Lemmy, for once defending heavy metal. "I mean, so-called heavy metal . . . I call it rock 'n' roll. If Eddie Cochran was around today, he'd be in a garage band. And he was, wasn't he? But it's the kind of music that they can aspire to do themselves, right? Might call it three-chord bullshit, but it isn't. There's just as much craft in making a three-chord song sound different than all the other three-chord songs, as there is in writing a 25-chord song. The passion is most of it, actually. And the volume; volume is very important. And we're good—we're a fucking good band. We deserve success. I don't care. It's not false modesty. I've got no false modesty. I have a certain amount of real modesty, but I don't want to show much. Fuck them. I'm proud of what I've done."

Lemmy—smoker, diabetic, drinker, hypertension and hematoma sufferer, abuser of a suspect ticker with a pacemaker—had been looking thin and fragile and far less mobile on stage as 2015 drew to a close. His enunciation was compromised but his bass was strong. Dates would be missed in America, but he completed a European tour. He played his last concert in Berlin, Germany, fittingly the nation Lemmy always called the band's best territory, on December 11. On December 13, back in his adopted L.A. home, Lemmy was thrown his last party, a star-studded early birthday celebration at the Whisky a Go Go. Two days later, he was admitted to hospital, checked out and released, with test results pending. On December 26, he was diagnosed with a particularly aggressive cancer of the brain and neck and given two to six months to live.

After the bad news, Rainbow owner Mikael Maglieri, sensing the end was near, delivered to Lemmy's sanctified and rent-controlled apartment his favorite video game, so that he could play it from his bedside. Lemmy loved the Rainbow, and his curious habit of hanging out there just showed how Lemmy could be misanthropic at the same time as he could be open and sociable. If you respected him and his space, he would respect you right back. It was in his eyes, his disarming politeness when you least expected it.

"It was a great place," mused Lem. "Stars like John Lennon and Keith Moon used to hang out there. Lennon went on a bender for about a year and he hung out there with Harry Nilsson. Ringo Starr and Alice Cooper used to hang out there. There is a great tradition there—rock 'n' roll is oozing out of walls. It is a legend that you can still visit. Plus they have a patio bar where you can smoke. I used to smoke in there but I didn't want to make them lose their license, so I stopped."

Recalls historian and label executive Rob Godwin, "I once put out a best of Motörhead box set. And around that time, I met Lemmy at the Rainbow and didn't even know he was going to be in there. I didn't know the legend of Lemmy at the Rainbow at that point, because this is back in the late '80s, early '90s. I'd seen him play twice with Hawkwind and I'd never met him before. I saw him in '72, and I saw him again when he guested with them in '87. I was on tour with a local Canadian band called Honeymoon Suite, and they were opening for Jethro Tull, playing Universal Amphitheater. Later on we went back to the hotel on Sunset Boulevard, and the hotel was like rock hell. I literally bumped into Stevie Ray in the lobby with a girl hanging off each arm. And Jon Anderson from Yes was sunbathing by the pool. And I went over to the Rainbow because the guys wanted to go over there. I'd heard all the Led Zeppelin stories about the Rainbow, so I said okay, let's go over there. We went over there, and there's Lemmy playing the bloody video game—I think it was Missile Command or something—standing at the bar. So I went over and just said a few nice things about Hawkwind to him and he was very gracious. He wasn't standoffish or gruff or anything, just like a normal nice guy. And he said, 'Do you want to play?' Because I was pretty good at Missile Command at the time, I played a game of Missile Command with him. The guys in Honeymoon Suite were more in awe, I think, at the fact that he was just standing at the bar because they had a different perception of him than me. To me he was always Hawkwind's bass player and I'd been more interested in what he had done with them."

Lemmy had no qualms about making the news of his terminal ticket to the other side public, but he would be dead before a proper press release could be drafted. On December 28, at 4 o'clock in the afternoon and four days past his 70th birthday, Lemmy died at his memorabilia-filled two-bedroom apartment two blocks from the Rainbow.

Motörhead manager Todd Singerman had been on the phone summoning Phil Campbell and Mikkey Dee to come visit him while he was still, seemingly, in relatively good shape. He was working quickly, despite the doctor giving Lemmy two months to live. It came as a shock to all, the diagnosis and Lemmy's quick passing, because there were any number of things that were going to kill him—just not cancer.

Lemmy would become the first rock star to have his memorial streamed live, garnering 230,000 viewers of the elegant event taking place on January 9, 2016, at Forest Lawn Memorial Park in Hollywood. Lemmy's son, Paul Inder, spoke memorably, as did Slash, Mikkey Dee, Lars Ulrich, WWE's Paul "Triple H" Levesque and Dave Grohl. Also in attendance were Rob Halford, Matt Sorum, Robert Trujillo, Bob Kulick, Todd Singerman, Scott Ian and Mike Inez. Notably absent was Phil Campbell. Ozzy Osbourne issued a statement of tribute, as did Alice Cooper, Tony Iommi and collectively Metallica and Iron Maiden.

Less publicized was the death, at 61, of Phil Taylor, who over a year earlier had suffered a brain aneurism that caused permanent complications. Taylor succumbed to his ailments on November 11, 2015, a short month and a half prior to Lemmy's demise.

I spoke to Eddie twice in the month before Phil passed, and a year earlier as well. In October 2014, there was even hope that somehow, Eddie could gerrymander some jamming with Phil to lift his spirits, perhaps even with Lemmy as some sort of informal and casual reunion. Relations had in fact been fine between all three of the guys for years, arguably relaxed and cordial, because once Lemmy had found Mikkey Dee and Phil Campbell, the guys were never going to have to deal with reunion talk.

"Yes, that's what I mean, you know, just a ride in the saddle one more time would be great. I mean, it's a bit of a dream at the moment, but, keep your fingers crossed. But I suppose Lemmy—I spoke to him last week, it's my birthday, I gave him a call—and he's not feeling too bad. Because the week before, I went up to Phil's 60th birthday, and I managed to text Lemmy to have him call Phil. Phil's had an aneurysm in his brain, when he was in Los Angeles. So we had that capped off. He's all right, but he varies. I'm trying to get him to play again now because he just spends too much time doing fuck-all and avoiding the world. So what I'm trying to do now is get him into playing again. I'm saying, 'Look man, you play and we'll get on stage together one last time.' So I'm trying to get him to do that at the moment. I don't mind, to be honest, I'll play any time. There's no one I'd like to play more with than Phil. Lem, I don't know. I didn't say anything to Lem. I told Lem that what I'm trying to do is get Phil working again."

Many thought that Phil had been struck with stroke, given reports that his speech was slurred. "No, not quite a stroke," qualified Eddie. "He's talking fine; he's just a little slow. His thought processes are a little hesitant. He's just a little damaged. That's all I can say. But he's generally okay. But he's not doing anything, and I think if he does something . . . you know, your brain is a marvelous thing; it can work things out. But he needs to do something. Just lays in bed all day, really avoiding everything. And yet he's fine when you sit and talk to him."

A year to the day later, October 8, 2015, Clarke's ambitions for the original Motörhead—himself and Phil and Lemmy—getting together, sadly, were more in the realm of visitation and reconnection rather than any thoughts of vigorous Motörizing. And on the horizon was the perfect occasion for something of that nature, even if it would become past the horizon for the band's dear leader, Lemmy Kilmister.

"They're having a 40th birthday concert at Hammersmith, in January," said a hopeful Clarke. "Which I'm quite looking forward to, because as you're probably well aware, Lemmy's having some ill health as of late, and so I don't know how long he's going to manage to keep going for. I think he's going to sort of rock until he drops, really. I did see him last year. I went to Birmingham and I got up on stage and we did 'Ace of Spades' together. That was November. And it was nice; that's the first time we had been together for years, sitting in the same room. Unfortunately, Philip's health is also on the wane. I went to see him; he lives in Darby, in England now, in the Midlands. I went to see him a couple of weeks ago, just to see how he is. He's not bad, but he won't be playing anytime soon. He's had the aneurism and that's damaged him a bit. So I don't anticipate him playing anytime soon, which is a shame. Because it would've been nice do one together."

Eddie says he certainly would have been at that 40th anniversary show, but he said, "I don't know about Phil. I think it depends on how he progresses in the next couple of months. He was quite ill in the summer, and that's why I went to see him. I was a bit worried about him, and so I went up there. He doesn't get up and around much. He spends a lot of time in bed at the moment. So I'm hoping that's going to improve, but they're not sure. The aneurysm has put a lot of pressure on his body and his liver and everything and he's struggling."

As for Lemmy and his bill of health, Eddie said, "I think he wants to die on stage. I mean, one of my quotes when I was in Motörhead—when I left Motörhead, was out of Motörhead, whatever, when I was not in Motörhead anymore—I used to say I was going to die, in Motörhead, onstage. In those days it was all gung ho and all for one and one for all sort of thing. A very dear friend of ours died last year on stage, at the Break for the Border, London. Micky Farren. He was a writer and poet, but he wrote some of our tunes on the first album and *Overkill*. He wrote with Lemmy and he's always been a great friend of Lemmy's and mine. And he died on stage. He went on stage and had a seizure or heart attack or something and he collapsed. And of course he never came out of it and died—he sort of died with his boots on.

"But we're hanging on with Phil," said Eddie as our chat grew to a close. "I'm going to check up on him this week and I might go and see him next week again. And just sort of keep an eye on him. God bless him, little fella. Because he's the baby of the band. He's kind of like a little kid. He was always breaking his foot or bashing someone's head in and breaking his hand. He did need a certain amount of care, Phil."

Not 11 days later, Phil passed on, leaving just Eddie and Lem, and then seven weeks on, that would be it for Lemmy as well.

"I have too many regrets to go into now, but overall I think I have been very fortunate to have met and played with all the people I have," reflects Eddie. "I do not think I would change a

Backstage at The Warehouse in Toronto, June 24, 2000. | © Martin Popoff

thing, as I would not risk losing the music and the memories I have. Whatever happens, I have no complaints. There is always gonna be things you would have done different, but who knows, it could have turned out worse!"

All for one and one for all, at least in the innocent days when it was all new. "Yes, it was always the three of us," agrees Clarke, defining the character of the classic lineup. "I'd say it was an equal share, to the three characters in the band. Like I was a character, Lemmy was a character, Phil was a character. The band wouldn't have been the band without him. Because he brought a lot of uniqueness to the band. He was very funny. He had loads of energy. And I always thought of him as one of the best drummers ever. Because it isn't so much technique or anything that for me denotes a great drummer. For me, it's someone who could fit in and make the music work. And Motörhead was not an easy outfit, really. We were all going fucking mad all the time. So everybody had to fit with everybody else."

As for his own role, Eddie says, "I never really thought about that. I would hope the fans just would've thought of me as Eddie, the guitarist in Motörhead. I played the guitar, I was just the third guy, another member. I always thought I was just an equal. The nice thing about having one guitarist and one drummer and one bass player—he does the guitar, he does the drums, he does the bass. Whereas with a band with two guitars, you get a problem. I always thought a three-piece was killer, you know? Killer. I've been very fortunate to have done this, to be honest."

So at least in the beginning, when it was pure (in contrast with Phil Taylor's demoralizing stories of his last days with Lemmy), the guys were equals with each other, but they were also equals with the fans. And, as has been a recurring theme throughout this book, Motörhead—at least the classic Motörhead of Eddie's day—would identify more with their crowd at the lip of the stage and hovering at their table in the pub than they would their musicianly peers, because, after all, keepers of the established industry thought they were miscreants. Or, as Lemmy would put it, "'Idiots with leather jackets on.' Fuck them, they are the dumb ones. I don't think about them at all."

"The fans loved us, which is all we really cared about," reflects Clarke. "In the fans' eyes we were respected, but not musicians'.

The fans loved us. But the musician elite people think, 'Oh, I'm a fantastic musician, man.' Musicians, a lot of them have their heads up their ass thinking that they're something closer to God. A lot of musicians are like that. That's why I haven't got many musician friends, because they think they're so fuckin' marvelous. But all they can do is play a fucking instrument. It's not like rocket science, you know what I mean? They're just playing a fucking guitar. You think, who are you cunts? And they were all, especially back then, 'Oh come look at me, I'm fucking . . .' And I'm sorry, I wasn't like that. We were like, 'Let's have another toot and a fucking drink and a joint, and fuck them, we don't care.' But these guys were walking around, 'I'm big, I'm fantastic.' Because they think if they're in a famous band, they have political views, you know? That their political views suddenly count. They forget that they're still essentially the cunt they were when they started. Playing the guitar hasn't turned them into a fucking messiah, you know? But that's what they were like. And we weren't like that. We didn't give a fuck. And plus they were scared of us because we looked like an angry bunch. Musicians are generally pretty weedy types. And of course, if you've got three guys standing in the corner with leather jackets and bullet belts and they look like death, you know, they're going to stay away from you."

Ask any old rock warhorse about the accolades heaped down upon him over the years from disciples that far outstripped any of their own achievements commercially, and the list will start coming. Ask Eddie, and he quickly answers, "No, not really. Ozzy was a good friend of ours. He seemed to like us. Apart from that, I can't really think of anything, no, not particularly. We were the black sheep, certainly back in the early days. I mean, we had Lars from Metallica; he would come to a lot of our shows. So he obviously appreciated what he saw and went off and did Metallica. So I think he was a big fan. I mean, I'm sure there are big fans out there, but it's been such a long time, so maybe I've forgotten a lot. But I know, as time is going on, Motörhead has become more acceptable. Back in our day, Motörhead wasn't acceptable. So what happened through the years, Motörhead has become the accepted norm, almost. It's quite fascinating, really. But the original band, it's also a badge for a time, isn't it? It was a moment in time."

As far as the most cherished of those moments in time go, Eddie picks "Motörhead playing the Hammersmith Odeon for the first time . . . I can still remember being on the side of the stage with Lem saying, 'Fuck, we are here!' Also, Fastway being courted by a couple of record companies and us having a choice. That was new to me, as we struggled a long while to get a deal for Motörhead. I did not have any preconceived ideas about the music business. The business is the same as all businesses, run by greedy people, many wearing suits. There was little to warm the heart. It also grinds you down, the backstabbing and the ripping off. Managers are not great, either. I think they think, 'You have the fame. I will have your fortune.' I still think the best thing was the fans and their dedication to the cause. Without them, none of us would be here. They made it all worthwhile."

"And so sure, we spent all our time with our fans before shows— always. We used to go to the bar, drink with them and all the rest of it. It was just something we did. And afterwards, we always set up a couple of tables, so after the show, we'd get dressed and we'd go out and take a picture and sign some things, chat with 'em. We did that every night. It was just that we knew that the fans gave us what we got, and we appreciated them as much as they appreciated us. And I think that has a lot to do with the sort of legend that is Motörhead, you know?"

Indeed, everything Eddie has just articulated has much to do with why millions of fans love Motörhead. But on a deeper, almost subconscious level, the appreciation of the band has much to do with the wild abandon emblematic of and represented by the music and the effortless freedom and lack of pretense that marked the personalities of Eddie, Phil and especially Lemmy, who has been the one left to espouse over 40 years of interviews and lyrics, the romance of ruthless individualism that is essentially the romantic notion of a biker outlaw. But the biker outlaw is at his most pure and most respected by his enemies when he pays the ultimate price for his freedom, a denouncement of attachments.

As alluded to earlier in our tale, neither Phil nor Eddie nor Lemmy ever married, and the only child between the three is almost an asterisk, notes Clarke. "Well, Lemmy had one from before I joined the band, going back probably six years before that; so obviously that was a Hawkwind baby. But he had nothing to do with the mother or anything. It was a baby at that time. He has since re-bonded with the lad, you know, and they're very close now. But of course, back in those days, you didn't have time for anything like that. You didn't have any money, you know what I mean? You didn't have a pot to piss in. You didn't have anything. So you had nothing to offer a kid. All you had was what you were doing, which was trying to survive, put some food in your stomach, buy some strings for your guitar and see if you can get a gig."

But none for Phil or Eddie.

"No, no. You see, that was the price you had to pay for being a great rock 'n' roll band. And nowadays, they all have children in the tour bus, all this; well, my idea of being a rock 'n' roller is it's full-on. It's the price you pay. And so as much as I admire these guys who manage to do both things, we were a bit more serious than that. We were literally just, you know, guys that loved our instruments, loved playing. We really loved it, and that's what people don't think about when they think about the guys in Motörhead. I loved my guitar, I lived for my guitar. I take it apart every day, I change it, I'd be looking around for bits, Phil would be looking around for new things every day. Lemmy on the other hand would be reading books all the time, but then of course his lyrics were second to none. So, you know, we really were into what we were doing, 110 percent, you know. It's every breath we took, really, was Motörhead. That's why none of us got married. And that's why we didn't have families—we had to be free to carry on."

Lemmy, June 24, 2000. Motörhead took the stage after support act Nashville Pussy, a firm Kilmister favorite. | © Martin Popoff

Selected Discography

A few points of style here. Track listings are for original U.K. issue albums only, and of course, this is a discography of the band as it existed with Lemmy, Phil and Eddie only, issued at the time they were still in the band. I haven't put quote marks around songs, simply for tidiness, even though that is the rule in the body of the book. I've included side one/side two designations given that all of these albums hail from the vinyl era. I've included no compilations; however, I have included singles and EPs (U.K. issue only) because of their significance to the industry and to Motörhead's career during this era. All songs written by Lemmy Kilmister, Eddie Clarke and Phil Taylor unless otherwise specified.

Albums

Motörhead

(Chiswick WIK2; August 21, 1977)

Produced by Speedy Keen

SIDE 1: 1. Motörhead (3:13; Lemmy Kilmister) 2. Vibrator (3:39; Dez Brown/Larry Wallis) 3. Lost Johnny (4:15; Lemmy Kilmister/Mick Farren) 4. Iron Horse/Born to Lose (5:21; Dez Brown/Phil Taylor/Guy Lawrence)

SIDE 2: 1. White Line Fever (2:38) 2. Keep Us on the Road (5:57; Lemmy Kilmister/Eddie Clarke/Phil Taylor/Mick Farren) 3. The Watcher (4:30; Kilmister) 4. The Train Kept a-Rollin' (3:19; Tiny Bradshaw/Howard Kay/Lois Mann)

Overkill

(Bronze BRON 515; March 16, 1979)

Produced by Jimmy Miller, except Tear Ya Down, produced by Neil Richmond

SIDE 1: 1. Overkill (5:12) 2. Stay Clean (2:40) 3. (I Won't) Pay Your
Price (2:56) 4. I'll Be Your Sister (2:51) 5. Capricorn (4:06)

SIDE 2: 1. No Class (2:39) 2. Damage Case (2:59; Lemmy Kilmister/
Eddie Clarke/Phil Taylor/Mick Farren) 3. Tear Ya Down (2:39)
4. Metropolis (3:34) 5. Limb from Limb (4:54)

Bomber

(Bronze BRON 523; October 27, 1979)

Produced by Jimmy Miller

SIDE 1: 1. Dead Men Tell No Tales (3:07) 2. Lawman (3:56) 3. Sweet
Revenge (4:10) 4. Sharpshooter (3:19) 5. Poison (2:54)

SIDE 2: 1. Stone Dead Forever (4:54) 2. All the Aces (3:24) 3. Step
Down (3:41) 4. Talking Head (3:40) 5. Bomber (3:43)

Ace of Spades

(Bronze BRON 531; October 20, 1980)

Produced by Vic Maile

SIDE 1: 1. Ace of Spades (2:49) 2. Love Me like a Reptile (3:23)
3. Shoot You in the Back (2:39) 4. Live to Win (3:37) 5. Fast and
Loose (3:23) 6. (We Are) The Road Crew (3:13)

SIDE 2: 1. Fire, Fire (2:44) 2. Jailbait (3:33) 3. Dance (2:38) 4. Bite the
Bullet (1:38) 5. The Chase Is Better than the Catch (4:18)
6. The Hammer (2:48)

No Sleep 'til Hammersmith

(Bronze BRON 535; June 27, 1981)

Produced by Vic Maile

SIDE 1: 1. Ace of Spades (3:01) 2. Stay Clean (2:50) 3. Metropolis
(3:31) 4. The Hammer (3:05) 5. Iron Horse/Born to Lose (3:58;
Dez Brown/Phil Taylor/Guy Lawrence) 6. No Class (2:34)

SIDE 2: 1. Overkill (5:13) 2. (We Are) The Road Crew (3:31)
3. Capricorn (4:40) 4. Bomber (3:24) 5. Motörhead (4:47;
Lemmy Kilmister)

Iron Fist

(Bronze BRNA 539; April 17, 1982)

Produced by Eddie Clarke and Will Reid-Dick

SIDE 1: 1. Iron Fist (2:55) 2. Heart of Stone (3:04) 3. I'm the Doctor (2:43) 4. Go to Hell (3:10) 5. Loser (3:57) 6. Sex & Outrage (2:10)

SIDE 2: 1. America (3:38) 2. Shut it Down (2:41) 3. Speedfreak (3:28) 4. (Don't Let 'em) Grind Ya Down (3:08) 5. (Don't Need) Religion (2:43) 6. Bang to Rights (2:43)

Extended Plays

The Golden Years Live EP

(Bronze BRO 92; May 8, 1980)

SIDE 1: 1. Leaving Here (3:02; Lamont Dozier/Brian Holland/Edward Holland) 2. Stone Dead Forever (5:20)

SIDE 2: 1. Dead Men Tell No Tales (2:54) 2. Too Late, Too Late (3:21)

Beer Drinkers and Hell Raisers

(Big Beat NS 61; November 22, 1980)

SIDE 1: 1. Beer Drinkers and Hell Raisers (3:27; Billy Gibbons/Dusty Hill/Frank Beard) 2. On Parole (5:57; Larry Wallis)

SIDE 2: 1. Instro (2:27) 2. I'm Your Witchdoctor (2:58; John Mayall)

St. Valentines Day Massacre

Credited to Motor Headgirl School

(Bronze BRO 116; February 1, 1981)

SIDE 1: 1. Motörhead/Girlschool: Please Don't Touch (2:49; Johnny Kidd/Guy Robinson)

SIDE 2: 1. Girlschool: Bomber (3:30) 2. Motörhead and Denise Dufort: Emergency (3:03; Denise Dufort/Enid Williams/Kelly Johnson/Kim McAuliffe)

Singles

Motörhead (3:13; Lemmy Kilmister)/City Kids (3:24; Larry Wallis/ Duncan Sanderson) (Chiswick S 13; June 1977)

Leaving Here (3:20; Lamont Dozier/Brian Holland/Edward Holland)/White Line Fever (2:38) (Stiff BUY 9; November 1978; withdrawn)

Louie Louie (2:47; Richard Berry)/Tear Ya Down (2:39) (Bronze BRO 60; August 25, 1978)

Overkill (5:12)/Too Late, Too Late (3:24) (Bronze BRO 67; February 23, 1979)

No Class (2:39)/Like a Nightmare (4:13) (Bronze BRO 78; June 15, 1979)

Bomber (3:43)/Over the Top (3:21) (Bronze BRO 85; November 30, 1979)

Ace of Spades (2:49)/Dirty Love (2:57) (Bronze BRO 106; October 27, 1980)

Motörhead (3:35; Lemmy Kilmister)/Over the Top (3:04) (Bronze BRO 124; July 11, 1981)

Iron Fist (2:50)/Remember Me, I'm Gone (2:26) (Bronze BRO 146; April 3, 1982)

Credits

Interviews with the Author

Bello, Frank. December 17, 2015.

Benante, Charlie. October 23, 2015.

Brabbs, Mark. May 26, 2015.

Brock, Dave. 2009.

Brock, Dave. August 7, 2013.

Byford, Biff. November 9, 2015.

Campbell, Phil. May 20, 2000.

Campbell, Phil. September 2, 2009.

Caris, Nick. July 10, 2015.

Chesters, Neville. 2009.

Clarke, Eddie. January 22, 2002.

Clarke, Eddie. March 21, 2008.

Clarke, Eddie. October 8, 2014.

Clarke, Eddie. October 8, 2015.

Clarke, Eddie. October 30, 2015.

Dee, Mikkey. March 2, 2002.

Dee, Mikkey. August 13, 2008.

Godwin, Rob. January 4, 2016.

Kilmister, Lemmy. 1998.

Kilmister, Lemmy. March 24, 1999.

Kilmister, Lemmy. June 26, 2000.

Kilmister, Lemmy. March 2, 2002.

Kilmister, Lemmy. February 28, 2005.

Kilmister, Lemmy. September 15, 2006.

Kilmister, Lemmy. August 13, 2008.

McAuliffe, Kim. October 2, 2008.

Pearlman, Sandy. 2009.

Riddles, Kevin. October 6, 2015.

Robertson, Brian. March, 2011.

Smith, Doug. April 28, 2016.

Snider, Dee. September 21, 1999.

Snider, Dee. October 16, 2015.

Taylor, Phil. December 10, 2009.

Turner, Nik. October 7, 2013.

Ward, Algy. May 17, 2015.

Additional Sources

Classic Rock Revisited. "Rock 'n' Roll is Supposed to be Fun—In Spite of Sting!" An interview with Lemmy by Jeb Wright. October 2006.

Classic Rock Revisited. Interview with Lemmy by Jeb Wright. April 2012.

Classic Rock Revisited. Interview with Eddie Clarke by Jeb Wright. April 2012.

Classic Rock Revisited. Interview with Eddie Clarke by Jeb Wright. 2014.

Dunn, Sam. Interview with Lemmy Kilmister. 2010.

Dunn, Sam. Interview with Phil Taylor. 2010.

Epstein, Dmitry. Interview with Gerry Bron. November 2004.

"Forced Exposure. Larry Wallis: The Complete Pink Fairies Story." Winter 1987.

Goldmine. "Pure Dumb Luck: An Interview with Lemmy Kilmister by Jeb Wright." Issue 800. Volume 37, No. 6. May 2011.

Kerrang! Iron Fist record review by Steve Gett. No. 13. April 8–21, 1982.

New Musical Express. "Blue Öyster Cult, Motörhead: Hammersmith Odeon, London" by Nick Kent. October 25, 1975.

Record Mirror. "Must We Fling this Filth at Our Pop Kids" by Ronnie Gurr. June 7, 1980.

Record Review. "Motörhead: Monsters of Metal Madness" by Jon Sutherland. October 1982.

RIP. "Lemmy at 'em!" by Chuck Eddy. Volume 11, No. 1. January 1997.

Sounds. "Motörhead: Roundhouse, London" by Geoff Barton. July

26, 1975.

Sounds. "Success? We've got it all tied up . . ." by Robbi Millar. February 21, 1981.

Steel Mill. "Joe Petagno" by Pete Alander and Kassu Kortelainen. October 2012.

Trouser Press. *Motörhead* record review by Ira Robbins. December 1977.

ZigZag. "Motörhead" by Kris Needs. September 1977.

About the Author

At approximately 7,900 (with over 7,000 appearing in his books), Martin has unofficially written more record reviews than anybody in the history of music writing across all genres. Additionally, Martin has penned 56 books on hard rock, heavy metal, classic rock and record collecting. He was editor-in-chief of the now retired *Brave Words & Bloody Knuckles*, Canada's foremost metal publication for 14 years, and has also contributed to *Revolver*, *Guitar World*, *Goldmine*, *Record Collector*, bravewords.com, lollipop.com and hardradio.com, with many record label band bios and liner notes to his credit as well. Additionally, Martin has been a regular contractor

to Banger Films, having worked for two years as researcher on the award-winning documentary *Rush: Beyond the Lighted Stage*, on the writing and research team for the 11-episode *Metal Evolution* and on the 10-episode *Rock Icons*, both for VH1 Classic. Additionally, Martin is the writer of the original metal genre chart used in *Metal: A Headbanger's Journey* and throughout the *Metal Evolution* episodes. Martin currently resides in Toronto and can be reached through martinp@inforamp.net or www.martinpopoff.com.

Martin Popoff -- A Complete Bibliography

Popoff Archive 2: Progressive Rock (2016)

Popoff Archive 1: Doom Metal (2016)

Rock the Nation: Montrose, Gamma and Ronnie Redefined (2016)

Punk Tees: The Punk Revolution in 125 T-Shirts (2016)

Metal Heart: Aiming High with Accept (2016)

Time and a Word: The Story of Yes (2016)

Ramones at 40 (2016)

This Means War: The Sunset Years of the NWOBHM (2015)

Wheels of Steel: The Explosive Early Years of the NWOBHM (2015)

Swords and Tequila: Riot's Classic First Decade (2015)

Who Invented Heavy Metal? (2015)

Sail Away: Whitesnake's Fantastic Voyage (2015)

Live Magnetic Air: The Unlikely Saga Of The Superlative Max Webster (2014)

Steal Away the Night: An Ozzy Osbourne Day-By-Day (2014)

The Big Book of Hair Metal (2014)

Sweating Bullets: The Deth and Rebirth Of Megadeth (2014)

Smokin' Valves: A Headbanger's Guide to 900 NWOBHM Records (2014)

The Art of Metal (co-edit with Malcolm Dome; 2013)

2 Minutes to Midnight: An Iron Maiden Day-By-Day (2013)

Metallica: The Complete Illustrated History (2013)

Rush: The Illustrated History (2013)

Ye Olde Metal: 1979 (2013)

Scorpions: Top of the Bill (2013)

Epic Ted Nugent (2012)

Fade to Black: Hard Rock Cover Art of the Vinyl Age (2012)

It's Getting Dangerous: Thin Lizzy '81–'12 (2012)

We Will Be Strong: Thin Lizzy '76–'81 (2012)

Fighting My Way Back: Thin Lizzy '69–'76 (2011)

The Deep Purple Royal Family: Chain of Events '80–'11 (2011)

The Deep Purple Royal Family: Chain of Events Through '79 (2011)

Black Sabbath FAQ (2011)

The Collector's Guide to Heavy Metal: Volume 4: The '00s (2011; co-authored with David Perri)

Goldmine Standard Catalog of American Records 1948–1991, 7th Edition (2010)

Goldmine Record Album Price Guide, 6th Edition (2009)

Goldmine 45 RPM Price Guide, 7th Edition (2009)

A Castle Full of Rascals: Deep Purple '83–'09 (2009)

Worlds Away: Voivod and the Art of Michel Langevin (2009)

Ye Olde Metal: 1978 (2009)

Gettin' Tighter: Deep Purple '68–'76 (2008)

All Access: The Art of the Backstage Pass (2008)

Ye Olde Metal: 1977 (2008)

Ye Olde Metal: 1976 (2008)

Judas Priest: Heavy Metal Painkillers (2007)

Ye Olde Metal: 1973 to 1975 (2007)

The Collector's Guide to Heavy Metal: Volume 3: The Nineties (2007)

Ye Olde Metal: 1968 to 1972 (2007)

Run for Cover: The Art of Derek Riggs (2006)

Black Sabbath: Doom Let Loose (2006)

Dio: Light Beyond the Black (2006)

The Collector's Guide to Heavy Metal: Volume 2: The Eighties (2005)

Rainbow: English Castle Magic (2005)

UFO: Shoot Out the Lights (2005)

The New Wave of British Heavy Metal Singles (2005)

Blue Öyster Cult: Secrets Revealed! (2004)

Contents Under Pressure: 30 Years of Rush at Home & Away (2004)

The Top 500 Heavy Metal Albums of All Time (2004)

The Collector's Guide to Heavy Metal: Volume 1: The Seventies (2003)

The Top 500 Heavy Metal Songs of All Time (2003)

Southern Rock Review (2001)

Heavy Metal: 20th Century Rock and Roll (2000)

The Goldmine Price Guide to Heavy Metal Records (2000)

The Collector's Guide to Heavy Metal (1997)

Riff Kills Man! 25 Years of Recorded Hard Rock & Heavy Metal (1993)

See martinpopoff.com for complete details and ordering information.

Get the eBook FREE!

At ECW Press, we want you to enjoy this book in whatever format you like, whenever you like. Leave your print book at home and take the eBook to go! Purchase the print edition and receive the eBook free. Just send an e-mail to ebook@ecwpress.com and include:

- the book title
- the name of the store where you purchased it
- your receipt number
- your preference of file type: PDF or ePub?

A real person will respond to your e-mail with your eBook attached. Thank you for supporting an independently owned Canadian publisher with your purchase!